Praise for *Family-Based Youth Ministry*

"The revised *Family-Based Youth Ministry* is must reading for pastors and youth workers. The additional insights build from the shoulders of his groundbreaking reframing of youth ministry done a decade ago. In so doing Mark DeVries integrates more than ten years of experimentation and reflection into a cohesive concept of family-based youth ministry."

MARK H. SENTER III, *Professor of Youth and Educational Ministries, Trinity Evangelical Divinity School*

"Mark DeVries has done us all a great and necessary favor by thinking through what's for too long been a missing link in youth ministry. When we fail to consider the primary role parents play in the spiritual nurture of their children, we can make the mistake of assuming we can fill that role. *Family-Based Youth Ministry* will challenge and guide you to build families and stimulate the spiritual growth of students by consciously engaging, rather than ignoring, student's families. I continually point youth workers to this valuable and timely resource."

WALT MUELLER, *Center for Parent/Youth Understanding*

"Mark is candid, honest, realistic, practical and down to earth! *Family-Based Youth Ministry* is a great resource and a must-read for all youth workers and parents."

RUSSELL J. SANCHE, *National Director, KKI Canada, Youth With A Mission*

"Mark DeVries has given us a very clear and readable rationale for rooting our youth ministry within the family structure. This will be one of those books that youth workers find they must read."

DUFFY ROBBINS, *Chairman, Department of Youth Ministry, Eastern College*

"This important book by a seasoned minister to youth argues for a Christian approach to young people by way of families—nuclear and ecclesial—rather than pied pipers. It is thoughtful, suggestive and groundbreaking."

THOMAS W. GILLESPIE, *President, Princeton Theological Seminary*

"Family ministry as a concept is spreading rapidly throughout the youth ministry culture. Mark DeVries's work demonstrates that he has been and will continue to be a pioneer and pacesetter for that movement."

RICHARD DUNN, *author,* Shaping the Spiritual Lives of Students

"I appreciate Mark's thoroughness and desire to risk as well as venture into uncharted territory. Effective youth ministry has always begun in this way. I endorse his premise and support the idea that youth ministry is in a new day requiring new approaches."

CLIFF ANDERSON, *Institute of Youth Ministry, Fuller Seminary Colorado*

FAMILY-BASED
YOUTH MINISTRY

REVISED AND EXPANDED

Mark DeVries

Foreword by Earl F. Palmer

IVP Books

An imprint of InterVarsity Press
Downers Grove, Illinois

InterVarsity Press
P.O. Box 1400, Downers Grove, IL 60515-1426
World Wide Web: www.ivpress.com
E-mail: email@ivpress.com

InterVarsity Press® is the book-publishing division of InterVarsity Christian Fellowship/USA®, a student movement active on campus at hundreds of universities, colleges and schools of nursing in the United States of America, and a member movement of the International Fellowship of Evangelical Students. For information about local and regional activities, write Public Relations Dept., InterVarsity Christian Fellowship/USA, 6400 Schroeder Rd., P.O. Box 7895, Madison, WI 53707-7895, or visit the IVCF website at <www.intervarsity.org>.

Design: Cindy Kiple
Images: Bob Thomas/Getty Images
ISBN 978-0-8308-3243-9
Printed in the United States of America ∞

Library of Congress Cataloging-in-Publication Data

DeVries, Mark.
   Family-based youth ministry/
   Mark DeVries.—Rev.
     p. cm.
   Includes bibliographical references.
   ISBN 0-8308-3243-2 (pbk.: alk. paper)
   1. Church work with teenagers. 2 Church work with families. I.
Title.
   BV4447.D45 2004
   259'.23—dc22
                                             2003027939

P	23	22	21	20	19	18	17	16	15	14	13	12	11	10	9	8	7
Y	24	23	22	21	20	19	18	17	16	15	14	13	12	11	10		

To Sušan,

who daily treats my trivia

as if it were the most important news in the world,

who lives with such infectious joy

that few can be with her long without laughing

and who has given me more in the past twenty-five years

than most men receive in ten lifetimes.

CONTENTS

FOREWORD

I remember hearing youth pastor Mark DeVries from Nashville First Presbyterian Church speak at a seminar in which he shared with a roomful of pastors his vision for ministry to youth. I thought at the time that what he was telling us was both refreshing and vitally important for the ministry to and among youth to which we are called as Christians. Now I have read his book and I still feel the same way.

Mark DeVries takes youth seriously, and, therefore, he does not see the role of the youth pastor as a steppingstone to larger ministries or what might be thought of as more important appointments. He sees youth ministry as a totally significant post, just as pediatrics in medicine is not an entry level into medicine that later evolves toward the "more important" responsibility of geriatrics.

I think Mark DeVries and his new breed of youth pastors will remain, in fact, youth workers all of their lives, wherever they are called to serve and in whatever use of their gifts to which the church lays claim. As a result the church, youth and their families will be the better for it. This is because we know that churches die down like forests when they fail to win the next generation to faith in Jesus Christ. The big question is, what is it that wins youth to faith and helps them catch their stride as growing Christians? It isn't playing at church. It isn't unfocused programs to occupy their time. It is the good news of Jesus Christ. He is the most winsome fact that we have to share with any generation.

The question of durability and strategy for our ministry with youth is the focus of Mark's book. He makes a profoundly important point as he argues that the most substantial ministry with the most long-lasting positive result is the ministry that relates to young men and women as members of families. This means we who do youth ministry are really involved in family ministry. The African saying puts it well: "It takes a village to raise a child," and the first village for every human being is the family of origin. Therefore, our ministry must encourage and strengthen that original village with friendly, nonexploitive adults for youth to borrow in their growing up and for families to borrow too. I salute Pastor DeVries for this notable book, which is a great gift to the church in helping us know how to stand alongside youth and their families.

Earl F. Palmer

ACKNOWLEDGMENTS

When I began this project, back in 1989, I never would have guessed how many different people would wind up adding their own unique contributions to my thinking about a new vision for youth ministry. I'd like to thank the following:

MY FORMATIVE FAMILY

My parents—for the unparalleled influence you had in setting the course for my life as a Christian.

My bonus parents (Richard, Louise and Caroline)—for embracing me as part of your own families.

John, Gene, Jerry and all the other ministers (and minister wannabes) in my parents' families—no one was ever surrounded by as rich a cloud of witnesses.

MY PASTORS

George and Trish Holland—for seeing through an obnoxious teenager and celebrating his gifts for ministry.

Dick Freeman—for loving Jesus Christ with a contagious passion and for not firing me when I drove a 14-foot bus under the church's 13-foot carport.

Don Childs—for letting a fly-by-night seminary student from another denomination practice on the kids in your church.

Bill Bryant—for giving me the freedom to experiment in youth ministry and for setting a standard of excellence that motivated me to look beyond my own limited perspective.

MY MENTORS

Robert Wolgemuth—for dragging us to Nashville, clinging to Christ when it would have been so simple to let go and giving us two of the greatest interns our church has ever seen. (Is it good?)

Weldon and Barbara Walker—for your wise counsel through all those years when we were trying to figure out what to do when we grew up.

Steve Eyre—for reading Jonathan Edwards with me and convincing me that I really could write a book.

Earl Palmer—for your vision for mentoring young pastors, your eager love for learning and your ability to bring out more in people than they ever knew was there (and for quoting C. S. Lewis as if you'd really been to Narnia).

Cindy "O Holy One" Bunch (IVP)—for laughing when I tried to be funny and giving invaluable suggestions about the manuscript. (Voicemail, anyone?)

Dick Armstrong and Ron White—for letting me make up classes that didn't exist.

MY PARTNERS IN MINISTRY

Larry Coulter—for getting me into this whole book-writing thing in the first place and for spending a week with me in Princeton to get the ball rolling. (Time for a Thomas Sweet?)

The Princeton Long-Term Youth Ministry Planning Team (Kendy Easley, Ron Scates, Robert Morris, Emily Anderson, Dayle Gillespie Rounds)—for listening and giving me feedback on my Family-Based Youth Ministry seminar more times than we care to remember (sui generis!).

Nan Russell, my teaching partner—for spending the past five years working the kinks out of our family-based curriculum and sharing your wild-ride journey with me. (Please don't get arrested again—at least not in front of the teenagers!)

Debbie and Kirk Freeman, Colyer and Drew Robison, Missy Schrader, Julle Tassy, Ginger Sheppard, Margaret Burnett, Chris Carson, and Emmett and Spick—for your teachable spirits and the secret encouragement your receptivity gave to my thinking.

The Cows, the Honchos, the Youth Committee, the Dad's Club, the interns, the prayer partners, the mentors, and my colleagues on the staff at First Presbyterian Church in Nashville—for creating the synergy that has become the means for God to do his surprising work among us here.

Our Dear Friends (you know who you are)—for your random acts of kindness that have empowered us to see a glimmer of what lies beyond our own blinders.

My Loyal Opponents (you know who *you* are too)—for challenging me to clarify my thinking and to broaden my perspective to include your point of view.

Trish "I've got some good news and some bad news" Callison—for putting your life on hold to complete my incomplete footnotes. (Leslie and John, thank you too.)

My team at Youth Ministry Architects—Jeff Dunn-Rankin, Chris Kelly, Carol DeLoach, Julian Bibb, Marti Burbeck and Jeff Flynn—for helping so many churches make the principles in this book come alive.

My bride, Susan, and my three children, Adam, Debbie and Leigh—for honoring me with your respect even when I deserve so much less.

INTRODUCTION

Several years ago I heard the surprising news that my good friend Jim, one of the most effective youth pastors I have ever known, was leaving youth ministry. Jim was no rookie. He had been in his church for almost ten years and had more than two hundred teenagers meeting weekly in cell groups with creative programming that drew young people from all over the city.

Now there is nothing shocking about youth workers changing jobs. But I did wonder *why* Jim was quitting—and not only his present position but youth ministry altogether. Did he get a better offer somewhere else? Was he moving on to become a "real" minister? Was he going to start a profitable curriculum business? Or make his own video series? I thought of all the possibilities, but his answer hit me cold.

"I am leaving," he said, "because I feel this overwhelming sense of failure."

Sense of failure? I sat stunned. This man had been a model for me, someone whose ministry I was actively seeking to imitate. And he tells me he feels like a failure? It just didn't make sense.

But since that conversation more than ten years ago, Jim's words have begun to make more and more sense to me. And I am starting to see that his experience may actually be more the norm than the exception. Whether it's the highly sought after youth pastor suffering from burnout in his booming, cutting-edge church or the highly acclaimed parachurch youth worker unable to recover from her chronic exhaustion, I'm seeing more and more of them suffering from a nagging sense of failure.

Youth ministers know the anxiety of a juggler keeping a knife, a bat and a fire stick in the air all at the same time. We know the temporary insanity required in moving directly from suicide counseling into an egg roulette competition and then into teaching a group of teenagers who are not afraid to yawn in public. We know the nagging feeling of inadequacy, always feeling like the runt of the litter on a church staff. And we've heard the not-so-silent whisperings, "Is he (or she) ever going to become a real minister?"

Youth ministers know they must always curb their enthusiasm about teenagers' testimonies. We have heard too much from too many who didn't follow through on their words. We know the frustration of being called disorganized because we forget to bring mustard for the otherwise perfect cookout. And we've fallen from the tightrope of listening to too much or too little criticism.

But whether from the call of God or from temporary insanity, we love this work. And even when things are at their worst, many of us still can't come up with anything else we'd rather do. Despite the frustrations common to all of us, I've met very few youth workers who are out of ideas. Most are out of time, energy, patience and money. But ideas? We have them by the truckload. Almost all of us know what we *ought* to be doing, but we just can't seem to keep all of the youth ministry plates spinning at once.

We would like to write great newsletter articles, prepare scintillating sermons, visit every kid in the group, boost attendance, work with parents, be available to handle crises at the drop of a hat, have a model family, keep praying and studying on our own, visit the schools regularly, disciple our volunteer leaders, train great teachers, find (or write!) curricula for Sunday school, build small groups, develop youth leadership, give stirring weekly reports, write letters to college students, teach guitar lessons, send personal birthday cards to each young person, involve youth in mission on a monthly basis, read the right youth ministry books and journals, plan great retreats and monthly fun trips, promote and fill all the trips, collect money, fill the sanctuary with well-groomed teenagers on Sunday morning, be the spiritual giant and fun-loving charisma machine we were hired to be, and of course *relax*—all at the same time!

But because we can't possibly keep all the plates spinning, youth ministry at its best involves a continual process of setting and adjusting priorities, of deciding what we will wring our hands about and what we will let slide. And let's face it, ministry to or through parents of teenagers has simply been one of the many things on our to do list that we've had to let slide.

In their extraordinary research into the youth ministry profession, Merton Strommen, Karen Jones and Dave Rahn discovered how true this phenomenon is. Many youth ministry professionals in the study indicated that priorities like "providing opportunities for teens and parents to interact" and "gaining parental involvement in the ministry" were *very* important. But these youth workers evaluated their own achievement of such family-based outcomes as the *lowest* of any category in the entire survey.[1]

Jim Burns, the most visible champion of family-based youth ministry, says the consensus is clear: Incorporating families into youth ministry is one of those things that everyone believes is important to do . . . next year!

The ironic truth is that we have at our fingertips the resource for vastly expanding the scope and long-term impact of our ministries. But many of us see this resource as something that gets in the way, so we lay it aside. We are like the would-be handyman who attempts to move a boulder from his yard with a screwdriver, all the while complaining that the sledgehammer and the pickax keep getting in his way. He may or may not get the job done, but exhaustion and frustration are certain.

This book is written for youth workers who are tired of quick fixes and easy answers. It's also written for anyone responsible for a Christian ministry to teenagers—pastors, youth committee members, parents, volunteer leaders and search committees looking for youth pastors. It is written for parents who want to understand the forces that most significantly affect their children's spiritual formation.

As the title suggests, this is also a book about families. Let me tip my hand a little. One of my working assumptions is that the contemporary crisis in youth ministry has little to do with programming and everything to do with families. Our culture has put an incredible emotional weight on the shoulders of the nuclear family, a weight that I believe God never intended for families to bear alone. One of the secrets you will learn about in these pages is the strategic priority of undergirding nuclear families with the rich support of the extended Christian family of the church. When these two formative families work in concert, we are most likely to see youth growing into a faith that lasts for the long haul.

This book explains a paradigm shift for youth ministry. It will challenge some of the assumptions underlying the way it's always been done and then offer an alternative. The first few chapters will identify what I see as the core deficiency in traditional youth ministry. The bulk of the book will offer a realistic, informed understanding of the primary factors that lead teenagers to Christian maturity. In the first edition of *Family-Based Youth Ministry*, the glaring omission was the obvious lack of an implementation strategy. It makes sense that the number one question people have asked me over the years has been, "We agree that it's a great idea. But how do we make it work?" This new edition ends with an implementation strategy that any church can successfully put in place. I have also provided a section at the end of each chapter called "Implications for Ministry." These ideas will give some practical handles for the application of the principles outlined in each chapter. In addition there is a smorgasbord of suggestions in the appendix.

The stories you will read are true. But, where appropriate, I have changed names and details to honor and protect the privacy of those whose stories I tell.

This is a book about a new way of approaching youth ministry that goes beyond the traditional formulas that seem, inherently, to set up youth leaders for failure. But this is not a "Shell Answer Man" handbook. You will not find in these pages the silver bullet to make ministry to teenagers a snap; working with youth will never be easy. What you *will* find is an approach that can vastly expand the long-term effectiveness of any Christian ministry to teenagers.

It's disturbing how few Christian teenagers actually grow toward a more mature Christian faith. A national study by Search Institute found that, in general, teenagers' church involvement and faith stagnate during high school.

JAY KESLER, *Energizing Your Teenager's Faith*

The health of ministries to high-school students in the United States is less than exciting. For the most part ministries which employ youth specialists are locked within the white middle class, as church boards urged by parents attempt to ensure the passing of Christian values from one generation to the next. . . . Parachurch agencies which attempt to reach the entire student population with a single strategy have ceased to grow.

MARK SENTER, *The Coming Revolution in Youth Ministry*

I have spent the past seventeen years working with youth toward one principal goal: to see a personal faith in Jesus Christ become the controlling reality in kids' lives. According to some standards for measuring success, my seventeen-year investment may be viewed as relatively ineffective. Although it is impossible to know what the long-term impact of my involvement in kids' lives really will be, at this time I can point to only small handfuls of kids and young adults with whom I have worked who bear the marks of being controlled by a personal faith in Christ. Though the personal rewards and joys of working with kids have been tremendous, these seventeen years have made one thing clear: Personal faith in Christ cannot be mass produced in adolescents' lives.

KEVIN HUGGINS, *Parenting Adolescents*

What the whole church must face—local congregations and parachurch ministries alike—is the enormity of the need. The facts speak for themselves: only 15 to 20 percent of American teenagers are significantly involved in a church.

DOUG BURLEIGH, past president of Young Life

It's one factor we haven't mentioned: our woeful inability as mainline Protestants to retain our young.

WILL WILLIMON, *Christianity Today*, August 17, 1997

1 ◆ SOMETHING'S WRONG

The Crisis in Traditional Youth Ministry

Traditional" youth ministry. It sounds like an oxymoron in a day when youth ministries pride themselves on being outrageous, wild, out of control—anything but "traditional." But as we stand on the backside of the turn of the millennium, such a clear pattern for youth ministry has emerged that no term describes it quite so well as "traditional."

What I am calling "traditional youth ministry" has little to do with style or programming or personality. It has to do with the place of teenagers in the community of faith. During the last century, church and parachurch youth ministries alike have increasingly (and often unwittingly) held to a single strategy that has become the defining characteristic of this model: the isolation of teenagers from the adult world and particularly from their own parents.

This traditional model has its roots in the turn of the century with the rise of the Christian Endeavor Movement, a church-based, interdenominational program created especially for youth. Undergirded by a culture in which teenagers had frequent interaction with adults and with their own parents, Christian Endeavor (and church imitations that followed it) flourished. Using a Sunday-night meeting format, these Christian Endeavor-type programs had uncovered a creative and quite effective model for reaching teenagers for Christ.

But when the popularity of the Sunday-night, church-based format began to wane in the 1940s, a new style of youth ministry appeared on the scene, a style popularized by Young Life and Youth for Christ. These organizations hit on the strategy of reaching young people apart from the traditional church setting. And during the next few decades these ministries expanded with explosive energy, reaching thousands of teenagers whom the institutional church seemed to be missing.

With the help of such resource groups as Youth Specialties, the cutting-edge creativity of these parachurch ministries became available to local churches. And in the last twenty years, hundreds of youth ministry resource organizations have been launched, making youth ministry more creative than ever, with an exceptional menu of products designed to reach teenagers more effectively. But despite the external improvements, youth ministry today is in crisis.

The things I did ten months ago aren't working anymore!

I was speaking at a conference not long ago and was asked to give a thirty-second explanation of family-based youth ministry. I reported simply what I have heard from many youth workers over the past five years: "What used to work ten years ago with teenagers is just not working anymore." I wasn't surprised to see the nods of agreement from this room full of experienced youth workers.

Later that evening, one of the conference participants pulled me aside and made a telling remark: "I agree that the things I did ten years ago don't work anymore," he said. "But the real shock for me is that the things I did ten months ago aren't working anymore either!"

SUCCESS: MATURE CHRISTIAN TEENAGERS?

The stereotypical guitar-playing youth leader with a set of idea books and a floppy Bible is no longer enough to attract the attention and enthusiasm of our youth. Long-term youth ministers who have followed the futures of their youth group members have begun to sense intuitively that something is wrong. Most veteran youth ministers I know have a busload of stories like my story about Jenny.

As a seventh-grader, Jenny began visiting our youth group with a friend during church basketball season. Quite honestly, I expected that she would disappear after the ten-game season was over. But was I ever wrong! At some point during that first year, Jenny responded to the claims of Christ and became a model youth group member. She was a regular fixture at our Sunday-morning, Sunday-evening and Wednesday-night youth programs. She sat in the youth section in worship and even showed up when missionaries gave their slide shows ("This is India—Land of Contrast [BEEP]").

Jenny came from a family in which the Christian faith was irrelevant at best. Her parents were supportive of her involvement in the church, but they made it clear that Jenny's spiritual priorities were not for them.

Whenever I had doubts about whether our ministry was having any impact, I would remind myself of Jenny and her amazing story. If anyone bore the marks of the success of our ministry, it was she. Like most youth ministers, I had trouble evaluating the success of our program strictly on the basis of how large a crowd we could gather for youth meetings. But Jenny's story gave me something to hang on to. I could point to her when I needed assurance that I was actually doing something right.

As Jenny grew older, I became more enthusiastic as I watched her precocious spiritual maturity develop. By the time she was a high school sophomore, she was a part of our student leadership team and someone I held up as a model for the younger members of our youth group. By anyone's standards, we had succeeded with Jenny. She was a mature Christian teenager, well ahead of most of her peers who grew up in Christian homes.

I left for seminary just before Jenny's junior year. That same year she moved away as well. I lost touch with her for several years; so when one of our mutual friends mentioned seeing her, I was anxious to hear how she had grown.

But I was deeply saddened by what I heard. Apparently, after leaving our active youth ministry, Jenny couldn't find a church she liked as well as ours, and gradually she gave up the search altogether. She has graduated from college and, after living with her boyfriend for a while, eventually moved on to a fast track in her career. Although she looks back on her youth group experience with nostalgia, she has shown little interest in pursuing her faith as an adult.

Jimmy, on the other hand, never quite connected with our youth ministry. We really worked to get him involved with our youth programs. He had no interest in retreats or mission trips; Sunday school bored him; and youth group seemed a little on the silly side for his taste. He sometimes attended another church across town. On my mental scorecard of kids we had been effective with, Jimmy was on the "loss" side.

But Jimmy had one thing going for him: Every Sunday he was in worship, either with his parents at our church or with his friends at another church. Jimmy didn't need our outrageous and creative youth ministry to lead him to faith maturity. For Jenny our youth ministry was her *only* Christian family. But unlike a real family, this one forced her to resign from the family when she was too old to fit the requirements. She now looks back on her youth group experience like she does on her high school Farrah Fawcett haircut— as a fun, even laughable part of her past, but as something that belonged exclusively in the realm of her teenage years.

I haven't closed the book on Jenny's story, but if it's shown me anything, it is that something was wrong with the way I was measuring success. We had *succeeded* in leading her to become a mature Christian *teenager*, but somehow we failed to place her on the track toward mature Christian *adulthood*. We were shortsighted, focusing on the short-term objective of keeping her involved and growing but forgetting the long-term goal of laying a foundation that would last for the long haul.

WHAT *IS* THE CRISIS?

For almost two decades now I have maintained the somewhat controversial position that youth ministry today is "in crisis." When I use the word *crisis*, many are quick to point out all the positive signs in youth ministry today. They point to the many churches that are reporting record numbers of young people active in their programs. They remind me of the parachurch organizations and national church ministries that have found ways of attracting unprecedented numbers to their events. And they document the staggering number of youth ministry practitioners who are drawn to national youth worker training events.

But when I speak of the crisis in youth ministry, I'm not suggesting that our traditional youth ministry models have failed to get students and their leaders to attend meetings. I readily admit that we have become quite proficient at that process. But I still insist that there is a crisis.

There is little doubt that there are more *successful* youth ministries today than there were twenty years ago. But take a look at the long-term, cumulative results of youth ministry:

- George Barna, in his *Index of Leading Spiritual Indicators,* documents that when thousands of believers were asked to rate what churches do best and what they do worst, "creating programs for teenagers" came in *dead last.*[1]

- William Willimon and Robert Wilson describe this crisis from the perspective of the United Methodist Church. They target their denomination's "inability to retain . . . young people, after their maturity, in the church" as one of the chief causes of decline in their denomination.

- Barna's research indicates that in spite of the fact that more and more youth are participating in our programs, those teenagers are not growing up to be adults who participate in church any more than they did almost thirty years ago. He writes:

    Since 1970, there has been no appreciable change in the proportion of adults who attend church services at any time during the week. This is true in spite of a growing number of churches, increased church spending for advertising and promotion, and the availability of more sophisticated techniques for informing people of a church's existence.[2]

- Most young people who disaffiliate with the church do so by the time they are sixteen. Research confirms that youth who drop out of the church do so not when they leave for college, as is often assumed, but while they are still in high school.[3]

- The struggles in my own denomination, the Presbyterian Church (USA), are symptomatic of the crisis in other mainline churches, all of which have had increasing difficulty hanging on to their youth once they become adults. Tom Gillespie, president of Princeton Seminary, has pinpointed this problem:

    The truth of the matter is that the chief cause of our membership decline is our inability over the past quarter of a century to translate our faith to our children. Put simply, we are unable to keep our children in the church when they become adults. As a result, we are not only a dwindling church but an aging church as well.[4]

The crisis in youth ministry is, simply put, that the ways we have been doing youth ministry have not been effective in leading our young people to mature Christian adulthood. Even with the massive increase in funding and training for youth ministry, even with the exponential increase in the number of resources available to those of us doing youth ministry, we are seeing no appreciable increase in the percentage of adults in our culture who are living out their faith for themselves.

Let's put it this way: How would we evaluate an automotive production plant that brought only a small percentage of its cars off the assembly line, ready to be shipped to customers? Managers could point to the efficiency of the workers on the assembly line, the new developments in technology or the increased morale of the staff. But if the company was not doing what it was created to do, namely, to produce cars, *crisis* would not be too strong a word to describe its situation.

> **The ways we have been doing youth ministry have not been effective in leading our young people to mature Christian adulthood.**

WANTED: MATURE CHRISTIAN ADULTS

We can't address this crisis simply by working harder to get more students to participate in our programs. The crisis is that we are not leading teenagers to *mature Christian adulthood.*

But what exactly is "mature Christian adulthood"?

I have found table 1 to be a helpful starting point as a contrast between the kinds of attitudes we hope our youth will grow out of and those we hope they will grow into.

If our youth programs are well attended, it's easy for us to be satisfied with childish faith. But attitudes of spiritual maturity are created as young people move out of the comfortable bubble of the youth program and live

Table 1. Comparison of Childish Faith and Mature Adult Faith

Childhood Faith	Mature Adult Faith
Good Christians don't have pain or disappointment.	God uses our pain and disappointment to make us better Christians.
God helps those who help themselves.	God helps those who admit their own helplessness.
God wants to make us happy.	God wants to make us into the image of Jesus.
Faith will help us always explain what God is doing (things always work out).	Faith helps us stand under God's sovereignty even when we have no idea what God is doing.
The closer we get to God, the more perfect we become.	The closer we get to God, the more we become aware of our own sinfulness.
Mature Christians have answers.	Mature Christians can wrestle honestly with tough questions because we trust that God has the answers.
Good Christians are always strong.	Our strength is in admitting our weakness.
We go to church because our friends are there, we have great leaders, and we get something out of it.	We go to church because we belong to the body of Christ.

out their faith through the challenging—and often monotonous—experiences of life.

Jim Rayburn, the founder of Young Life, is frequently quoted as saying, "It's a sin to bore a kid with the gospel." Being, in many ways, a product of Young Life myself, I have a deep appreciation for what Rayburn was getting at; namely, that the traditional structures of the church are often obstacles rather than windows through which we see Christ.

But keeping teenagers from ever being bored in their faith deprives them of the opportunity to develop the discipline and perseverance they need to live the Christian life. Oswald Chambers was right when he

If our youth programs are well attended, it's easy for us to be satisfied with childish faith.

said "Drudgery is the touchstone of character." It is precisely in those experiences that teenagers might describe as "boring" that the Christian character is often formed. In that sense, I wonder if it isn't more of a sin to imply to young people by our programming and our style that the Christian life is always fun and never boring.

Christian faith may begin on the mountaintop, but Christian character is formed in the crucible of pain. We should not be shocked, then, to discover that the depth of faith maturity among Christians in our country pales in comparison to that of Christians who have lived out their faith under the shadow of persecution.

If our programs are training teenagers to be reactive, immature Christians, we can expect those young people will eventually become discouraged by the difficulty and boredom of the Christian life.

Mature Christian adults, then, are those people who no longer depend on whistles and bells to motivate them to live out their faith. They have become proactive Christians—not reactive ones. When young people grow up to be *reactive* Christian adults, they are constantly waiting for someone or something to attract them, to involve them, to impress them. A reactive Christian always puts the responsibility for his or her spiritual life on someone else.

If our programs are training teenagers to be reactive, immature Christians, we can expect those young people will eventually become discouraged by the difficulty and boredom of the Christian life. Could it be that the much of our effort in programming and publicity may, in fact, move teens away from, rather than toward, mature Christian adulthood?

THE RIGHT NUMBERS

What a great night it had been! It seemed like young people were crammed into every corner of the room. We had pulled out all the stops for this first

Sunday night after Easter. For the first time in my six years at this church, we had more than one hundred young people together. Parents and church colleagues patted me on the back, and I drove home satisfied that we had finally begun to get this program off the ground. But even as I breathed a satisfied sigh of self-congratulation, a vague uneasiness came over me.

I began to wonder, *What was Jesus feeling when the crowd gathered on Palm Sunday, less than a week before his death? Was he thrilled by the attendance and their enthusiasm, or could he see through the crowd to the process of what they were already becoming? What do numbers really tell us anyway?*

We may live in a culture in which bigger has become synonymous with better, but we serve a Lord who spoke of his kingdom in terms of a mustard seed, a widow's mite and a single lost sheep. I love building a crowd. It makes me feel good. It makes me look good. And because of what building a crowd does for me, I have often mistaken short-term success for long-term effectiveness.

The shortsighted standard of success of traditional youth ministry reminds me of a "Hagar the Horrible" cartoon. Hagar has his men in a Viking ship rowing with all their might, but they are in complete confusion. After several frames, they finally begin to stroke together. In the next to the last frame, Hagar praises his men, "You've finally gotten it! Now we're going somewhere!" And the final frame shows the enthusiastic group of soldiers rowing themselves . . . off the edge of the earth. Ultimately, Hagar didn't know where he was leading his group. In fact, his enthusiasm about their "progress" in many ways blinded him to the frightening result of the direction they were going.

But as ironic as it may sound, my complaint is not that we are too concerned with numbers. My concern is that we don't take numbers seriously enough. The truth is that avoidance of numbers certainly isn't characteristic of the New Testament writers.

- Jesus knew exactly how many disciples he had. Often they are referred to not as the disciples but simply as "the Twelve."

- Jesus sent out seventy disciples to minister.

- More than four thousand people were fed miraculously at one event and more than five thousand at another.

- Luke tells us that in the early days of the church three thousand were saved in a single day.

- Paul reminds us that Jesus appeared to more than five hundred people after his resurrection.

- The shepherd in Jesus' parable would never have known about the one missing sheep if he had not been obsessed with numbers.

As biblical Christians, we don't need to be embarrassed about using numbers. But frequently youth workers and churches evaluate their success or failure by the *wrong* numbers.

I interviewed the pastor of a small church recently. I could tell by the tone in his voice that he felt their youth ministry was a failure. He expressed his disappointment about their youth program—about how hard it was to get teenagers to come, and about how few of their youth programs had actually worked. I asked about his numbers, and he explained despairingly that the church had eighteen young people. As I pressed him further, I learned that of that group, fifteen were involved in the life of the church *every week!* The pastor, somewhat embarrassed, explained that most of their involvement was not with other youth but with adults in the church. He evaluated his youth ministry as unsuccessful because he couldn't get roomfuls of teenagers together for a youth meeting.

On the same day I visited a church in the same city that had more than ten thousand members. I spoke to its youth minister as he was on his way out the door and only had time to ask him a few questions, so of course I asked about numbers. "How many young people do you have in your group?" I asked.

"About two hundred," he responded, without an ounce of arrogance, but with an obvious air of success.

"And how many students are on your rolls?"

"About four hundred." He hesitated and explained, "We have decided that the best way to build our group is to have about twice as many on the rolls as we expect to see come. We spend our time with the ones that show up. It *works*."

Both of these youth leaders were looking at the wrong numbers. The one who had fifteen out of eighteen involved weekly felt like a failure because, compared to other churches in town, he just didn't have many teens attending youth meetings. And the youth worker whose ministry was essentially ignoring two hundred students felt like a success, simply because of the size of the group.

The ironic fact for most of us is that we spend huge amounts of energy getting *more* teens involved while ignoring most of the ones God has already given us. It's no coincidence that once Jesus chose the Twelve (the ones for whom he would be responsible), he didn't go out looking for more!

THE SEARCH FOR NEW MODELS

Mark Senter, in his comprehensive history of youth ministry in the United States, suggests that every fifty years or so, one or two major youth ministry agencies are recognized as the pacesetters for that era. Although the history doesn't fall out into exact fifty-year stages, Senter traces a definite pattern that can help us understand the current state of flux in youth ministry in the United States:

- 1830s-1850s: Sunday School Union and Young Men's Christian Association

- 1890s: Society for Christian Endeavor

- 1940s: Youth for Christ and Young Life

- 1990s: ????

Not only does Senter identify an approximately fifty-year pattern between stages, he also documents a clear pattern within each stage. Each of these movements is carried along for the first twenty or thirty years by a wave of excitement and constant innovation. By the thirty-year point, each begins to become institutionalized, its strategies codified into planning manuals and many of its methods adopted by the church. And by the end of the fifty years, the once cutting-edge ministries have become tame institutions, setting the stage for a new movement to begin.

If Mark Senter is right (and I think he is), we are in a time ripe for the emergence of new movements to lead the way in the next youth ministry cycle. The shape of youth ministry is in transition across the United States. The Young Life and Youth for Christ ministries both had significant turnover in their senior leadership in the 1990s. Although teens in some locations are attending these groups in record numbers, these parachurch groups are themselves in a process of identity clarification, as each transitions from an identity as a "movement" to an identity as an "institution."[5] Senter explains:

> A study of history suggests we are about to see a fundamental departure from what we have understood to be youth ministry during the closing decades of the twentieth century. Though most parachurch agencies and denominational programs will continue to exist and make contributions, . . . their strategies have become flawed. . . . A new movement is about to appear and may already be emerging.[6]

Mike Yaconelli, in an address at the National Youth Workers Convention, seemed to be suggesting the same thing:

> Kids today are unlike any other generation of kids we've ever had to work with in youth ministry. All of the techniques, all of the strategies, all of the philosophies that we all are using and grew up with don't work any more. But if we don't wake up in the church and begin to radically alter and change what it is that we're doing with kids, we've lost them.[7]

Traditional youth ministry in the church today may have become little more than a hodgepodge of the structural remains of youth ministry dinosaurs. Every church has a youth Sunday-school program. Why? Because every church has always had a youth Sunday-school program. Almost every church also has a Sunday-night youth program. Why? Because we can't seem to let go of the structure that worked so well at the beginning of the 1900s. And nearly every church youth ministry has developed a fragmented collection of parachurch resources and ideas about youth discipleship groups, special events, mission trips and so on.

The next stage of youth ministry will not be found by returning to a primary dependence on any of these structures. The answer to the crisis in youth ministry does not lie in infusing our tired structures with life. We need an entirely new way of looking at youth ministry.

IMPLICATIONS FOR MINISTRY

1. Now, more than ever, churches need to concentrate on numbers, making every effort to be faithful in providing a ministry to the students God has given to the church.

2. Realistically, only a limited number of teenagers can be given leadership in the youth program. But most teenagers can be given a ministry alongside an adult in the church, a ministry that benefits someone other than the youth.

3. It is time to think about youth ministry in a new way. Invite a friend or a group of stakeholders to read through this book with you.

WILD HAIR IDEA

These are years for bold experimentation in youth ministry. Churches should not be afraid to step back from some of the sacred structures of Sunday school and youth group in order to develop a ministry to teenagers that is clearly designed to build long-term faith maturity. At the end of each chapter I will give one Wild Hair Idea for those churches willing and able to step radically away from what is expected.

*The thing that impresses me most about America
is the way parents obey their children.*

EDWARD, DUKE OF WINDSOR (1895-1977)

*Adolescence has become a waiting period
of enforced leisure with few responsibilities and
little or no meaningful contact with adults.*

ADOLESCENT ROLELESSNESS IN MODERN SOCIETY,
A REPORT OF THE CARNEGIE COUNCIL ON ADOLESCENT DEVELOPMENT

*Ours is the only era in the entire history
of human life on this planet in which the "elders"
of the tribe ask its newer members what the tribal rules
and standards of expected behavior would be.*

PAUL RAMSEY, ETHICIST, PRINCETON UNIVERSITY

*More often than not, children are learning major value systems in life
from the horizontal peer-culture. The vertical structure is not there
in adequate increments of time or intensity to do the job.*

GORDON MacDONALD,
THE EFFECTIVE FATHER

*When peers have dialogue primarily with peers,
they fail to be exposed to those with more advanced insights
and more highly developed faculties. . . .
Our children, who are constantly engrossed in peer-centered activities,
interact minimally with those more mature than themselves.*

STEPHEN GLENN AND JANE NELSEN,
RAISING SELF-RELIANT CHILDREN IN A SELF-INDULGENT WORLD

*The culture of the electronic media prescribes perpetual adolescence
and consumption as developmental ideals.
Indeed, perpetual adolescence and consumption constitute the
twin-pronged gospel of these media.*

QUENTIN J. SCHULTZE ET AL.,
DANCING IN THE DARK

2 Is Anybody Out There?

The Growth of Teenage Isolation

Teenagers today are in trouble. And what they don't know can literally kill them. We are sending our kids into adulthood ill prepared for the increasing demands of our complex society. Like so many children in the Middle East who defend themselves only by throwing rocks at soldiers with machine guns, this generation of teenagers enters the confusing battleground of adulthood armed with nothing more than vague values and innocuous religious experiences.

As in any war, there have been casualties. Teenagers are dying at a higher rate than they were forty years ago—victims of accidents, suicide, homicide, drugs and alcohol. While the members of every other age group are more likely to *live* than they were forty years ago, adolescence has become for many a life-and-death obstacle course.

Most of us who work with teenagers have heard the negative statistics. But we don't have to read them to know they are true. We work with the teenage boy who has been in and out of rehabilitation three times. We visit the hospital where one of our college girls rotates comatose on a board for months because of an accident after drinking at a fraternity party. And we've stood beside enough premature graves to know that something is very wrong.

Social scientists and armchair politicians all seem to have their explanations, from the deterioration of public education to the breakdown of the American family. Without a doubt, no single factor is entirely responsible for the deteriorating developmental environment our teenagers face. But I'm convinced that a single trend in our culture has precipitated the crisis more than any other factor. And until our approaches to youth ministry begin to take this trend seriously, our ministry to young people will be severely limited in its impact.

THE ROOT OF THE CRISIS

We can point to any number of secondary reasons for our inability to lead our young people to mature Christian adulthood. We could point to the fact that most youth ministries today are funded for failure, setting aside just enough money to guarantee a frustrated staff and an ineffective ministry.[1] We could point to the fact that most churches hire youth staff members and recruit volunteers only for the short haul, making it impossible for youth in the church to develop friendships with durable, available adults.[2]

Granting our children the "privilege of being left alone" has served, in part, to create a wholesale epidemic of adult neglect of the next generation.

I believe that each of these causes is only background noise. We can find the primary cause of the current crisis in youth ministry in the ways that our culture and our churches have systematically isolated young people from the very relationships that are most likely to lead them to maturity. Granting our children the "privilege of being left alone"[3] has served, in part, to create a wholesale epidemic of adult neglect of the next generation. This audacious claim is precisely the thesis of Patricia Hersch in her groundbreaking study of adolescence in America, called *A Tribe Apart*. She writes,

> A clear picture of adolescents, of even our own children, eludes us—not necessarily because they are rebelling, or avoiding or evading us. *It is because we aren't there.* Not just parents, but any adults. American society has left its children behind as the cost of progress in the workplace. This isn't about working parents, right or wrong, but an issue for society to set its priorities and to pay attention to its young in the same way it pays attention to its income.[4]

The television series *Dawson's Creek* comes as close as anything to demonstrating how *adults* perceive the teenage experience. The producers of the show (I'm guessing there's not an adolescent in the bunch) leave viewers with the impression that the town of Capeside would change little if there were no parents or other adults present. In the make-believe world of *Dawson's Creek*, it is, in fact, the youth who are the dispensers of wisdom about their world. And those older than eighteen are either hopelessly out of touch or have little else to occupy their time than interfering with Dawson and his friends.

It's clear that young people grow to maturity in general, and to maturity in Christ in particular, by being around people who exhibit such maturity themselves. Margaret Mead, a renowned anthropologist, warned of the dangers of what she called a co-figurative culture, a culture in which all learning is horizontal, and little or no learning comes from an older and wiser generation.[5]

The obvious limitation of a co-figurative culture, or what Robert Bly calls a "sibling society," is that each generation has to relearn (and often incorrectly) a value system that can give them coherence and meaning. And Mary Pipher (of *Reviving Ophelia* fame) even goes so far as to pinpoint this phenomenon as the cause of much of our current social ills:

> A great deal of America's social sickness comes from age segregation. If 10 14-year-olds are grouped together, they will form a *Lord of the Flies* culture with its competitiveness and meanness. But if 10 people ages 2 to 80 are grouped together, they will fall into a natural age hierarchy that nurtures and teaches them all. For our own mental and societal health, we need to reconnect the age groups.[6]

ARENAS OF ISOLATION

In a recent research project, a group of seventy-five suburban teenagers were given beepers and belts and asked to write down exactly what they were doing and feeling at the exact moment the beeper sounded. After several months of observation, the results gave a frighteningly accurate portrait of how teens spend their time.

The single most disturbing conclusion, as recorded in the book *Being Adolescent* by Mihaly Csikzentmihalyi and Reed Larson, was the unprecedented unavailability of adults in teenagers' lives. The study revealed that teenagers spend less than seven percent of their waking hours with *any* adults, while spending approximately half of their time with peers.[7]

Increasingly isolated from the adult world, more children and youth simply fend for themselves, often under the dispassionate care of television and other technology, sometimes under the thumb of shameful abuse and neglect. Emotionally available neighbors, grandparents, teachers or coaches are quickly moving to the endangered species list, as the pace of life topples over itself and the number of children who need care vastly outpaces the number of adults who choose to be available to them. And even when young people are with adults, it's usually in a large group setting in which the teenagers are being entertained, informed or directed by those adults, leaving little opportunity for the dialogue and collaboration required for youth to learn adult values.

Cornell University's Urie Bronfenbrenner cites nine cultural shifts that have taken place during the past generation, changes which have increasingly separated children and youth from the world of adults, especially the adults in their own families:

1. fathers' vocational choices that remove them from the home for lengthy periods of time

2. an increase in the number of working mothers

3. a critical escalation in the divorce rate

4. a rapid increase in single-parent families

5. a steady decline in the extended family

6. the evolution of the physical environment of the home (family rooms, playrooms and master bedrooms)

7. the replacement of adults by the peer group

8. the isolation of children from the work world

9. the insulation of schools from the rest of society

This last factor has caused Bronfenbrenner to describe the current U.S. educational system as "one of the most potent breeding grounds for alienation in American society."[8] Though he wrote these words in 1974, the trend toward isolation has not been significantly checked since that time. In neighborhoods, schools, social activities, their own families and even at church, young people are afforded less and less opportunity to be with adults.

NEIGHBORHOODS

I grew up in a Presbyterian manse. Next door to our home was Mr. Flanders's Schwinn bike shop. When I had nothing to do (which was often), I would travel the sidewalk over to Mr. Flanders's shop and look at his coin collections or run my fingers over the new bikes. Honestly, I don't remember one thing he ever said to me, but I do remember he was someone who let me peek into what it was like to be an adult. I was not close to Mr. Flanders; he was not a mentor. But he was a part of my developmental landscape—an entrée into the adult world.

The closest thing some children have to an available adult is 911.

By 1990 the number of Americans who say they never spend time with their neighbors actually doubled, and seventy-two percent of us indicated that we didn't know our neighbors at all.[9] Children and teenagers in our culture are more and more removed from the "Mr. Flanders" kind of adult—an adult whom they can know for free, not a tutor or a teacher or a parent or a babysitter or even a youth leader.

Many children have their schedules so packed that even if adults were available there would be little opportunity to spend time with them. From organized sports leagues to the growing amount of homework schools are pressured to give, teens have little time to do anything but check their schedules and run. Most young people grow up in neighborhoods populated by wandering children and dogs but very few visible adults. Sadly enough, the closest thing some children have to an available adult in their neighborhood is 911.

SCHOOLS

Schools too have increasingly isolated junior high and high school students from the adult world. In some schools, teachers now have classes with as many as forty students. With the classes and teachers changing every fifty minutes, it's rare, if not impossible, for the average student to have individual time to talk with his or her teachers.

Schools are no longer places in which the less mature have the opportunity to interact with the more mature. Students are intentionally stratified to limit class groupings to only those within a certain range of ability. This horizontal peer structure may be a more *efficient* way to teach, but this pattern prevents youth from developing *effective* vertical relationships that will promote their maturity.

Though a growing number of very committed teachers have a tremendous impact on the values of their students, teachers have little or no time for nondirective conversations with their students. The majority of the time teenagers spend in school is dedicated to isolated work alone and periodically with peers, but seldom in meaningful conversation with adults.

SOCIAL ACTIVITIES

Teenagers are also increasingly "on their own" when it comes to choosing social activities. From Pulaski, Tennessee, to New York, New York, resident teenagers complain that there is "nothing to do."

"Hanging out" with friends or partying in an adult-free home has become the norm for adolescent social life. At one such party, a fight broke out between kids from rival high schools. In the process a high school boy was stabbed and subsequently died. Reporters asked the parents who hosted the party, "Where were you that evening?"

Their answer offers a telling metaphor. They said, "We were upstairs. *We just didn't want to get in the kids' way.*" When adults choose to stay out of the kids' way, the consequences can be fatal.

When I was a college student, my friends and I discovered an unusual place where children and teenagers could "try on" being adults. On Friday nights, we would load up in my 1962 VW bug and drive twenty miles to the American Legion Hall in Elk, Texas, for a night of two-stepping, with an occasional waltz or polka thrown in. Not only did the trip to Elk break the pizza and movie monotony, but I realize now that we had stumbled into one of the few places on the planet where we could be next to eighty-year-old sweethearts and eight-year-old puppy lovers having fun together. I'm sure there are places like Elk, Texas, where our kids can go for fun, but I'm hard pressed to think of one in my city.

FAMILIES

Without question, the most damaging isolation that teenagers in our culture experience is within their own families. American parents spend less time with their children than do parents in any other country in the world, according to Harvard psychiatrist Armand Nicholi. Fifty years ago, families worked and ate together by necessity. Teenagers and parents had little choice but to spend hours and hours together. In the process, young people couldn't avoid observing and listening in on the adult world, giving youth exposure that laid a natural track into adulthood.

As families prospered, they no longer found it necessary to work and eat together. The natural bridge from childhood to adulthood was severely weakened, and in some homes, removed altogether. With one in four young people now indicating that they have *never* had a meaningful conversation with their father,[10] is it any wonder that 76 percent of the 1,200 teens surveyed in *USA Today* actually *want* their parents to spend more time with them?[11]

Andrée Aelion Brooks, in her eye-opening book *Children of Fast-Track Parents,* describes her interviews with scores of children and parents who seemed to have it all: "If there was one theme that constantly emerged from my conversations with the children it was a surprising undercurrent of aloneness—feelings of isolation from peers as well as parents despite their busy lives."[12]

THE CHURCH

It might be hoped that churches would stand in the gap and provide an environment in which children and youth could dialogue and collaborate with adults. But sadly enough, for many teenagers active in church, this is the one place where they may just be the most segregated from the world of adults. And the more "successful" the youth program, often the more exacerbated the isolation becomes.

Most "successful" youth ministries have their own youth Sunday school, youth missions, youth small groups, youth evangelism teams, youth worship, youth budget, youth interns, youth committees, youth offering, youth Bible studies, youth "elders" (like "jumbo shrimp?"), youth centers, youth choir, youth rooms, youth discipleship programs, youth conferences, youth retreats, youth fundraisers and (my personal favorite) youth ministers.

Even when families do worship together, almost inevitably the parents sit together, the children are shuffled off to "children's church," and the youth sit in the balcony. The church, the one place where teenagers could logically be linked to the world of adults, has missed the opportunity.

Stuart Cummings-Bond has creatively referred to this isolation as the "one-eared Mickey Mouse." He uses figure 1 to describe how, in most churches, the program of the church and the youth ministry make only tangential contact.

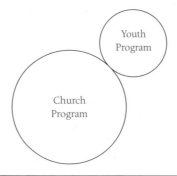

Figure 1. The one-eared Mickey Mouse. Stuart Cummings-Bond, "The One-Eared Mickey Mouse," *Youthworker,* Fall 1989, p. 76.

I was fortunate enough to grow up in a church small enough that it could never sustain a "successful" youth ministry for more than a few months. We had moments when things went beautifully, but for the most part, we struggled along, year after year, with our ten- to fifteen-member youth group.

We spent a lot of time reinventing the wheel, figuring things out by ourselves. In our sporadic youth group meetings, we played a lot of football, talked about sex more than a few times and had more lock-ins than I care to count. And because our Presbyterian church had trouble hanging on to our part-time Baptist youth directors for very long, our pastor wound up spending a lot of time with the teenagers. He knew all of our names. He knew our parents. And he helped us as we muddled along together. But, on the whole, almost every teenager in our youth group was in church every week. *Every* one of us knew that we belonged.

Our little church's youth ministry wasn't successful enough to experience the "one-eared Mickey." But through my relationship with the pastor and even in the "boring" worship service, I saw and heard the gospel. As a matter of fact, it was in this church, after our typically mediocre "Youth Sunday," that an elderly woman, Edna Lou Sullivan, pulled me aside and said, "Honey, you are going to be a minister someday." Almost thirty years later, I still consider her words the first step in my call to the ministry.

The less capable the church is at programming, the more responsibility the youth and adults in the church will be required to take, and the more time they wind up spending together to make the program work. There are worse things a church can do for its teenagers than providing miserable programs for them—patently isolating them from Christian adults is at the top of that list.

MECHANIC OR SURGEON?

Churches that use the traditional model for youth ministry approach the task of working with students much like a mechanic would. When a mechanic sees a problem in an engine, he isolates the problem, and then he fixes it.

When leaders in American churches began to see teenagers' growing disinterest with the church, they responded like a good mechanic: isolate and fix. Church leaders assumed that by isolating the youth department into its own independent subgroup, they could create a curriculum that would instill all the values necessary for youth to grow to mature Christian adulthood. But the Christian community is not a machine. In fact, the "solution" of isolation itself created a much worse problem.

Because teenagers are an integral part of the *body* of Christ, perhaps we would be better off to approach this problem less as a mechanic would and more as a physician would. When an organ is removed from a living body, that organ dies, and often the body dies along with it. The same principle is true in the body of Christ. Whatever new models for youth ministry we develop must take seriously the fact that teenagers grow toward mature Christian adulthood as they are connected to the total body of Christ, not isolated from it.

IMPLICATIONS FOR MINISTRY

1. Try to go one month without isolating teenagers from the rest of the church. Instead, integrate them with adults in every typical youth ministry setting— youth could join different adult Sunday-school classes or an adult small group, help in the nursery and help teach the children's classes.

2. Leaders could learn a great deal simply by finding out how many and which adults their teenagers spend their time with. A simple survey at the beginning of class, asking kids to list every adult they talked with over the past month and how long they spent talking, would be an informative tool for youth leaders.

3. Establish a task force to determine ways that the church can provide more opportunities for the teenagers in the church to build relationships with adults in the church. Choose one priority to implement each year for the next three years.

WILD HAIR IDEA

Instead of youth group one night, assign the kids the job of having a half-hour visit with some adult outside of their family. Wait to have youth group again until each student has told you a little something about his or her visit.

Lack of dialogue and collaboration between
the more mature and less mature threatens the bonds of
closeness, trust, dignity, and respect that hold our society together. . . .
People are basically tribal creatures.
Human beings have never done well in isolation.
STEPHEN GLENN AND JANE NELSEN,
RAISING SELF-RELIANT CHILDREN IN A SELF-INDULGENT WORLD

The generation that knows only itself
is destined to remain adolescent forever.
SIGN IN THE UNIVERSITY OF COLORADO LIBRARY

Over the years, the tone of discourse on adolescents
has become shrill and frightened. . . .
Maybe if we just tell adolescents to say no, no, no to
everything we disapprove of, maybe then they will be okay.
But the piecemeal attempts to mend, motivate, or rescue them
obscure the larger reality: We don't know them.
PATRICIA HERSCH, *A TRIBE APART*

Never forget that the children of over-committed, harassed,
exhausted parents are sitting ducks for the con men of our time.
JAMES DOBSON, *CHILDREN AT RISK*

The young are in character prone to desire and ready to carry
any desire they may have formed into action.
Of bodily desires, it is the sexual to which they are most disposed
to give way, and in regard to sexual desire they exercise no self-restraint.
They are changeful too, and fickle in their desires
which are as transitory as they are vehement;
for their wishes are keen without being permanent,
like a sick man's fits of hunger and thirst.
ARISTOTLE, 4TH CENTURY B.C.

The inattention to children by our society poses a greater threat to our
safety, harmony and productivity than any external enemy.
MARIAN WRIGHT EDELMAN, CHILDREN'S DEFENSE FUND

In a way it's a good thing adults don't know much about teens.
If they knew all about us, they'd puke.
FOURTEEN-YEAR-OLD STUDENT QUOTED IN THE *CHICAGO TRIBUNE*

3 THE DEVELOPMENTAL DISASTER

The Impact of Teenage Isolation

One of the summer highlights for our Texas youth group was its annual tubing trip, three or four hours down the highway to the southern Texas town of New Braunfuls. Even with having to collect, inflate and load fifty inner tubes onto the top of the church bus, I loved everything about this trip. I loved the things that happened on the bus on the way down. I loved being catapulted down the river chute with the kids. And I loved ending the day with a leisurely three-mile float downriver.

But between the raucous screams of the chute and the relaxing sighs of the float, there was a challenge: making it over that simple three-foot waterfall. Most of us were simply thrown out of our tubes, head over heels into the rushing water. But often those who weren't thrown from their tubes found themselves stuck at the bottom of the falls. No matter how vigorously they paddled, no matter how frantically they tried, they found themselves immobilized by the relentless pull of a current that actually drew them back toward the falls. The peculiar hydraulic current of that place kept tubers stuck, unable to move forward. Unless they got out of their tubes or had someone who had already made it through the falls help them, there was simply no way out.

I can think of no better image for the developmental treadmill our culture has created for its young people. Paddle as they might to move away from childhood and toward independence, the current of their own culture conspires to pull them back, keeping them tied to immaturity and dependence.

As the bridge from childhood to adulthood gets longer and longer, young people find themselves mired in a peer-centered culture that no longer moves them naturally into adulthood. And unless they can find the footing to step out of that culture, they can be stuck in a perpetual adolescence.

Imagine what would happen if a group of inexperienced middle school students were given the task of teaching each other how to scuba dive. One boy might assure the group that he understands how it's done, since he's seen it a hundred times on television. One of the girls might remember a book about sea explorers she checked out in the third grade. And a third person might brag that his dad has the entire *Sea Hunt* series on DVD. They might even all agree that one or more of them know what they are talking about. But if they actually attempted to teach each other to scuba dive, the consequences could be fatal.

The bridge from childhood to adulthood is getting longer and longer.

Teenagers won't learn the skills required of mature adults in a peer-centered youth Sunday-school class. They won't learn these skills by talking with their friends. The maturation process occurs as the less mature have repeated opportunities to observe, dialogue and collaborate with the more mature. By denying teenagers opportunities for this kind of involvement with adults, our culture sends its youth into the adult years relationally, mentally and morally unprepared for the challenges of adulthood.

RELATIONAL RETARDATION

A film producer described the crisis among today's youth in this way:

> For too long, young people have been told that their greatest problems are drugs, sex, alcohol, etc. . . . These are, in fact, only symptoms of a much greater disease. The disease of youth is [that their key relationships] are in disarray, their relationships with God, self, parents, friends, and the world.[1]

The movie *The Breakfast Club* gives a clue to the cause of this "disease" in relationships. In the movie, a group of mismatched teenagers are serving detention together on a Saturday morning. The only significant adult in the movie is the curiously absent assistant principal, who, apart from periodically barking threats, keeps himself safely outside the detention room.

After some uncomfortable moments (and a few joints of marijuana), the group begins to talk. Soon the intimacy of the group grows intense. They have a taste of transparent, honest relationships. But they admit that when they go back to school on Monday, there is little chance these friendships will continue. Often, the best our culture has to offer its youth relationally is a series of fragmented experiences of intimacy that can seldom be sustained.

Characteristically, teenagers seldom have the natural relational and developmental capacity to maintain committed relationships for extended periods of time. They flow in and out of relationships with their peers. This year's enemy may be next year's best friend. And even in more "committed" relationships, the focus is on the often-superficial skills of "dating," "going together" and "breaking up."

> Often, the best our culture has to offer its youth relationally is a series of fragmented experiences of intimacy that can seldom be sustained.

But one of the keys to successful adult relationships beyond the superficial level (for example, parenting, marriage and church membership) is a commitment to demonstrate love in spite of pain, conflict or frustration. Young people learn to love through the long haul as they are surrounded by adults who, over and over again, demonstrate this kind of enduring, long-suffering love. Could it be that one of the reasons for the Western nations' devastating divorce rate is that the current of our culture works against its young people ever developing the skills of genuine love?

I recently talked with a man whose wife decided that their marriage was "not going to work out." She was not interested in counseling. She just wanted their marriage to end. Her final words to him as he walked out the door sounded hauntingly reminiscent of the words a teenager would use to break up with her boyfriend: "I just want to be friends."

If a teenage boy stops feeling love for his girlfriend or he is attracted to another girl, he can simply break up and go out with someone else. In a marriage, when a man stops feeling love for his wife or is attracted to someone else's wife, the mature Christian adult behaves very differently.

In youth culture, the natural, God-ordained process of attraction—"falling in love"—has been elevated to consume a young person's understanding of what real love is. Teenagers have naturally absorbed the belief that they are simply victims of feelings that come and go. Consequently, they learn to obey "that loving feeling" (or the lack thereof) at all costs, leaving them lacking the relational maturity to establish long-term relationships.

COGNITIVE FRAGMENTATION

Because teenagers now have less time in dialogue with adults, the door has been opened for the media to play a much more powerful role in the formation of their values. Even *TV Guide* has acknowledged that the more children are isolated from their parents, the more susceptible those children are to the power of the television:

> The children who are more inclined to go along with television, to lap up its messages uncritically, are those who have received little in the way of guidance at home, hence their susceptibility to whatever the big tube sends their way.[2]

What makes the television's impact so potent is the radical change that has taken place in the way we process information. Neil Postman, in his challenging book *Amusing Ourselves to Death,* claims that American society has actually gone through a transformation in the way we think, having moved from a word-centered culture to an image-centered culture. It's likely, Postman argues, that in their time, most of the first fifteen U.S. presidents would not have even been recognized if the average American had passed them on the street. But by contrast, when we think of George Bush, Billy Graham or Albert Einstein, what comes to our minds is an image, and most of us have few words to link with that image.

Postman points to the inherent danger of this new kind of thinking:

> You can only photograph a particular fragment of the here-and-now—a cliff or a certain terrain, in a certain condition of light; a wave at a moment in time, from a particular point of view. And just as "nature" and

"the sea" cannot be photographed, such larger abstractions as truth, honor, love, falsehood cannot be talked about in the lexicon of pictures.[3]

Our culture's growing dependence on images for thinking has limited our ability to make moral decisions or even understand abstract moral concepts. When our young people are taught to speak and think primarily in the language of images and not of logical thoughts, moral principles and Christian values may sound to them like so much babbling in a different language. Living in an image-centered culture produces adults who are moved more by impression than by rational thinking.

The ability to sustain a logical, linear argument is developed primarily in the context of extended discourse with thinking adults. But because of their isolation from the world of adults, even in our educational system, teenagers seldom have opportunity to learn and practice the skills of assessment and judgment with those who actually *have* those skills. As a result, most teenagers learn to think and argue only anecdotally (and to respond most energetically to anecdotal proofs), using fragmented images and emotional stories instead of logical argument.

Adults in an image-centered culture are moved more by impression than by rational thinking.

As a professor of history at Smith College, R. Jackson Wilson has had twenty-five years to observe students and their abilities. His observation of his current students' abilities confirms this thesis: "Students are ready to tell you how they feel about an issue, but they have never learned how to construct a rational argument to defend their opinions."[4]

Teenagers' isolation from adults leaves them severely limited in their ability to think critically. They are easily swayed by what feels right at the moment, whether it's going to church, buying a $200 pair of tennis shoes or having sex. Without the habit of critical thinking, our teenagers become easy prey to anyone who has something to sell.

MORAL HANDICAP

The haunting story of fourteen-year-old Rod Matthews serves as a warning to a culture gone adrift. Rod was not interested in the things that normally interest teenagers. Neither sports nor books were enough to quench his insatiable boredom. Only one thing excited him: death. He spent hours watching the video *Faces of Death*, a collection of film clips of people dying violently. Rod's curiosity about death led him to want to see death personally, not just on the television or movie screen.

Eventually he found a way to satisfy his curiosity. One winter afternoon he lured a friend out into the woods and proceeded to beat him to death with a baseball bat. During his trial for murder, a child psychiatrist made the most telling remark. When asked to give a clinical evaluation of Rod's condition, the doctor's assessment was that Rod was not insane in the conventional sense but that he simply didn't "know right from wrong. . . . He [was] *morally handicapped.*"[5]

Rod's story represents the extreme result of a society that abandons its responsibility for teaching moral values to its children. A horizontal peer culture is not enough. When the vertical structure connecting children with adults has eroded, should we be surprised that our children grow up having difficulty establishing any firm values of their own? It only makes sense, then, that a recent study of seventh and eighth graders revealed that those who spent more time with peers were much more likely to be abusers of alcohol and drugs than those teens who spent more time with family.[6]

The "Just Say No" campaign of the 1980s was indicative of the moral (in)abilities of our young people. After spending millions of dollars on drug education campaigns that focused on giving young people rational reasons for not taking drugs, the U.S. government determined in the 1980s that a rational approach was not the way to reach this generation of young people. The "Just Say No" campaign was developed at least partly because leaders recognized that this new generation makes major moral decisions not by rational argument but by being "sold" a certain standard.[7]

The young people who are fortified with significant relationships with adults are consistently the ones who are able to resist involvement in negative behaviors. Their relationship with these adults gives teenagers perhaps the most compelling argument for making healthy moral choices. Stephen Glenn and Jane Nelsen's research confirms this thesis:

Peer influence correlates closely with the rise in rebellion, resistance, chemical abuse, and promiscuity. Children who have strong perceptions of closeness and trust with significant adults are highly resistant to peer influence and are more heavily influenced by those adults who validate them for who they are.[8]

Our kids are growing up in a culture that keeps them trapped in immaturity, training them to react to what is sold, rather than think and act proactively. As a result, their relational, cognitive and moral deficits have become the most common characteristics of this at-risk generation.

THE HIDDEN HAZARDS OF YOUTH CULTURE

Though the statistics and studies on this isolation are legion, they often mask the desperate aloneness that so many teenagers feel, an aloneness acted out in the self-destructive actions of millions each year. The following journal entry of a teenage girl writing several years ago for her high school English class portrays the pathos of this "alone" experience in all of its intensity:

No one is there . . .

My wounds are green and throbbing.
I can't scream any louder.

If they were here now
They would see
That the beauty that was out is now in
And the rottenness that was in is now out.

But no one will come.

Perhaps the most tragic shift during the past fifty years has been that we have begun to treat adolescents as adults rather than as those in the process of completing their childhood, in transition toward adulthood. Although there are many things about being a teenager that are to be honored and enjoyed, adolescence, like childhood, is transitional in character. The end result of adolescence is to no longer be an adolescent.

But for teenagers in our culture, the lines between childhood and adulthood have become increasingly blurred, so much so that many adults well into their twenties and thirties still behave in ways characteristic of adolescents. With few clear rites of passage, teenagers are in the double bind of being expected to make adult decisions in a world that persistently juvenilizes them.

When we idolize youth as an end in itself, we remove the healthy protection that growing things require. George Will pinpoints this problem: "In Randall Jarrell's novel *Pictures from an Institution* a foreign visitor says, 'You Americans do not rear children, you incite them; you give them food and shelter and applause.' The problem is juvenophilia."[9]

Cultures, by definition, pass on the best of what has been learned so that the best of that culture may be maintained. In other words, one of the prime functions of a culture is to perpetuate itself and its values. In the same way, the development of a separate youth culture has functioned to perpetuate adolescence.

> Teenagers are expected to make adult decisions in a world that persistently juvenilizes them.

The very existence of a youth culture places teenagers at cross-purposes with their own development. They need to leave the world of youth, but during their teenage years they are indoctrinated into a culture that functions to maintain their attachment to it.

Youth culture, like most youth ministries, is essentially an orphaning structure. It does not carry its members through life; rather, it orphans them at the very time they are most in need of a stable culture. Stephen Glenn has estimated that by the time an average American teenager is sixteen years old, he or she is "as morally mature as a 1950's 12-year-old, and five years behind European kids in abstract thinking."[10] The structures that carry young people to adulthood must become the focus of youth ministry for the next generation.

Street gangs provide the most blatant picture of the dysfunctional power of a youth culture. In a gang, there is authority, strict rules and punishment, and a shared sense of values. But all of these norms are determined by a group of young people not yet mature enough to make wise decisions consistently. The first and often only solution to a problem is violence (exactly what we might expect if we left a pre-school group to govern itself). We can ex-pect that any system run by children or teenagers (including a youth ministry) will be dysfunctional.

The very existence of a youth culture places teenagers at cross-purposes with their own development.

In many of our churches, if groups of more than ten young people are sitting to-gether in worship, they tend to act, at best, like children. They snicker, rattle candy wrappers, and often simply get up and leave. But if those same youth are sitting with their parents or divided up among the total congregation, they, almost without exception, imitate the behavior of the adults they are with.

We recently completed a six-week confirmation class for a group of thirty sixth-graders. The boys in the class were so energetic that they came to be affectionately labeled the "Young Nazis." Even with two pastors and three older high school youth in the group, the boys were successful in disrupting the class every week.

But on the day that the members of the class were introduced to the session by their "Elder Friends" (who, incidentally, sat next to them), we wondered if we were in a different class. The boys were quiet, attentive and respectful, imitating the values of the adults in the group.

A seven-year-old child went through his parents' devastating divorce. And for months after the divorce he was wetting his pants. His father tried everything to get his son to correct the problem. He read books. He took his son to the doctor. He sent off for programs. Nothing worked. Finally the father sat his seven-year-old child down and said, "What's going on? Babies do this!"

The boy answered back, "And their daddies hold them."

Often teenagers don't have the clear insight of this seven-year-old boy. But most want the same thing—they want to be held in a family where the love is secure, where they know they belong, where there is someone older and stronger to carry some of the load.

Increasingly, the message of adult culture to its youth has become "you're on your own." And this isolation (intentional or unintentional) has placed our culture squarely atop a demographic time bomb, and more and more voices are reporting that they can hear it ticking.

Our modern fascination with the professionalization of youth ministry may have kept us blissfully ignorant of our growing proficiency at rearranging deck chairs on the Titanic. Any approach to youth ministry in the new millennium must move beyond a myopic focus on programming and "relational ministry" done by a few enthusiastic, inexperienced, short-term, early-twenties youth leaders who stay around only long enough to "wow" our kids. Unless our new models of ministry can help our culture restore the "generational threads that used to weave their way into the fabric of growing up,"[11] our ministries will be severely limited in their long-term effectiveness.

Are we connecting our kids to nurturing relationships that will last them after they complete their teenage years?

The question we must ask is, "Are we connecting our kids to nurturing relationships that will last them after they complete their teenage years, or are we simply exploiting them as public relations tools to make our ministries appear successful?" I submit that unless we are making intentional, focused efforts at connecting kids with mature Christian adults in the church (not just their youth leaders), we are more like the vultures preying on kids at rock concerts and less like spiritual leaders praying that their children's lives would be founded upon the most eternal things.

IMPLICATIONS FOR MINISTRY

1. The most important priority a church can have in its work with teenagers is providing them with opportunities for significant dialogue and relationships with mature Christian adults. This priority does not require a massive budget or an extensive program. It does require a group of adult leaders in the church who will make the creation of relationships between adults and teenagers the central priority of the youth ministry.

2. Churches must not depend on the communication vehicles of youth culture (television with its frantic change of scenery for the chronically

bored, "contemporary" music with its "make me feel good" priority, and successful athletes with their stories of freedom from failure) to carry the demanding claims of the gospel. All of these means may be helpful thresholds to the Christian life, but they are not sufficient to carry the responsibility for developing spiritual maturity.

3. We must not be afraid to instill the value of participating in weekly corporate worship with the entire church family as a central priority for the youth ministry.

WILD HAIR IDEA

Challenge the youth and their leaders in the church to fast from the cultural vehicles of value transmission (television, recorded music, movies) for one month and share their experiences at the end of the month.

While you wait for your teenagers to grow up,
you can take comfort in the fact that by the time young people
reach their mid-twenties, their lines are almost always identical
to the lines their parents drew. . . . So perhaps the point is
not how we can get our kids to behave as we want them to,
but how can we be the kind of parents we ought to be so
that when our kids are like us, we'll like what they are.
JAY KESLER, *ENERGIZING YOUR TEENAGER'S FAITH*

It is no coincidence that all twentieth-century totalitarian orders
labored to destroy the family as a locus of identity and meaning
apart from the state. Totalitarianism strives . . . to require that
individuals never allow their commitments to specific others—
family, friends, comrades to weaken their commitment to the state.
To this idea, which can only be described as evil,
the family stands in defiance.
JEAN BETHKE ELSHTAIN, IN *REBUILDING THE NEST*

It is common wisdom to suggest that churches lose a
great many of their youth to non-affiliation during their college years.
Studies have shown, however, that the greatest share of disaffiliation
among youth occurs before college, and it is related to
how important religion is to the parents [and] the amount of love
and affection given a child (i.e., more love associated
with a greater tendency to affiliate).
MILTON COALTER, QUOTED IN *THE PRESBYTERIAN (U.S.A.)*
GENERAL ASSEMBLY REPORT OF THE TASK FORCE ON MEMBERSHIP

But if strangers and strange sights can shake the world of children, it takes the
people they know and love best to pull it out from under them like a chair.
FREDERICK BUECHNER, *SACRED JOURNEY*

Nothing has more power to influence a teenager's life—
for good or ill—than home and family.
Every youth ministry hour spent equipping parents to nurture faith
in their teenagers is like giving money to public television:
your gift is almost always doubled by a matching grant.
Parents will always out-influence even a great youth leader,
so it makes sense to invest where you'll get the best return.
RICK LAWRENCE, *TRENDWATCH*

4 SITTING ON A GOLD MINE

The Power of the Nuclear Family

I loved talking to Jay. And why wouldn't I? It seemed as if every time we talked, he had something positive to say about my work as his youth director, now more than twenty years ago. Jay always seemed to find his way to the heart of our youth ministry all through his junior high and high school years. In fact, he even went on to join the youth ministry staff of the church at one point. As I look at Jay now, as a husband and father in his mid-thirties, I see a man who has, without question, grown into a proactive Christian adult.

A decade or so ago, I decided to check out some of my thinking about family-based youth ministry theory with Jay. So I asked him, "How would you compare the impact your youth directors had on your Christian life with the impact your parents had?"

He said, "You guys were great and everything. . . . But honestly, I think if you had never been around, I would still be in the same place spiritually that I am today. My parents had a huge impact on my relationship with Christ."

It's time for a reality check.

THE HIDDEN CURRICULUM OF THE FAMILY

In the movie *Karate Kid,* Mr. Miagi, the wise old mentor, takes on the task of teaching karate to Daniel, an impatient young teenager who has asked for help. Facing the immediate pressure of bullies at school, Daniel is eager to become an expert in martial arts as quickly as possible. But Mr. Miagi has other plans.

Instead of teaching his student karate moves, the master teacher begins rather unconventionally. The old man gives Daniel laborious tasks to accomplish, tasks that take days to complete—"paint de fence," "wax de car," "sand de floor." But Daniel simply wants to learn karate. After days, perhaps weeks, of monotonous labor, his predictable frustration boils to the surface. Overcome with the reality of aching muscles, wasted hours and the fact that he has yet to learn a stitch of karate, Daniel storms off, only to be called back immediately by Mr. Miagi's authoritative summons: "Danielsan!"

What Daniel doesn't realize, until Mr. Miagi takes a surprising swing at him, is that he *has* been learning karate, without even realizing it. The mundane, repetitive, painful work has trained his muscles to move instinctively, teaching him more karate than any set of formal lessons could have ever taught. Beneath the apparently unrelated activity, the master teacher has a hidden curriculum.

Parents have this sort of formative effect on their children. All of the youth group and Sunday school lessons on "Communication," "Getting Along with Your Parents" and even "Discipleship" have minuscule impact compared to what children learn on a day-to-day basis as they "paint de fence" in their families.

Though social scientists have trouble agreeing on much of anything, most are clear in their recognition of the incomparable power (for better or for worse) of moms and dads in the faith and character formation of their children. Take, for example, the results of a study done recently by the National Center on Addiction and Substance Abuse (CASA). The survey of 1,115 teenagers revealed a clear link between certain types of parental behaviors and children who are likely to be free of chemical dependency. Here's a sampling of those parental habits:

1. They are engaged in their teens' lives, including helping with homework or attending teens' extracurricular activities.

2. They have at least five sit-down meals together weekly.

3. They attend religious services together with their teens.

4. They set curfews.

5. They see drug use as dangerous and morally wrong.[1]

But those of us older than thirty-five don't need to see the studies. The reality of our own parents' influence is all too obvious. I still remember the day several years ago when I looked into the mirror in horror, realizing for the first time that I looked less and less like the guy in my high school annual and more and more like my father.

I now realize that I developed most of my emotional, relational and spiritual reflexes in my family. And despite all I have read and taught about parenting and communication, I, like most adults, find myself doing the very things my parents did, even though I promised myself I would never do some of them. Without a single lesson from my parents on adulthood, my muscles were trained.

When I ask adults in the church to consider the influence their parents had on their own faith formation, the vast majority of them have little difficulty describing the immensity of that influence. And it is staggering that whenever I ask a group of Christian youth leaders how many of them came from a home in which at least one Christian parent was present, an average of 90 percent of the folks in the class raise their hands. And even in families in which neither parent was a Christian, the adult children confess that they bear some undeniable marks of the value system they grew up with.

Across the nation, churches are beginning to wake up to the fact that often the most faithful, long-term leaders of youth can actually be parents of youth themselves. Here's why: No one has more long-term interest in the students I work with than their parents do.

I have a friend who is a psychiatrist for adolescents who says, "I always start with the family. If a child is coming to see a psychiatrist, it's usually not just the child who has the problem." The point of this chapter is not whether parents *ought* to have such a formative effect on their children (though I do believe that the tremendous power of parents' influence *is* part of God's design). But just as gravity pulls objects toward the ground, whether we want it to or not, so families exert unparalleled influence on the development of their children's lives and character.

Many are under the illusion that peers have as much influence in teenagers' lives as their parents do. With the increasing isolation of youth from the world of adults, peer influence may indeed be significant, but such influence is almost always short-lived. Kevin Huggins is right:

Although peers sometimes do exercise more control over an adolescent's choice of dress, music, entertainment, etc., only when parents are extremely negligent do peers exercise more control over the teen's choice of beliefs and relational styles than [the parents] do. In the vast majority of cases parents remain the single most important influence in the development of an adolescent's personality.[2]

A *USA Weekend* survey of more than 250,000 teenagers indicated that 70 percent of them identified their parents as the *most important* influence in their lives. Comparatively, only 21 percent of them rated peers in this way.[3]

In my work, I get to do quite a bit of premarital counseling.[4] As a general rule, I spend a great deal of time with each couple talking about each of their parents—how they argued, how each partner is like or unlike his or her parents, and so on. I *always* ask about the parents. But in seventeen years of doing this kind of counseling, I've never found it relevant to ask about their best friends (or even about their youth minister!).

Seventy percent of teenagers identified their parents as the most important influence in their lives.

Because of the extensive exposure parents have to their own children,[5] they leave an indelible impression that radically affects how receptive their children will be to the gospel. There is overwhelming evidence that parents are, almost always, the single most significant determining factor in the development of their children.

FOR BETTER . . .

Research has repeatedly shown the strong correlation between healthy family ties and positive social behavior in teenagers. Merton and Irene Strommen, in their broad-based adolescent-parent study involving almost 20,000 youth and parents, confirmed this connection. They discovered that the strength of the relationship between parents and their teenagers fortifies teenagers with the courage to make wise choices. The study discovered that teenagers from close families were the least likely to be involved in high-risk behavior.[6] Not surprisingly, a similar University of Minnesota study involving 12,000 youth came to the exact same conclusion in 1997.[7] And still a third study revealed that the teenagers who are *least likely* to engage in at-risk behaviors are those who also describe themselves as having good relationships with their parents.[8]

We also know that there is an identifiable correlation between the amount of time parents spent with their teenage children and the teenagers' ability to resist sexual pressure. Sixty-one percent of those young people who described their parents as "seldom or never" spending time with them had experienced sexual contact, compared to only 39 percent of those whose parents frequently committed time to be with them.[9]

Parents' influence extends even beyond personality and moral development to the world of academics. The National Merit Scholars organization recently completed a study in which they sought to identify the factors that influence these teenagers' high achievement. The research indicated that the vast majority of these students have one subtle and somewhat surprising factor in common: they eat dinner with their families almost every day.[10]

Laurence Steinberg, professor of child and family studies at the University of Wisconsin, completed an extensive study on academic performance. He found, not surprisingly, that parents who developed close ties to the schools were the parents of children with the strongest academic records.[11]

Building a level of family closeness that fortifies children and youth is much less complicated than we might expect. Glenn and Nelsen estimate that building a structured ritual or activity into a family may take as little as *thirty minutes a month* with older children. Evidence indicates that those families that have built some traditional times to be together have children who experience much less difficulty than children who come from similar families but spend no intentional time together.[12]

And when it comes to faith formation, the impact of parents is dramatic. Research now shows that parents who simply talk about faith in the home and who involve their children in serving alongside them can actually double and sometimes triple their children's chances of living out their faith as adults.[13] Martin Luther's five-hundred-year-old words speak with pinpoint accuracy:

Most certainly father and mother are apostles, bishops, and priests to their children, for it is they who make them acquainted with the gospel. In short, there is no greater or nobler authority on earth than that of parents over their children, for this authority is both spiritual and temporal.[14]

. . . OR FOR WORSE

I grew up watching Herman, Lily, Grandpa and Little Eddie on the seventies sitcom *The Munsters*. Herman was a tall, Frankensteinesque character with green skin and railroad spikes protruding from his neck. Everyone in this family looked as if they had just stepped out of a horror movie. Everyone, that is, except one.

Little Eddie had an older sister (or was it a cousin?) who, by our society's standards, was beautiful: blond, vivacious and attractive in every way. But this young adult, whose name most of us have trouble remembering, *felt* inferior. Her family talked about her in whispering, sympathetic tones, silently embarrassed by her "disabilities." Her primary negative image of herself did not come from her friends or her work or society in general, but from her family.

Parents' power to build up is matched by their power to cause harm.

In God's eyes, all of the teenagers we work with are valuable and gifted. But if their family discounts those gifts, those young people may have difficulty believing us when we acknowledge them. Power is always a two-sided coin. Parents' power to build up is matched by their power to cause harm. And the evidence is equally convincing on both sides. Armand Nicholi captures the essence of this double-edged sword of parental power:

> If one factor influences the character development and emotional stability of a person, it is the quality of the relationship he experiences as a child with both of his parents. Conversely, if people suffering from severe non-organic emotional illness have one experience in common, it is the absence of a parent through death, divorce, a time-demanding job or absence for other reasons.[15]

A study of violent rapists conducted in 1987 revealed that 60 percent of them were from single-parent homes. And a Michigan state study of teenagers who had committed homicides found that 75 percent of them were from broken homes.[16] We now know that of the 1.5 million children who have at least one parent in prison, 50 percent of them will commit a crime before they even turn eighteen.[17]

For these young people, alienation from religion had little to do with their churches' programming.

Bob Laurent, in attempts to discover why certain teenagers feel alienated from the church, found a strong connection between problems at home and adolescents who felt acutely alienated from the church. He found that those who showed an across-the-board alienation from religion responded as follows to these statements:

"There are many conflicts and arguments in our family."—agree

"In our family we respect each other's privacy."—disagree

"Our family members are critical of each other."—agree

"We do not forgive each other easily in our family."—agree

"The members of our family hardly ever hurt each other's feelings."—disagree.[18]

For these young people, alienation from religion had little to do with their churches' programming. These youth were alienated despite the quality of their churches' youth ministries. The conclusive factor for them was their family of origin.

THE LABORATORY OF THE SOUL

In my childhood, my faith was formed as much around the dinner table as it was in the pew. Although my father is a pastor and my mother was a missionary, I don't remember hearing my parents talk much about God or about their own faith. What I do remember is our family meal.

Sometimes we would sing, sometimes pray a psalm; other times my dad would assign my brother or me to say "God is great." And it was in this seemingly minimal mealtime ritual, perhaps more than any other place, that my parents passed on the baton of their own faith.

As Christmas approached, we had a daily Yule log with candles that we lit as a family in the evenings. And during Lent, my brother and I watched with pride as the cardboard One Great Hour of Sharing bank became heavier and heavier with our nickels and pennies. Along the way, with family prayer, spiritual traditions and weekly offering envelopes, my parents taught me that following Christ was a priority.

From ancient times, the family has always been the central faith-nurturing structure. As Edward Hayes points out,

> The first altar around which primitive people worshipped was the hearth, whose open fire burned in the center of the home. The next altar shrine was the family table, where meals were celebrated and great events in the personal history of the family were remembered. The priests and priestesses of these first rituals were the fathers and mothers of families.[19]

The teenagers in my church may be impressed by my stirring message on "be quick to listen, slow to speak and slow to become angry" (Jas 1:19), but my children are the ones most likely to absorb the "lesson" on this topic that they observe in my life. In the crucible of the family, pious masks evaporate before the fire of human frailty. In our families, our grand theologies boil down to how we live amid the frustrations of our most intimate relationships. Parents do not need to give lectures to their children in order for those children to learn what their parents believe. Their children will know soon enough. And children almost always catch the beliefs of their parents.

Some have described the family as "the laboratory for soul work."[20] And study after study has proven the accuracy of this title.[21] Roger and Margaret Dudley from Andrews University studied the transmission of religious values from parents to their teenage children in the Seventh-day Adventist Church. Their conclusion? Even though the teenagers as a whole were slightly less traditional than their parents, the teenagers' values did, in fact, parallel the values of their own parents. The study concluded, "Youth tend . . . to resemble their parents in religious values held . . . and even the independence of adolescence cannot usually obliterate these values completely."[22]

The Search Institute's National Study of Protestant Congregations indicated that the first predictor of adolescent faith maturity was the level of "family religiousness." The particular family experiences most tied to greater faith maturity were the frequency with which an adolescent talked with mother and father about faith, the frequency of family devotions and the frequency with which parents and children together were involved in efforts, formal or informal, to help other people.[23]

As might be expected, the Search study's first recommendation for change in Christian education was to "equip mothers and fathers to play a more active role in the religious education of their children, by means of conversation, family devotions and family helping projects."[24]

More than two hundred years ago, Jonathan Edwards made this same recommendation:

> Every Christian family ought to be as it were a little church consecrated to Christ, and wholly influenced and governed by his rule. And family education and order are some of the chief means of grace. *If these fail, all other means are likely to prove ineffectual.* If these are duly maintained, all the means of grace will be likely to prosper and be successful.[25]

Christian families provide one of the two most effective lifelong nurturing structures to carry young people to mature Christian adulthood.

SITTING ON A GOLD MINE

Traditionally, we youth ministers have viewed parents as an interruption, as obstacles to success in ministry. There's Darin's mom who corners us for "just a minute" to launch into a thirty-minute advertisement for the latest Christian book or tape. There's Gerald's dad who won't let Gerald come to youth group because it's "too silly." And there's Jennifer's mom who wishes youth group could be more fun, and she does the youth minister the favor of calling fifteen other parents to get their "objective feedback."

In many ways, a youth pastor's job would be much simpler if he or she didn't have to deal with parents. But doing youth ministry without parents is like driving a car without the engine. From the top of a hill, this kind of car can coast at high speeds. But only for a while. Eventually it will stop. Without an engine, it has no lasting power.

Most long-term youth ministers have resigned themselves to working like Sisyphus, the greedy king in Greek mythology, doomed to push a huge rock up a mountain only to watch it roll down again and to repeat the cycle over and over again throughout eternity.

But the roller-coaster syndrome of youth ministry is not a necessary part of the job.

Jed Clampett and his *Beverly Hillbillies* family owned millions of dollars in oil for years as they struggled to stay alive in their mountain shack. They were sitting on a gold mine and didn't even know it.

Doing youth ministry without parents is like driving a car without the engine.

Traditional youth ministers work themselves to the bone to hold their ministries together "with Scotch tape and paper clips," while at the same time ignoring the most powerful resource they may have—teenagers' parents. We can no longer continue to view parents as neutral factors in our ministry to their teenagers. Parents, simply by the way they raise their children, will either empower our ministries or sabotage them. Parents play a role second only to that of the Holy Spirit in building the spiritual foundation of their children's lives.

IMPLICATIONS FOR MINISTRY

1. Programming for parents of children and teenagers should be understood by the leadership of any church as central and foundational for the youth ministry. Christian education and youth committees can be just as intentional about this kind of programming as they are about the recruitment of Sunday school teachers or the search for the right youth staff or program.

2. Intentional family-based programming does not need to replace age-specific youth programming. But unless family-based programming is

given priority, it is likely that the church will never get around to the task of building this solid foundation for its youth ministry.

3. Youth ministers can orient parents to the youth program each year by documenting for them the incredible power they have in their children's lives and asking them to join the church as covenant partners in the Christian nurture of their children.

WILD HAIR IDEA

Make it a priority of the youth ministry that all of the parents receive a personal visit from some representative of the church each year to strategize together about the Christian nurture of their sons and daughters.

To me it seems clear that our society is seriously malfunctioning
in its role of preparing children for adulthood.
The upheaval and disarray we are seeing in childrearing patterns
are unprecedented in modern times.

VANCE PACKARD, *Our Endangered Children*

Statistically, no other parents in the industrialized world spend less time
with their children than American fathers and mothers.
According to the Wall Street Journal, American parents spend, on average,
"less than 15 minutes a week in serious discussion with their children."

DENNIS RAINEY, *Family Reformation*

My kid's all screwed up from heavy metal music and exposure to sexual
videos at an early age. Don't blame me for his problems. . . . I'm never home!

A PARENT, QUOTED IN BOB DEMOSS, *Learn to Discern*

The dreariness of the family's spiritual landscape passes belief.

ALLAN BLOOM, *The Closing of the American Mind*

If America were a parent, it could be prosecuted for child abuse.
So say the members of the Carnegie Council on
Adolescent Development . . . after years of intensive study.
The council's report, titled Great Transitions, found that while
three-quarters of third-graders' parents claim high or medium involvement
in their kids' lives, only about half of eighth-graders' parents do.

RICK LAWRENCE, *Trendwatch*

An emerging frontier in youth ministry is family ministry.
While ranking it high in importance, few youth ministers evaluate
themselves as having done well in strengthening family relationships.

MERTON STROMMEN, *Youth Ministry That Transforms*

The movie [Home Alone] touched a nerve of American families
who too often feel inept at providing care and can only hope
that their young children can cope on their own.

DIANA GARLAND, *The Journal of Family Ministry*

5 THE CRITICAL CARE UNIT

The Peculiar Crisis in Today's Christian Family

Our fixer-upper." That's how we referred to it as we signed on the dotted line to buy our first home. We were sure that all this house needed was just a little TLC. We could easily finish out a room here, build a fence there, add a little paint, a little wallpaper, and we'd have the house like we wanted it in no time.

So, armed with the arsenal of construction skills I had gained on youth mission trips, I took a week of vacation to build a simple fence around the backyard. I threw myself into the project with abandon. By the end of the first day, I had made three trips to Home Depot, read through the handy "How to Build Your Own Fence" instruction book, and begun measuring and putting stakes in the ground for the fence posts. I have to admit it—I impressed myself. And as I put the tools away at the end of the day, I was already putting together my mental list of the home improvement projects I would begin with all the vacation time I would have left over after I finished the fence.

But the next morning I awoke to a mid-March snowstorm, followed by several days of freezing rain. By the end of the week, I found myself with one day of "vacation" remaining, with the fence project barely begun. So I went back to the drawing board.

I set myself the more realistic goal of simply getting all the fence posts in place by the end of the day. And by noon, I had finished digging every post-hole, except the final one. But before I could finish congratulating myself, I hit rock. Now I had run into plenty of rocks in this process already. I knew exactly what to do. I would dig around it, find the edges and pull it out. Simple process. Or so I thought.

Three hours later, with my sledgehammer and pickax at my side, I found myself looking down at a hole six feet wide and a foot and a half deep. And I still hadn't found the edge of the rock. I did then what I should have done two hours and forty-five minutes earlier. I left the rock where it was and moved the hole.

There comes a time when we have to give up moving an obstacle and adjust our plans to the landscape we are given to work with. For many years of my ministry with teenagers, I tried to move the rock of parents' failing to give attention to the spiritual growth of their children. I would complain, "If parents would just do their job, my work would be done."

I have given guilt-laden lectures to parents about their failures, comforting myself by blaming the parents for the natural frustrations of youth ministry. But simple solutions are usually no solution at all. My pushing parents to work harder was not the silver bullet for youth ministry that I thought it was. The more I dug around, the more I saw how deep the problem really was.

The simple solution of involving more parents in youth ministry can be much more difficult than it sounds. The fact of the matter is that almost half of the parents of high school students stay away from virtually *every* school function, from open houses to school plays, from football games to parent/teacher nights, with their participation decreasing as their children get older.[1] Youth leaders shouldn't be surprised, then, to find this same pattern of parental noninvolvement repeated when they first seek to engage parents in a partnership in the Christian nurture of their teenagers.

Parents do have incomparable power in the faith formation of their children, and we are foolish not to access this power in our youth ministries. But we live in an age of intense pressure on the family, and this pressure has produced a new pattern for parenting teenagers that severely hinders many Christian parents from positively influencing their children's faith. Any model that attempts to base itself on families must take seriously three factors affecting today's parents.

THE IMMATURE CHRISTIAN PARENT

When I first began applying the principles of family-based youth ministry, I held to the single strategy of letting parents take responsibility for the Christian nurture of their children. It wasn't long, though, before I realized that this simplistic focus only created frustration both for me and for the parents. The first obstacle I had to face was that many of the parents of the teenagers I was working with were not mature Christian adults themselves.

According to the 1990 Search Institute report, only *15 percent* of men between the ages of forty and fifty-nine have a mature, integrated faith.[2] Stated another way, it is likely that *85 percent* of our young people come from homes without a father to set an example of faithful discipleship. Is it any wonder, then, that 83 percent of ninth- and tenth-grade boys have an undeveloped faith?[3]

The same Search Institute report indicated that more than half of sixteen- to eighteen-year-olds rarely or never participate in family projects to help others, have talks with their fathers or other relatives about faith or God, or share in any type of family devotion.[4] The report went on to document huge deficits among the Christian adult population of our churches: 61 percent of adult church members *do not* give significant time or money to help others; 66 percent of adult church members *do not* devote time to reading or studying the Bible; 72 percent of adult church members *are not* involved in Christian education.[5]

If youth attendance is all we're interested in, we will scarcely even notice a problem.

The roots of the crisis in youth ministry, therefore, reach far beyond a simple analysis of the attendance patterns of our youth. If youth attendance is all we're interested in, we will scarcely even notice a problem. But attendance doesn't necessarily produce faith maturity.

In our church of more than three thousand, we have about four hundred teenagers on our rolls. On any given Sunday, the parents of more than three hundred of those youth are not in worship.

One church I am familiar with had an adult Sunday school class that took several months to allow its members each to talk about their profession and how their faith related to their profession. The idea was for the doctor to teach about being a Christian doctor and for the lawyer to teach about being a Christian lawyer—a different Christian professional each week.

What became immediately obvious was that all of the professionals understood their professions quite deeply. They spoke in animated ways about their work and its challenges. But as it came time for them to speak about their faith, most spoke nervously and resorted to the kinds of clichés they had learned in children's Sunday school. For most, although they had continued growing and learning in their vocation, their spiritual development had stagnated.

Mature Christian parents, for the most part, no longer undergird our youth ministries. And unless we pay attention to the significant spiritual deficits in our teenagers' families of origin, much of our creative programming and frantic organizing may be no more than rearranging deck chairs on the *Titanic*.[6]

THE HELPLESS PARENT

The announcement boomed over the airport intercom:

> We have a lost child . . . No . . . Check that . . . Six-year-old Jennifer is here with us. What we have are *lost parents*.

Walt Mueller has said it well: "There is another 'lost parent' announcement echoing through North American youth and young adult culture."[7] Many parents, particularly parents who are active in the church, are feeling lost, helpless and plainly out of their league when it comes to the task of providing for the Christian nurture of their own children.

Even those Christian parents who start out intentionally nurturing the faith of their children often find that more "urgent" demands derail the priority of faith formation, as Merton and Irene Strommen's interview with this Christian couple indicates:

> "Do we have family devotions?" Janet repeated the question after the interviewer. Then she looked over at her husband Bob and they exchanged a helpless laugh.
> "I haven't heard that word for a long time," said the husband. "We had it when I was a kid."

"Don't you remember, Bob," said his wife, "we started out having something like that when the children were small?"

"Yeah, we were idealists, then, I guess."

"There are problems, aren't there?" The interviewer was tentative, waiting for a response.

"You bet there are," said Bob. "The last years I've traveled a lot in my business—days at a time, so Janet is alone with the kids."

Janet chimed in quickly. "I work part-time now, and when I get home, I'm a chauffeur. First I bring Betty to her cheerleader practice—it's every day after school, you know. John's in cub football now and then he'll have hockey. There's no time for *anything,* let alone something structured like family devotions. We scarcely eat together. I'm a short-order cook."

Bob was a bit meditative. "I can see where it would be a good thing. I hardly know what my kids are thinking anymore. But," and he gave that helpless little laugh again, "time is the problem. Time."[8]

Today's parents have become victims of their own schedules. They feel helpless—no longer in control of their own priorities. It is not surprising, then, that coordinators of Christian education programs across the country named "busy schedules of teenagers" as only the second most common problem in Christian education. The most common problem was the "busy schedules of adults."[9]

In our family of five, we have started the "regular" habit of family devotions more times than I can count. As the children have gotten older and their schedules increasingly complicated, the smallest diversion can throw our new habit off track. It is sometimes months down the road until we realign our priorities and start again.

This generation of parents seems to feel increasingly powerless over their children. Many parents have taken to heart the warnings of well-meaning friends, "Enjoy your kids now, because they'll be teenagers soon!" The net result is that parents are intimidated by the natural growth of their own children and paralyzed in setting priorities for them.

Like nervous drivers letting go of the wheel when something frightens them, many of these parents have let go of the wheel of giving guidance to their children. They simply close their eyes and hope they live through it. As Ben Patterson writes,

> Parents in the church today feel threatened and out of their depth when it comes to communicating the message of the Gospel to their children. They are not only insecure in their grasp of the Gospel, they are insecure in their grasp of their children. My congregation is filled with parents who would not dream of allowing their children to stay home from school because their children considered school boring. Yet they fold up when their kids tell them they think church is boring.[10]

Unfortunately, many parents have simply thrown up their hands in despair. These defeated parents may be among the 75 percent of letter writers who indicated to a newspaper columnist that if they could do it over again, they would not repeat the hassle of having a family.[11]

THE CRISIS OF THE AMERICAN FAMILY

The helpless parent syndrome is not caused primarily because of laziness on the part of the parents. These parents are products of cultural forces that are just beginning to be acknowledged. Rutgers sociology professor David Popenoe has his finger on the pulse of the trends affecting the American family when he writes:

> During the past 25 years, family decline in the United States, as in other industrialized societies, has been both steeper and more alarming than during any other quarter century in our history. Although they may not use the term "decline," most family scholars now agree, with a growing tinge of pessimism, that the family during this period has undergone a social transformation. Some see "dramatic and unparalleled changes," while others call it "a veritable revolution."[12]

In an extensive collection of essays on the American family titled *Rebuilding the Nest,* editor David Blankenhorn discovered two noteworthy areas of general agreement among family scholars from a variety of different perspectives:

1. As a social institution, the family in America is increasingly less able to

carry out its basic functions. The family, in short, is becoming weaker as an institution in our society.

2. The quality of life for America's children is declining. On this point, consensus really is the proper word. Scholarship tells us plainly that it is becoming harder each year to be a child in the United States. Surely, such an alarming fact should be widely known in our society. It is not.[13]

A youth worker can no longer say with integrity, "I was their age once." Certainly, we have been teenagers, but we have never had to face the kind of world that these teenagers face. Several summers ago, a Young Life camp offered a one-hour optional seminar titled "Families in Crisis." Students were asked to come only if they were struggling with some difficult issue in their family and needed someone to talk to about it. The leaders expected only a few teens to interrupt their free afternoon to come to the group. But for each of the four weeks of camp, the "Families in Crisis" seminar was *packed out*. Students told story after story of brokenness and crisis in their families. Hiding beneath the surface of these young people who looked like they had it all together was the incredible pain and fear that their families were falling apart.

The typical youth minister now works in a church where family values are embraced. But even in the most conservative churches, youth leaders deal with teens whose parents are openly having affairs, teens whose parents have committed suicide, teens whose parents are in prison, teens whose parents are alcoholics, sexaholics, workaholics and drug addicts. *Bankruptcy, embezzlement, court battles* and *custody disputes* are terms that are becoming more and more familiar to those called to Christian ministry with teenagers.

But this crisis has been a long time coming. *Newsweek's* special issue "The 21st Century Family" suggested that between 1960 and 1986 the time a parent was able to spend with a child fell approximately ten to twelve hours per week.[14] And the vacuum created by the frantic pace of the American family is filled by the electronic "nurture" of television and other media. As early as 1978, the *Saturday Review* cited the results of a two-year study in which a college researcher asked children ages four to six, "Which do you like better:

TV or Daddy?" Forty-four percent preferred television![15]

A sign spotted in a toy shop window in the late 1980s captures the attitude of hopeless confusion this generation of parents has inherited when it comes to what to do with their own children and teenagers:

1920—spank them

1930—deprive them

1940—ignore them

1950—reason with them

1960—love them

1970—spank them lovingly

1980—to hell with them!

Although the jury is still out on what the new millennium will bring, we can anticipate that the increasing speed of change will continue to place tremendous pressure on families.

The cumulative result of these changes is that the tried-and-true formulas for parenting—the way our parents did it—are not always reliable road maps anymore. Kevin Huggins is right: "Any honest parent who is after more than outward appearances knows that formulas don't work. Detailed instructions are good for assembling toys; they're useless for raising kids."[16]

THE CRISIS AS OPPORTUNITY

The cultural trends present churches with an unparalleled opportunity to affect entire families and thereby exponentially increase their ministry to teenagers. In my twenty-five years of youth ministry, I have never seen parents more hungry for help than they are now. They want to spend more time with their children. They feel acutely the need to be better equipped as parents. As a result, the climate is ripe for parents to become increasingly involved in programs that can equip them in the spiritual formation of their children.

These parents feel helpless, not only with their children, but with their lives as a whole. For many parents, the years of having teenagers in the home are by far the most stressful. As their children go through the developmental crises of adolescence, many parents are experiencing an identity crisis of their own.

At its worst, this kind of parental desperation can be a nightmare for youth leaders. Parents who feel lost and afraid of losing their children can blame the youth program for not doing enough. But this desperation also represents a teachable moment with parents that churches must not ignore.

The popularization of the "dysfunctional family" phenomenon over the past decades has caused many adults to reconsider the mistakes and limitations of their own families of origin. Parents today, for the most part, are exceedingly interested in finding ways *not* to repeat the mistakes of their own parents. The vision of family-based youth ministry is to harness the incredible motivation of these parents and direct it toward solutions that can have a lasting spiritual impact for their children.

In and of itself, the nuclear family is not enough, particularly in light of the tremendous pressures of our time. Every teenager needs an extended Christian family of significant adults. For the minority, that extended family will simply affirm the healthy Christian values they find at home. But for the majority, an extended Christian family is imperative to allow them to overcome the spiritual deficits of their families of origin. For many, the church may be the only Christian family they ever know.

Every teenager needs an extended Christian family of significant adults.

IMPLICATIONS FOR MINISTRY

1. Nuclear families can play a significant role in the Christian nurture of teenagers in the church. But it is unrealistic to expect that all parents will be equipped and prepared, in and of themselves, to lead their children toward Christian maturity. Youth workers need to find ways to equip parents without basing the success or failure of the youth ministry on those parents' faithfulness.

2. The years of parenting an adolescent, particularly a young adolescent, are years when parents feel an acute motivation to learn to be more effective fathers and mothers. Every church can do at least one thing a year to communicate to these parents that they have a supportive partner in their church family.

3. Seminars on recovering from divorce, preparing for parenting an adolescent, enriching your marriage, teaching your children Christian values and understanding your teenager can all serve as windows to building faith maturity in the parents of teenagers.

WILD HAIR IDEA

Create an "Introduction to Christian Parenting" class for all parents of sixth-graders to take just before their children become a part of the youth group.

Somebody has to be crazy about the kid.

URIE BRONFENBRENNER, QUOTED IN *FAMILY RESEARCH TODAY*

It may well be that the sociological phenomenon
that makes modern marriage [so] different . . . is . . .
the attenuation of extended family connections.
Even 2000 years ago the human institution of marriage
would not have been able to carry the load of
emotional satisfaction it is expected to bear today.

EDWIN FRIEDMAN, *GENERATION TO GENERATION*

The youth ministries which will have the greatest impact
in the coming revolution will be those which successfully
recruit and equip lay people to bear the primary
responsibility for reaching the current generation of
junior and senior high school students.

MARK SENTER, *THE COMING REVOLUTION IN YOUTH MINISTRY*

If I have seen further . . .
it is by standing upon the shoulders of giants.

SIR ISAAC NEWTON

I still remember, as a junior high school student,
refusing to go out with my friends on Friday nights because
I would much rather stay home for my parents' neighborhood Bible study.
I loved listening to them laugh and argue and study the Bible together.
Surrounding your children with good people is one of the
great gifts parents can give their children.

MIKE YACONELLI, *THE WITTENBURG DOOR*

Those who believe that student leadership in youth ministry
is simply about adults getting out of the way so kids can take over
are wrong-headed and short-sighted.

DAVE RAHN, *YOUTHWORKER*, JANUARY-FEBRUARY 2001

STACKING THE STANDS

The Power of the Extended Christian Family

He grew up in a neighborhood where kids going to Harvard only happened in pipe dreams and miracle stories. So one might naturally assume that after getting his Ivy League ticket out of the gang-infested world of his childhood, Gene Rivers would never look back. But now, at age forty-eight and after attending both Harvard and Yale, he is beating the odds again.

He's back in his old neighborhood of Dorchester, one of the poorest areas in Boston, giving hope to a generation of would-be disposable children. And this maverick minister has caused the media and political experts to ask, "Can religion fight crime and save kids?" *Newsweek* describes the appeal of his unconventional approach to transforming communities where traditional strategies, both conservative and liberal, have failed:

> Now both sides are beginning to form an unlikely alliance founded on the idea that the only way to rescue kids from the seduction of the drug and gang culture is with another, more powerful set of values: *A substitute family* for young people who almost never have two parents, and maybe not even one at home. And the only institution with the spiritual message and the physical presence to offer those traditional values, these strange bedfellows have concluded, is the church.[1]

Gene Rivers' story isn't just a story about urban youth ministry. In fact, his strategy may contain the key to providing a lasting ministry to teenagers in all of our churches, suburban, rural and urban alike. His strategy? Help the church build supportive, nurturing relationships across the generations—

providing an intentional, extended Christian family for our teenagers.

We may assume that spending money on a "youth house" or a state-of-the-art "youth room" is exactly what our kids need. But far too often, such traditional "youth-serving" practices serve only as a quick-fix, patronizing solution to isolate kids from the very people they need to be around to develop a maturity in Christ.

We may assume that spending money on a "youth house" or a state-of-the-art "youth room" is exactly what our kids need.

How, then, can our youth ministries be more than isolation wards for teenagers? How can the church go about the task of building an extended Christian family for its children and youth?

A VIEW FROM THE STANDS

Like most youth ministers, I get to attend more than my fair share of high-school football games. I often arrive at games shortly after halftime but soon find myself cheering with the rest of the crowd. I get caught up in the spirit of the game, just as if I'd been there from the opening kickoff. Cheering the team on is one of the things I do best.

I never made it far in my own football career, though. I logged about twenty seconds of game time on the seventh- and eighth-grade teams. By the time I got to high school, I'd realized that football was no place for a 5' 9", 110-pound class clown to shine. Instead I found my cheering crowd by being on stage. After hours of tedious rehearsals, I remember the energy of the opening night. The air became electric as the auditorium began to fill up. No dress rehearsal could compare to the thrill of the show with a real audience.

The author of the book of Hebrews obviously understood something about the power of standing in an arena filled with a roaring crowd. Relying on a familiar athletic image, this writer paints a picture of a competition in which the stands are packed with fans who have moved beyond being mere spectators; their very presence calls out a different kind of performance:

Therefore, since we are surrounded by so great a cloud of witnesses, let us also lay aside every weight and the sin that clings so closely, and let us run with perseverance the race that is set before us. (Heb 12:1 NRSV)

Every teenager needs an extended family of Christian adults—adults who can be a part of the cloud of witnesses that cheers him or her on. And the church can and should be the primary vehicle through which teenagers are exposed to the adults who make up their extended family in Christ.

Adults can be a part of the cloud of witnesses that cheers teenagers on.

THE RADICAL ALTERNATIVE

As powerful as the influence of parents is on the faith development of the young, there is another influence that can be equally as powerful, and in some cases, even more so. It is this influence on which we must lean heavily, particularly as our youth ministries become increasingly populated with teenagers who don't come from Christian homes.

The book *Faithful Parents, Faithful Kids* documents a study of Christian adults that sought to identify which home-based faith-nurturing practices were most likely to have the greatest long-term impact on children. The study found that there was no single, across-the-board practice that worked in even a slim majority of families. Some effective parents required their teenage children to attend church, but the majority didn't—more than 50 percent of teenagers quit going to Sunday school in high school. Only 25 percent of families reported having devotions together. And surprisingly few of these adults (15 percent) reported praying fairly often with their parents during their teenage years. For the researchers looking for a barn-burning discovery, the results had to be frustrating.

What the study did discover, almost accidentally, *was a single faith-nurturing factor that was present in more than 90 percent of the families surveyed.* The authors write, "While we didn't come up with a sure-fire formula, one thing was obvious: *Those who stuck with their faith . . . had a half-dozen "mentors" present during their growing up years."*[2]

Emmy E. Werner, from the University of California at Davis, has come to a similar, well-documented conclusion. Since 1955 she has been studying resiliency in a group of five hundred Hawaiians who were born into difficult circumstances, such as poverty and addiction. Her work was one of a small number of studies included in Radcliffe College's "Landmark Studies of the 20th Century" conference. Her "landmark" conclusion? The strongest predictor of resilience (of children who grow up in abusive situations and then go on to live happy and productive lives) was "an adult mentor outside the immediate family—grandmother, a minister [for example]—who gave them a sense of being loved and important."[3]

As adolescents go through the acute changes of their developmental years, they are likely to go through any number of psychopathologies. But in the vast majority of cases, these imbalances don't last. During these years when the ability to offend and stumble clumsily along is so great, teenagers need adults who will know the wisdom of waiting and remaining connected as the process evolves on its own timetable.

It's when the church and family abandon their role of helping young people navigate that passage to adulthood that teenagers become most susceptible to the influence of their friends, their music and the media as surrogate (and often tyrannical) mentors. For too many kids, the media steps into the gap created by our cultural neglect and gives youth a map of reality, telling them who they are and what they need to think about. And there they learn the frightening lie that the only ultimate arbiter of truth is oneself. Alone again.

> By and large, the age-driven transience of twenty-something youth directors severely limits their long-term availability.

Unfortunately it's often the students who need mentors the most who have the most difficulty finding one. As Judith Wallerstein discovered in her highly acclaimed study of the children of divorce,

> Children of divorce, who need help most of all, may find it even harder than other children to find mentors. . . . There aren't many mentors in the shopping mall. Where are modern youngsters going to

find them? Of all the children in our study, only very few found and made use of mentors.[4]

When a student makes it to mature Christian adulthood, he or she can almost always point to either the influence of godly parents or that of at least one available, durable, nonexploitive Christian adult who modeled for them what being an adult Christian was all about. Sometimes twenty-something youth directors can make this kind of long-term, ongoing investment in a handful of students, but by and large, their age-driven transience severely limits their long-term availability.

WHAT IS AN EXTENDED CHRISTIAN FAMILY?

An extended Christian family is a community of believers who affirm and encourage growth toward Christian maturity. Although having a set of peers who affirm one's Christian faith is important, teenagers particularly need adults who can help provide a consistent, lifelong structure of Christian maturity. Apart from the family (and perhaps the media), the church may be the only lifelong nurturing structure left. Only the church and the family can provide Christian nurture from birth to old age—even death. Almost all other groups students are involved in are essentially orphaning structures, including parachurch youth ministries, schools, scouts *and youth groups.*

> Only the church and the family can provide Christian nurture from birth to old age and even death.

Orphaning structures provide support and connection for people only so long as they fit into the age group of that particular organization. Many orphaning structures provide teenagers with a high degree of support and involvement. But, in the end, without a connection with lifelong nurturing structures like the family and an extended family, a young person's life can easily become a fragmented and rootless search for identity.

Each time a person leaves an orphaning structure, he or she may feel confused and lost, looking for a new matrix for reality, a new place to belong. The rise in popularity of Twelve-Step groups reflects one way that disoriented people have been able to create for themselves lifetime support structures. Unfortunately, contemporary churches have often been much more effective in providing young people with meaningful connections to the orphaning structure of the youth group than to the lifelong structure of the church. As Ben Patterson argues,

> It is a sad fact of life that often the stronger the youth program in the church, and the more deeply the young people of the church identify with it, the weaker the chances are that those same young people will remain in the church when they grow too old for the youth program. Why? Because the youth program has become a substitute for participation in the church. . . . When the kids outgrow the youth program, they also outgrow what they have known of the church.[5]

Wherever a mature Christian adult is found, chances are that a strong connection to an extended Christian family will be found as well. Sometimes, even when the parents are antagonistic to the Christian faith, young people are able to continue to flourish in their faith. Almost always this kind of growth happens not because of the charisma of a youth leader or the insight of a curriculum but because of a web of connections to an extended Christian family that offers a different set of faith values.

My experience has been that a young person who makes a commitment to Christ through a traditional youth program, but who comes from a family that is apathetic or antagonistic toward the Christian faith, really only has three options for his or her faith future:

1. Many will simply reject their faith altogether as adults and follow the faith course set by their parents.

2. Others will make a connection to the adult extended Christian family of the church and live out their faith for the long haul.

3. And interestingly enough, a sizable group will create their own extended Christian family by *becoming ministers themselves.* For example, teenagers who come to know Christ through Young Life will often become Young Life leaders. New Christians who were nurtured in Campus Crusade will join the Crusade staff. And teenagers who were nurtured in the youth group become youth ministers or marry one. Why? The primary Chris-

tian models for these young adults from non-Christian homes were Christian ministers.

NOTHING BUT THE FACTS:
THE EXTENDED FAMILY'S IMPACT

Researchers at the University of California at San Francisco sought to determine why some young people are destroyed by the deficits of their home environment while others seem to thrive under the very same set of circumstances. In reviewing these studies, Earl Palmer uncovered one constant factor among resilient teens:

> They all experienced the non-exploitive interest, care and support of at least one adult during their childhood years—a parent or grandparent, uncle or aunt, older brother or sister, coach or teacher, pastor or youth leader—an adult with no hidden agenda or exploitive design on the youngster.[6]

The Search Institute has discovered that young people who thrive experience certain key assets that help them overcome adverse situations. And church or synagogue involvement tops the list of assets that promote resilience.[7] In *Children of Fast-Track Parents,* Brooks reports, "Studies of resiliency in children have shown time and again that the consistent emotional support of at least one loving adult can help [children] overcome all sorts of chaos and deprivation."[8]

Steven Bayme, director of Jewish Communal Affairs Department, documents the impact of the community of faith on the stability of Jewish families:

> More interestingly, among Jews affiliated with synagogal movements—Orthodoxy, Conservatism, and Reformed—the chances of marriage ending in divorce are approximately one in eight. Among Jews unaffiliated with the Jewish community, the chances of divorce rise to one in three.[9]

Grandparents also provide this kind of stabilizing influence for children. In his study of children of divorced parents, John Guidibaldi discovered that young people who lived close enough to their grandparents to seek help from them performed significantly higher academically. He found that the same positive academic results were typical of children who had regular contact with the relatives of their custodial parent.[10]

I remember Sunday lunches at my aunt's house with a table full of relatives, laughing and arguing around the table until it was time for supper. I remember a backpacking trip in Colorado with one high school friend and four of our Young Life leaders. I still recall the Sunday nights around the prayer altar at First United Methodist Church in Waco, Texas, with teenagers and little children and balding old men praying side by side. Those experiences have filled my arena with a cloud of witnesses. In each of those settings, I was told in some way that my life mattered, that my faith was significant. Although I had a number of wonderful experiences with Christian friends who were my own age, none of them seem to have carried the long-term weight or given me the security that these connections with Christian adults did.

Of course it's only logical to believe that the best way to reach teenagers is by creating a youth ministry. But in the long run, the teenagers in our churches will be affected by significant experiences with adults much more than by the mountaintop youth-group experiences that we spend so much energy creating. Everything we do in our youth ministries should be, first and foremost, about helping to give kids excuses to build connections with Christian adults.

THE SHRINKING EXTENDED FAMILY

Unfortunately, many of our young people run their race of faith in essentially empty arenas. Oh, there may be the fourth-grade Sunday school teacher or the pastor from the town they used to live in, but for the most part, the stands are empty. As teenagers are cut off from their extended families of support, they often enter the less-healthy environment of peer dependence. It's no coincidence that the rise of the peer-centered youth culture has paralleled the shrinking of the extended family.

Parent educators H. Stephen Glenn and Jane Nelsen report,

- In 1940, at least one grandparent was a full-time, active member of approximately 60 to 70 percent of all households. Today, fewer than 2 percent of our families have a grandparent available as a resource.[11]

- The child culture [of a generation ago] consisted of interactions with siblings, cousins, friends and classmates—children of all ages rather than age mates in a single peer group. In short, childhood in those days was an internship for life.[12]

Today teenagers have less access to the natural extended family structures that lead to mature adulthood. And they have such limited connections with adults that it has become a novelty for a teenager and an adult to have more than a passing conversation together. Merton and Irene Strommen conducted a seminar for pastors on youth counseling a number of years ago. Part of the training involved the pastors actively listening to a single teenager for forty-five minutes. The Strommens write,

It has become a novelty for a teenager and an adult to have more than a passing conversation.

> We were impressed by the fact that many friendships were formed between the pastors and youth, friendships that often continued through the years via letters. When several youths were queried about these friendships, one said, "You don't understand. Never before in my life have I had an adult listen to me for forty-five minutes. It's a good experience." We came to realize there are few times an adolescent is able to speak freely to an adult without being stopped short by a reprimand or correction.[13]

The Search Institute reported that less than a third of the youth in mainline churches had felt the love and support of an adult in the church more than ten times during the past year.[14] What a tragedy that many of our young people have to pay an adult to listen to them!

NOW THERE'S A GREAT IDEA

The body of Christ is the extended family par excellence. From the birth of the church, Christians were called "brothers and sisters." Early believers understood that to be a Christian meant being involved in a new family. The extended Christian family (that is, the church) is not simply a safety net for those people who don't grow up in Christian homes. It's a new family, a family that affirms and focuses our identity as believers. It's ludicrous to think that a person could be a Christian without being connected to Christ's body.

Marjorie Thompson's paradigm for faith nurture in the family firmly roots the Christian family in the larger context of the church when she writes,

> It is inconceivable to treat the family as an insular unit, just as it is impossible to isolate an individual from the matrix of relationships shaping his or her individuality. The church is the context for our entire discussion of family spirituality. Without this context we will indeed reinforce the cultural idolatry of the nuclear family.[15]

Only in the church will young people move from the idealistic pseudo-faith of individualistic Christianity into the real world of following Christ alongside other imperfect people. I remember well how it felt coming home from my first Young Life camp as a teenager. How I wished the world could be like it was in Colorado—a world where everyone loved and listened to everyone else, a world where people didn't care what others looked like but loved them anyway, a world where everyone always got along. It took quite some time for me to realize that I would never find a church as wonderful as camp and that God was calling me to live through an often frustrating maze of relationships.

When I first arrived at my church in Nashville, Mary Price Russell was the only girl in a seventh-grade class of ten very active boys. Over the years, her parents were marvelously intentional about nurturing their children's faith, making their home a place for gatherings of teenagers and adults alike. Mary Price, now a mother in her thirties, is one of those young people who have grown to be independent in Christ.

She decided early on that she wouldn't simply follow the faith of her parents, but would find her own way of knowing God. As a result, she frequently chose to attend another church, where she sang faithfully in the youth choir. She almost never came to our Sunday school group, and she attended another youth group more than her own. On the surface, our ministry with Mary Price was a failure.

But during her junior year in high school, she got into a typical, but explosive, argument with her parents. The argument was interrupted when she, in typical teenage style, grabbed the car keys and left. Of all the places she could have run, Mary Price chose to knock on the door of one of her old youth leaders from our church. Having someone who would listen to her and understand gave her the courage to return home. And because the youth leader was no stranger to the family, Mary Price invited him to return with her and help her say what she needed to say to her parents. Into the wee hours of the morning, the four of them talked and listened and cried their way to a renewed commitment to each other. Clearly, we had failed at getting Mary Price to come to our meetings, but we had succeeded in the more important task of surrounding her with significant relationships with mature Christian adults. No wonder she used to come home from college and say, "I love coming back to a place where the first three pews of the church celebrate my homecoming."

After high school graduation, she joined a team from our church on a mission trip to Jamaica, where she experienced the body of Christ in even more vivid terms. One day she stayed late with a few other teenagers to finish pouring concrete at the Jamaican infirmary, which she described simply as "a place where people go to die." As she waited for the bus, Mary Price talked with an old man on crutches, who played song after song on the harmonica. As he finished playing "Amazing Grace," Mary Price and her new friend talked about their faith. Finally, in her best Jamaican accent, she asked, "Bruce, Mon, you really do love the Big Guy, don't you?"

As tears came to his eyes, he answered this young woman who had over the past week become his friend: "Price, Mom (Ma'am), today you are white and I am black. But someday," he pointed toward heaven, "someday, that will not matter, and we will be together."

Though some might be tempted to edit her adolescent spiritual vocabulary, there is little doubt that Mary Price gained a priceless addition to her cloud of witnesses that day. She will likely never talk to Bruce again, but he has become a part of her "great cloud of witnesses." Her faith has been powerfully undergirded through a chance connection with this adult from a very different world as a part of her extended family in Christ. Since that trip,

Mary Price has worked as a summer intern in our youth ministry and she went on to become a youth director at a church halfway across the country. Coming full circle, she not only became part of the extended family for her students but also made family-based youth ministry her priority for her own ministry, implementing the philosophies of this book much more seamlessly than I could have.

STACKING THE STANDS

Often the extended Christian family surprises our teenagers. They find, as Mary Price did, the serendipity of meeting an adult who validates their own faith experience. These experiences don't have to happen accidentally.

We have some friends whose six-year-old son recently made his own decision to follow Jesus. His parents asked him what adults he would like them to tell about his decision. He listed off the names of ten or twelve families, and now his parents have asked each of us to write him a letter (one letter a month) celebrating with him his decision to follow Christ. They want him to know that he now belongs to a much richer and larger Christian family.[16]

A number of drug and alcohol abuse prevention organizations have designed a parental contract that creates a sort of extended family of support for positive values among teenagers. With very little effort, parents can be connected with other parents to affirm baseline standards concerning curfew, drug and alcohol use, and serving drugs and alcohol in the home.

Many churches have designed Elder Friend programs that match up young people being confirmed with one of the officers of the church. A friend of mine recently went through a very painful divorce. During the separation process, his teenage daughter ran away to Colorado. When her father found out where she was, he realized that she was in the very town where the elder who had stood with the family at this child's baptism happened to live. Late one night, after receiving a phone call from his frightened daughter, my friend called across the country and said to this elder friend, "Fifteen years ago you stood with a little baby being baptized, and tonight she needs you."

This teenager had been involved in her church's youth program, but her experiences there pale in significance to the power of being connected to this elder friend. This kind of connection gave her a lifelong nurturing structure, even when she had run away from her own Christian family.

If our youth ministries are going to have lasting impact, we must move away from a traditional model of viewing highly programmed youth activities as the key to long-term discipleship. Instead, we must see all of our programming as an opportunity to connect young people to their own great cloud of witnesses.

IMPLICATIONS FOR MINISTRY

1. Establish a prayer partner program that matches every one of the church's teenagers with an adult in the church.
2. Provide annual four-week courses for parents and teens together dealing with topics such as communication, decision-making, drugs and alcohol, sex, preparing for college, and so on.
3. Strive to involve the parents of every young person in some volunteer capacity in the youth program during the year.
4. When teens take mission trips, commission them before the entire congregation as missionaries being sent out by the church.

WILD HAIR IDEA

Have an extended-family scavenger hunt or road rally during youth group one night. Each group would have a list of kinds of adults in the church to find (for example, an adult in the church whom you call by his or her first name, an adult in the church who knows the name of everyone in your family, an adult in the church whom you've never met but whose name you know). Teams load up in cars (driven by an adult, of course) to collect signatures from as many adults on the list as possible.

*There is one thing stronger than all the armies in the world;
and that is, an idea whose time has come.*
VICTOR HUGO

*Without a mentor, somebody who can kick around in a kid's head,
talk to him about attitudes, about why he does what he does,
about how important it is to meet other people halfway . . .
a kid won't make it.*
BRUCE RITTER, *SOMETIMES GOD HAS A KID'S FACE*

*I am convinced that the very foundations upon which we engage
in Christian education are shaking. And while a host of builders
attempt with varying degrees of success to shore them up,
there is a dearth of architects engaged in designing new structures.
The church's educational problem rests not in its educational program,
but in the paradigm or model which undergirds its educational ministry.*
JOHN WESTERHOFF, *WILL OUR CHILDREN HAVE FAITH?*

*I take a very low view of climates of opinion.
In his own subject every man knows that all discoveries are made and
all errors corrected by those who ignore the climate of opinion.*
C. S. LEWIS, *THE PROBLEM OF PAIN*

*The day of the broadcast is over.
Narrowcasting has become essential for radio and television to survive.
The day of youth ministry broadcasting is over as well.*
MARK SENTER, *THE COMING REVOLUTION IN YOUTH MINISTRY*

*When one part of [an] organism is treated in isolation from its
interconnections with another, as though the problem were solely its own,
fundamental change is not likely. The symptom is apt to recycle,
in the same or different form, in the same or different member.
Trying to cure a person in isolation from his or her family . . . is as misdirected,
and ultimately ineffective, as transplanting a healthy organ into a body
whose imbalanced chemistry will destroy the new one as it did the old.
It is easy to forget that the same family of organs that rejects a transplant
contributed to the originally diseased part becoming foreign.*
EDWIN FRIEDMAN, *GENERATION TO GENERATION*

7 IT ONLY MAKES SENSE

The Vision of Family-Based Youth Ministry

I enjoyed my years as an expert on teenagers. When parents came to me for counsel or church leaders looked to me for advice, it was nice to have the detachment and authority that being an "expert" brings. But with a growing youth ministry staff and increasing responsibilities in other areas, it had been, in the pointed words of the little girl in *Ferris Bueller's Day Off*, "a long time since I smelled the inside of a real school bus."

But all that changed when my son joined the junior-high group. And now as a parent of two youth-group kids myself, I can't help but see youth ministry through a radically different lens. I realize now that what I want my children to gain from our youth ministry is exactly what parents of the youth I have worked with for years have wanted.

I don't want another program to fill up my kids' calendars or another place for them to be isolated from "interfering adults." I want a place that can give me the help I desperately need—that means providing my children with a place where they desperately want to be and relationships with adults and peers who call them into more eagerness and faithfulness about following Jesus Christ.

It's no surprise, then, that the principles of family-based youth ministry began to crystallize around the same time that our oldest child stepped into our youth ministry himself. It was the added role of "youth-group parent" that put me in a position to see what I had never seen before.

THE NASHVILLE STORY

When I came to First Presbyterian in Nashville seventeen years ago, I inherited a small but strong Sunday-night program—a core group of youth who came fairly regularly and who seemed to love being together. Most of this core group went to the same two schools. And actually, since one of these schools was only for boys and the other only for girls, students from these two schools moved in almost identical social circles.

I soon realized that despite the homogeneous nature of that active group, there were young people from twenty-one different schools on our church rolls. So naturally, my first plan was to try to expand the Sunday-night program so that it included teenagers from as many different schools as possible.

I worked with our volunteer leaders to come up with fun, engaging programs for each week. And after several years of diligent planning and work, the group had grown from about thirty to about . . . well, thirty. True, I was engaging different youth. But I had simply exchanged the "old guard" with a "new guard." The Sunday-night program seemed to be going nowhere.

With passion, I began trying new program after new program. But it seemed that each new program I tried basically hit the same ceiling. Whether we were only having fun or having more diligent Bible study or doing service projects or some combination of the three, the group would settle into a ho-hum pattern that seemed to be going nowhere.

In the world of nature, things grow by two means: either by being planted or by being pruned.

As I tried to keep the Sunday-night program alive, I began to see the need for small groups for young people who wanted something a little deeper than we could give in Sunday school or youth group. So we created "house groups," which met for a year. The young people involved in these groups had some great experiences building friendships with Christian adults, but all in all, the house-group plan met with only limited success.

I was several years into my ministry in Nashville—and thinking daily of what new program I needed to create—when God placed Earl Palmer in my path. I don't remember what his message was about that year at the youth ministry event at Princeton Seminary, but his illustration about growth opened up a new way of thinking for me. He simply said, "In the world of nature, things grow by two means: either by being planted or by being pruned."

I had attended scores of youth ministry training events and read dozens of youth ministry books, but no one had ever suggested "getting rid of something" as a solution to a growth problem. Since the time I arrived in Nashville several years earlier, I had created new program after new program, but I seldom got rid of any of the old ones. Could it be possible, I wondered, that the multitude of programs were choking each other out? Before I left Princeton, I determined that something in this programmatic jungle had to go.

I returned to Nashville with a new vision. Program-hacking machete in hand, I began to examine our ministry for some place to cut. The problem was that there was something good about everything we were doing. Youth group had an appeal to some; the house groups were definitely meeting a need. I could try to cut Sunday school, but only if I was interested in rapid relocation. Clearly this was not going to be a choice of cutting something bad from the program. That task would have been easy. But I knew that too many "good things" were choking our ministry out.

I was also beginning to recognize that our "plain old vanilla" youth group had hit an invisible ceiling. We were trying to reach such a broad spectrum of young people in that weekly meeting that for the majority it was not an effective doorway to involvement.[1]

Eventually I settled on getting rid of the Sunday-night youth group (a sacred tradition of most Southern churches). More than any other of our programs, it simply wasn't going anywhere. And it was becoming increasingly difficult to have a program that would be meaningful for both the "Mother Teresas" and the "Al Capones" of our group.

At the same time, I was beginning to develop some preliminary ideas about a family-based youth ministry. My initial research confirmed over and over again that real power for faith formation was not in the youth program but in the families and the extended family of the church. In my mind, removing the Sunday-night youth group was the obvious choice. I was confident that, once they understood the rationale, the church would love this idea as much as I did. Was I ever in for a surprise.

Let's just say that the idea of "nuking" our Sunday-night youth group was not immediately embraced by everyone in our congregation. A group of parents lobbied strongly for the status quo. My colleagues on the church staff kept giving me those "I'm-sorry-you're-going-to-the-gallows" looks. And the rumor began to circulate around town that we had simply given up on our youth ministry because no one ever came.

For two years, we actually did go without Sunday-night "youth group" (and lived to tell about it). By the end of our second year, weekly attendance had increased to almost sixty teenagers. Since we now had only one weekly youth program (Sunday school), instead of three or four, we were able to increase significantly both the quality of our programming and the number of young people involved.

We used Sunday nights primarily for focused special events for the six classes. For example, one Sunday the tenth-graders would go to the soup kitchen; the next Sunday, the ninth-graders and their parents would ride go-carts. The structure allowed for flexibility in scheduling without the expectation that every student be involved every week on Sunday nights. In addition, a few youth-initiated discipleship groups began meeting every Sunday afternoon.

Of course, not everyone was pleased, and many were vocal about their concerns. During these two years, it seemed as if I spent every Youth Committee meeting defending our current program and arguing about whether or not we should "go back" to having traditional youth group.

But by the middle of the second year, I began to realize a tremendous (unexpected) byproduct of our minimal programming: I now had a huge group of parents more eager to be involved than ever. Without knowing quite how I had gotten there, I was now exactly where I wanted to be—with a group of enthusiastic parents willing to invest in our youth ministry.

As 1992 began, I started to meet weekly with an incredible group of eight parents who went to work with a passion to create a broad-based vision for our youth ministry. After two hundred hours of work, the group made an extensive, thirty-page recommendation that provided for significant involvement by both the parents and the teenagers in the ongoing planning process for our ministry. They designed a flexible program that didn't lock us into any one activity for too long.

Since the first edition of *Family-Based Youth Ministry* was published in 1994, the one question I have been asked more than any other is, "How has your perspective changed since you wrote the book? Is there anything you would have done differently?" My response always begins the same: "If I had to do it over again, I wouldn't traumatize the church so much."

Though I still believe—more than ever—that the vision is right, and I still believe that sometimes the best way to grow a ministry is by pruning programs, I also believe that I could have implemented change in a way that didn't create so much resistance from parents and church leaders. And as I have watched others implement family-based youth ministries around the country, I've seen my error repeated over and over again. Youth pastors, sold on this new vision of ministry, push changes on their churches without first getting buy-in from the key stakeholders in the youth ministry. Unintentionally, they have found themselves distracted from ministry, mired in battles over youth ministry philosophy. But it doesn't have to be this way.

People also ask me what our youth ministry looks like now. We still don't have a weekly Sunday night "youth group," though there's plenty of activity going on with teenagers at our church on most Sunday nights. If I have learned anything over these past two and a half decades in youth ministry, and particularly recently as I have found myself consulting with a wide variety of churches, it is that effective youth ministries come in all kinds of packages, using all kinds of models. The secret is not what the program looks like, but what is strategically built beneath that program.

THE TWOFOLD STRATEGY

When I left the church in Texas where I had served in youth ministry for six years, the teenagers and their parents decided to have a celebration roast for my wife, Susan, and me. As is expected at such an event, people spoke warmly from their vast store of selective memories about the "success" of our youth ministry. Hearing their words led me to consider exactly what success in youth ministry might really look like. And so, in my final article for the church newsletter, I raised that very question for the church.

I explained that we really wouldn't know how successful our program had been for about a decade or so. Would these young people still be growing in Christ? Would they have chosen to be proactive Christians, taking the initiative in knowing and serving God? I knew that all of our exciting programs would be like mist in the wind unless we had given our teens something that lasts.

It is now twenty years since I left Waco. Almost without exception, those young people who are growing in their faith as adults were teenagers who fit into one of two categories: either (1) they came from families where Christian growth was modeled in at least one of their parents, or (2) they had developed significant connections with an extended family of adults within the church.[2] *How often they attended youth events (including Sunday school and discipleship groups) was not a good predictor of which teens would, and which would not, grow toward Christian adulthood.*

When a church makes the first priority of its youth ministry attracting teens, those churches will choose almost exclusively young, enthusiastic, good-looking adults as youth workers. Typically that strategy works beautifully in the short run. But I agree with Ben Patterson when he argues that young Christians need more:

> A twenty-year-old youth worker may be effective in getting the kids' attention, but he or she often isn't able to bridge the gap between kids and the adult community, primarily because the youth worker isn't yet a full member of that adult community. That's not the youth worker's fault; it is, however, a serious limitation.[3]

Beginning a family-based youth ministry involves a shift in perception. Our goal is no longer simply to have a "strong youth program." When, for example, having a Sunday-night youth group was not helping our teenagers move toward mature Christian adulthood, we made the decision to get rid of that regular event—even if it meant weakening the "youth program."

A startling study done by the United Church of Australia documented the long-term impact of dividing the church into age-specific groups. The researchers discovered that people who grew up in church attending worship and not Sunday school were much more likely to be involved in church as adults than were those young people who had attended only Sunday school without attending worship.[4]

The results of this study clearly call into question our myopic focus on creating a successful youth ministry. If this conclusion is transferable to Christians of other nations (and I know of no reason why it wouldn't be), there is no such thing as successful youth ministry that isolates teenagers from the community of faith.

There is no such thing as successful youth ministry that isolates teenagers from the community of faith.

PRIORITY NUMBER ONE: EMPOWER PARENTS

Our isolated youth programs simply cannot compete with the formative power of the family. Over and over again, I have seen the pattern. Young people may pull away from their parents' influence during their teenage years, but as a general rule, as adults, they return to the tracks their parents laid. I picture it like the canal illustration in figure 2, in which the water flows naturally toward mature Christian adulthood, because of the walls that are in place.

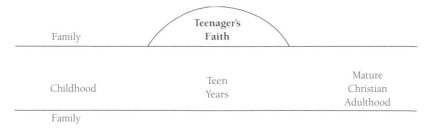

Figure 2. The family as a primary faith-nurturing structure

I pulled away from my parents during my teenage years by becoming (what I assumed was) "more spiritual" than they were. I was sure that because I carried my Bible more often than they did, I took it more seriously than my Presbyterian-minister father and my missionary mother. During my college years especially, I stretched as far as I could to get away from the traditional Christianity they practiced.

But now, as a minister in the same denomination as my father, in a church very similar in style to those he served, I recognize that much of my pulling away was only temporary. And although there are a few significant differences (created through my connections with an extended Christian family), for the most part I have returned to the core values of my family.

When teenagers become adults, they will ordinarily return to the core values of their parents.

Like a rubber band, young people may stretch away from their parents' faith during their teenage years. But when they become adults, they ordinarily return to the core values of their parents.

These parents need help in learning how to provide for the Christian nurture of their children. We, as youth workers, can never replace the influence of a teenager's primary socializing structure (the relationships that surround them when they wake up in the morning, go to bed at night, and will likely spend holidays with for the rest of their lives). What we can do is partner with those parents, support them and equip them to pass on their faith to their teenagers as effectively as possible.[5]

Equipping parents for their work as the primary nurturers of their children's faith has been an essentially untapped resource in youth ministry.[6] Churches can learn to be as intentional about equipping parents as they are about developing programs for children and youth. Chapter twelve offers a strategic process for making this kind of equipping ministry happen.

PRIORITY NUMBER TWO: EQUIP THE EXTENDED FAMILY OF THE CHURCH

The isolation of American teenagers may be a symptom of the rootlessness of the American family. Many parents, in a desire to build security for their children, choose to isolate their families into worlds of their own, a world in which "family always comes first."

But this "my family first" attitude, especially among Christians, has, in fact, often served to sever nuclear families from the very structures most likely to give their children a faith that will last for the long haul. Without strong ties to specific extended families, nuclear families can themselves become self-perpetuating breeding grounds for rootlessness and alienation.

When Jesus was told that his mother and his brothers were outside looking for him, he could have said, "I'm sorry to end this teaching time, but my family comes first." Instead he responded, "Who are my mother and my brothers?" He looked around at the people sitting with him and said, "Here are my mother and my brothers! Whoever does God's will is my brother and sister and mother" (Mk 3:31-35). Jesus redefined the nature of the family for the Christian, placing a high priority on the extended family of brothers and sisters in Christ.

In even more radical terms, he challenged his listeners to resist the natural temptation to place family loyalty on a par with loyalty to God: "Whoever comes to me and does not hate father and mother, wife and children, brothers and sisters, yes, and even life itself, cannot be my disciple" (Lk 14:26 NRSV).

Of course, Jesus was not advocating a wholesale rejection of the nuclear family. His concern was that those who follow him understand clearly the nature of their first family. The unswerving, ultimate priority of the Christian is the glory of God and his kingdom. Sometimes the nuclear family will support these priorities and other times not. The standard by which the nuclear family is to be judged is by the new family of brothers and sisters in Christ.

In his book *The First Urban Christians,* Wayne Meeks points out that one of the most stinging critiques the ancient Romans made about Christianity was that it destroyed the family. There was no more cherished value in Roman society than the family. Every Roman institution depended on it.[7] The Romans rightly understood the Christian faith as a threat to the family, because Christianity advocated the subordination of family loyalty to one's loyalty to the new Christian family.

Therefore, the second priority of family-based youth ministry must be to provide an extended Christian family for our teenagers by allowing them to experience the extended family of the church community (not to be confused with a peer-centered extended family of teenagers in the church). Though there are obvious benefits of these kinds of relationships for young people who grow up in Christian homes, the extended Christian family provides particular benefits for youth who come from homes in which neither parent shows interest in the Christian faith. These teenagers need more than their youth leaders. They (even more than young people from Christian homes) need the secure lifelong structure that a web of relationships with adults in the entire church can provide.[8]

If this church is ever able to create a successful youth program, it may destroy its youth ministry.

A retired Air Force pilot reminiscing to young people about his fearful and faith-demanding flights in World War II is more than just an old man telling stories. A Sunday school teacher who invites her students to pray with and for her through her battle with cancer gives her class much more than a curriculum could ever provide. But those stories can be the gospel made real, good news "with skin on it." As youth hear adults speaking of their own faith experiences, they begin to develop a faith vocabulary of their own to describe their own experience of God.

There are many ways for adults to be with teenagers without being their teachers. One of the churches I described in chapter one was accomplishing this goal quite successfully without even knowing it. That Texas pastor lamented that his church had virtually no youth program. But in his small church, 15 out of 18 young people were active in some program of the church *weekly*—ushering, singing in the adult choir, helping in the nursery or teaching children's Sunday school. This church had, without even planning to do so, created multiple opportunities for its young people to be influenced by Christian adults in the church. If this church is ever able to create a successful youth program, it may destroy its youth ministry.

THREE MODELS FOR YOUTH MINISTRY

In struggling to determine what to do about our ministry to teenagers, I discovered that most churches are frustrated with their youth programs. Not only are church leaders not getting what they want, but those same leaders can't seem to agree on exactly what they *do* want.

As I looked for churches that were doing youth ministry effectively, I discovered a distinct pattern. Every church I looked at was using one of three distinct models. I haven't seen a youth program yet that doesn't fit into one of these three categories. The principles of family-based youth ministry can be implemented in any of them. Either of the first two can be quite effective. The third is the model used by the majority of churches and almost always results in a sense of frustration and failure.

FORTUNE 500—THE WAL-MART APPROACH

I call the first model the "Fortune 500" youth ministry. In a Fortune 500 program, the congregation and the church expect excellence in everything—great communication, great pastoral care, great student leadership development, great missions, great education, great volunteer recruitment and training, great youth music program, excellence in everything. The favorite phrase heard around a Fortune 500 youth ministry is "We can do it better."

This model of ministry has many advantages. It tends to produce a high-quality, visible program with many teenagers involved and very creative programming. The church becomes known around the community as a church that makes youth ministry a real priority.

One disadvantage of this kind of program is that the high level of programming can inadvertently train the youth of the church to be good consumers, to grow up to be adults who demand superior programming before they will take the effort to pursue their own faith. The other disadvantage is that this type of program is fairly expensive. According to my rough estimates based on general research of churches with this style of program, a church can expect to pay between $1,000 and $2,000 annually *for each student* active in the program on a weekly basis. In other words, if a church wants a Fortune 500 program with one hundred teens involved weekly, it will cost the church between $100,000 and $200,000 annually (with the majority of the budget typically going to staffing).

A typical Fortune 500 youth ministry has a large full-time youth ministry staff (usually three or more full-time workers). Some of these churches have extensive intern programs with scores of paid workers investing in the youth of the church.

STICK TO YOUR KNITTING—
THE STARBUCKS APPROACH

I call the second model of youth ministry "Stick to Your Knitting." This type of program revolves around a single element of the youth ministry. It could be the youth choir, the mission program, Bible study, evangelism, Sunday school or small groups. With this model, the church simply chooses (intentionally or accidentally) the focus of ministry for its teenagers and strives to do that one thing very well. Around a church that has a Stick to Your Knitting style of youth ministry, the favorite phrase is "We may not do everything, but we sure have a great . . ."

The advantage of this kind of program is that it can be less expensive than the Fortune 500 model, while involving just as many young people. Teens are likely to feel involved on a deeper level if they are invested in a single program rather than dabbling in a variety of events.

The single disadvantage to the Stick to Your Knitting model is that it lacks the balance teenagers need as they are developing a clear understanding of the Christian life. Young people can come to equate the whole of the Christian life with a single focus. For example, a church whose "knitting" is the youth choir may find that for some young people the choir makes up their entire faith identity. Or a church that makes missions a primary emphasis might neglect worship or Christian education or discipleship.

The Fellowship of Christian Athletes and Youth With A Mission are two ministries that have developed this model of youth ministry well. Both of these groups have a single focus and emerged from the youth ministry confusion of the 1980s with a consistently growing ministry to teenagers.[9]

COMPARATIVE CONFUSION—
THE GOING OUT OF BUSINESS SALE

No model can provide everything, and any model a church chooses will have disadvantages. But while either of the first two approaches will work effectively if embraced fully, most churches, in an unrealistic effort to avoid all the disadvantages, opt for a youth ministry with no clear vision at all. They then almost inevitably fall into the model I call "Comparative Confusion," the worst of all possible choices.

The church with a Comparative Confusion youth ministry places great demands on its youth program. These demands are not based on what is realistic for that church considering its budget. Rather, the expectations are based on the fact that "not enough teenagers are involved in our church," while other churches seem to be reaching young people much more successfully.

The favorite question of the Comparative Confusion church is, "Why can't we just do what *they're* doing?" Since the focus is not set, this style of program has the apparent advantage of flexibility and the potential for constant change. But leaders in Comparative Confusion youth ministries have difficulty acknowledging or enjoying their own accomplishments as long as another church seems to be doing more.

The obvious disadvantage is that this approach produces a perpetual attitude of frustration and failure. When the identity of a program is based solely on how it compares with other churches, frustration almost always results. Does the church across town have a great youth choir? The Comparative Confusion church will work like crazy to "stay competitive." Whether it's concerts, small groups, missions or the latest youth ministry fad, the Comparative Confusion youth ministry remains in a reactive posture, responding to the loudest voices or the priorities of the newest staff or volunteers, never sticking with any one priority long enough to let it work. Because of the constant sense of failure that is a part of this style of ministry, the Comparative Confusion church can expect a rapid turnover of youth workers.

Family-based youth ministry works best with either of the first two models. A "Fortune 500" youth ministry needs the undergirding that comes from involving families and the extended family of the church. And a "Stick to Your Knitting" youth ministry will need the broad-based foundation that a family-based perspective can bring. The key is that a church become intentional about choosing its youth ministry model and then undergird that model with family-based programming. To assist churches in this decision-making process, I have included a description of nineteen possible models of youth ministry in appendix C.

A CHANGE IN MINDSET

Jenny had been a youth pastor for just a year and a half when she started looking for a new position. It wasn't the "problem kids"—she loved working with them. It wasn't the pressure to produce numbers. It wasn't even the ubiquitous adminis-trivia that threatens to overwhelm all of us in this business.

It was, she said simply enough, the parents. She explained, "It's not that they're critical. It's that they just don't get it. Whenever I talk about the incredible influence parents can have on the faith of their children, I might as well be talking about calculus. They just tell me what a great a job *I'm* doing with their kids, like I'm the spiritual drive-through, just another service provider right alongside their soccer coaches and piano teachers."

She described some of the programs she had tried: "Two years ago, we did a class for parents and youth together. It was embarrassing. We have 125 kids in the room for this "parent/youth" event and twenty-five parents show up! Last year, we did a big-deal parenting seminar that thirty people came to—and of course those were the very parents who needed it the least. I've got a church full of drop-off parents!"

As I told Jenny that day, the secret to engaging "drop-off parents" is not likely to be found in "parent-focused" programming. Those programs are often just as likely to repel parents as attract them. What we do need is a new mindset, a few new ways of thinking about working with parents that can, in the long term, help them to move alongside us as partners rather than as spectators.

MINDSET CHANGE NUMBER 1: THINK PANAMA—CANAL, THAT IS

The Panama Canal gives a picture of a brilliantly designed process for moving a ship from one elevation to another. Rather than hoisting, pulling or dragging the ship to higher levels, the engineers created a series of locks, and in each lock, ships are lifted *naturally*, simply by raising the water level.

Let's face it. Trying to push, pull or drag parents into taking initiative for the Christian nurture of their own children can easily become an exercise in frustration. What we can do, though, is "raise the water level" and create a new sense of what's normal for parents in the church.

I learned this lesson the hard way. You may recall that I was excited and absolutely convinced about the unparalleled power of parents in the faith formation of their children, and so I made an immediate shift from "traditional" youth programming to a more parent-focused approach. I reduced regular programming and exchanged those programs with cajoling exhortations and expectations that parents take a larger role in the faith formation of their children. And I met predictable resistance from all sides.

I was violating the "Panama Principle." I've seen it in our church and in scores of family-based youth ministries across the country. The churches that practice the Panama Principle by focusing on what their parents are doing well, who tell the stories of the small victories those parents *are* having in their homes, who "raise the water level" to a new normal, are the youth ministries whose parents are beginning to "get it." But those who violate this principle and focus instead on parental passivity reap an epidemic of resistance and spiritual inactivity among those parents.

So how do we "raise the water level"? A few ideas:

- Pass along to your pastor the stories of parents in your church who *are* being intentional about the faith formation of their children, and ask that those stories be used in a worship service.

- Create a team of parents responsible for supporting and empowering other parents in the church and ask them to "experiment" with home-based faith-nurturing practices.

- Pull together a group of parents (half of whom could be typical "drop-off" parents) to help with a specific event just for parents. You could easily use twenty parents to help with food, decorations, promotion and prayer. The *process* of creating the event can itself draw parents in, even if the event itself is far from perfect.

MINDSET CHANGE NUMBER 2: THINK CANINE

Just by the way Dr. Johnson introduced himself, I could tell this would not be a pleasant call. He wanted to know why he had not yet received the information on the upcoming retreat. He had, he explained, requested the information three days earlier and had not yet received it.

On this particularly normal week, I was up to my eyeballs in crises and deadlines, so I simply asked whether Dr. Johnson had any particular questions I could help him with. "Actually, there is," he began with intensity, "I want to know if this is going to be one of those proselytizing things . . . because if it is, I want you to know that I will not permit Katie to be a part of it."

It seemed like I had just hung up the phone with Dr. Johnson when I got a call from a mother of a teenage boy in the church. She wanted to know if we had plans to give the kids any real spiritual "meat" on this same retreat, because her son Tom "quite honestly" didn't really have time for a weekend full of fun and games.

Enter the "Canine Principle." Different breeds of dogs behave in different ways. Different breeds of parents do too. And we would be foolish to respond the same way to all of them. Over the years I have observed at least four different "breeds" of parents: the pit bull, the terrier, the Golden retriever and the sheepdog. And though my descriptions will be inexact at best, they might just provide a framework for understanding how to reach the different types of parents we work with effectively.

- *Pit bulls—the fighters.* Jeff was a kid who came to church in spite of the biting criticism of his mother. When he sang a solo in the church musical, she refused to come. Nothing could soften her—until Jeff started failing algebra. When one of Jeff's youth leaders started coming over on Tuesdays to work on algebra, she remained cold and distant. But when his six weeks' grade moved from an F to a B-, she saw in the youth ministry an ally, not an adversary. Jeff's mom is a long way from being willing to attend a parenting seminar at church, but there is no question that this ministry was successful in reaching this drop-off parent.

- *Terriers—the skeptics.* When Jerry's mom, Marie, stormed into the living room where we were to have our youth meeting one Sunday night, she immediately asked for the person in charge and started drilling me with questions. It was an uncomfortable few minutes, but Marie finally allowed Jerry to stay for that night's program (and a hundred or so more), and eventually became my one-woman "terrier-response team," answering questions from other skeptical parents.

- *Golden retrievers—the encouragers.* When I first met Al, he was the typical Golden retriever parent. He picked up his son outside my house after a

Table 2. The "Canine Principle"

Parent Type	Pit Bull	Terrier	Golden Retriever	Sheepdog
Attitude	Antagonistic	Skeptical	Open	Eager and active
Need	Results	Trust-building consistency	Encouragement and exposure to sheepdogs	Training and opportunity to lead
Definition of Successful Youth Ministry	"There's something different about my kid . . . and I like it."	"My child is safe in this group. They know what they're doing."	"My child wants to be there."	"My child is growing toward maturity in Christ."
Desire for Their Kids	Happy, well-behaved kids	Positive peer group	Moral children	Godly children
Common Mistakes	Turning kids against parents	Breaking promises	Blaming and criticizing	Excluding from the youth ministry
Opportunity	Demonstrating the credibility of the gospel	Connecting to contagious believers	Personally following Jesus Christ	Partnering in the gospel

Super Bowl party. He was excited about Jimmy actually *wanting* to be involved, even though he and his wife had not been in a church consistently since they were married. During the next year, Jimmy became a regular, and one morning as I was heading to Sunday school, I ran into Jimmy's parents in the hallway . . . on their way to try out an adult Sunday school class for themselves. I have no doubt that Al and his wife are moving in the right direction.

- *Sheepdogs—the doers.* My friend John is a parent of two teenage boys at a church in another city. I know him well enough to know that he "gets it" (to borrow Jenny's phrase) when it comes to leading his own children spiritually. Recently he called and said, "I just want to know if this is normal. I volunteered to teach youth Sunday school at my church, and the youth director basically gave me the 'don't-call-us-we'll-call-you' response. Is that normal?"

As strange as it may sound, it happens all the time. Available, eager, committed Christian parents often try to volunteer only to receive an apathetic response that leaves them scratching their heads. Sure, not every parent is cut out to be a youth Sunday school teacher. But if you've got sheepdog parents in your church who are ready to help and you ignore them, you're barking up the wrong tree.

It goes without saying that these different breeds of parents have very different needs. Our mission in reaching them is to help them make incremental steps toward living into their God-given responsibilities with their children. Depending on the type of parent, they may not care about the gospel or our program. But what they do care about is their kids, and our common love for their kids can provide a profound starting point for partnership. For more on the canine characteristics of parents in your church, see table 2.

MINDSET CHANGE NUMBER 3: THINK HINGES

An oft-quoted verse from the Old Testament—"Talk about them when you sit at home and when you walk along the road, when you lie down and when you get up" (Deut 6:7)—is often used to help parents understand how they can best pass on their faith to their children, but interestingly enough, some of the very same principles apply to our work with those parents. What I love about this text is its strategic focus on what I call "hinge moments." As a parent, I know that often the most receptive times for my own kids are during these moments when we are changing gears—sitting down to eat, getting up to go somewhere, at bed time and at the beginning of a new day.

In working with parents, we can watch for hinge moments, times when parents are most likely to be receptive to our ministry. It may be leaving for or returning from a church trip, a graduation, a confirmation or even a birthday.

This past summer we took Jan, a fifteen-year-old girl, on one of our mission trips. Her mother was somewhere between a pit bull and a terrier, skeptical at best. After having at least one tense phone conversation before the trip, I knew that I wanted to make every effort to connect with her when she picked up Jan at the church.

When we stepped off the van, I kept my eye out for Jan's mom, and told her how impressed I had been with her daughter, what a great contribution Jan had made to the trip. As this mom looked over my shoulder at the expressions of exhausted delight on her daughter's face, I could see the ice melting. It was a hinge moment.

When a new minister comes to the church, when a new adult Sunday school class begins, when the new school year begins . . . they're all hinge moments, opportunities for us to forge again and again in this partnership we share with the parents of our youth.

> *The partnership has to begin with us. If we expect parents to join us in our mission with their kids, we need first to join them in theirs.*

But the partnership has to begin with us. If we expect parents to join us in our mission with their kids, we need first to join them in theirs. None of us are called to churches where the parents are consistently "getting it." We are missionaries to a strange and multilayered tribe of teenagers and their unpredictable moms and dads, called to watch for the unfolding work of God's Spirit in their lives as well.

THE FOUNDATIONAL FOCUS

Jesus ends his Sermon on the Mount (Mt 7:24-27) with a marvelous parable about two houses. From what Jesus tells us, we can assume that the houses were structurally very similar. Nothing about the buildings themselves determined their destiny. But one of them crashed under the weight of the wind, and the other withstood the storm. Only one thing made the difference: the foundation.

Family-based youth ministry is not a "new wing" to be added to a church's youth ministry "house." It is not an optional enrichment program. Family-based youth ministry is a foundational model.

Much that has been done in traditional youth ministry during the past fifty years has been highly effective; the houses have been well designed. But because the foundation has often been limited, so has the long-term impact.

What family-based youth ministry has to offer is less a blueprint than a vision for youth ministry that lasts for the long haul. Like Jesus in the parable, I am advocating a different foundation, not a different floor plan.

Colossians 1:28-29 expresses the goal of family-based youth ministry:

> We proclaim him, admonishing and teaching everyone with all wisdom, so that we may present everyone perfect in Christ. To this end I labor, struggling with all his energy, which so powerfully works in me.

The first principle of family-based youth ministry is this primary goal: to equip young people to grow toward mature Christian adulthood (that is, to present them "perfect" or "complete in Christ").

Making this goal our first priority—rather than the short-term objective of getting students to come to meetings—may radically transform our attitudes about youth ministry. Instead of trying harder and harder to make the old "tried and true" programs work, we can be open to a myriad of new possibilities that can lead us more directly to our primary goal.

Steven Covey tells a wonderful story that provides us with a picture of how easy it is to confuse our short-term objectives with our long-term goals. Covey invites us to imagine a man going to the eye doctor for the very first time. The man explains how much trouble he is having seeing things; everything is blurry.

After a cursory look into the patient's eyes, the doctor takes off his own glasses, gives them to his patient and says, "Here, try these." The patient puts the glasses on, takes a moment for his eyes to adjust to the new lenses and quickly realizes he cannot see a thing. He responds, "It's worse now than before!"

The doctor answers in an obvious tone of frustration, "Hey, they've worked great for me for ten years. Just try a little harder and I'm sure they'll work."

Simply trying harder and harder at the same old things we've done in youth ministry over the past few decades will not address the foundational crisis in youth ministry. Family-based youth ministry, on the other hand, offers a structure in which each church can develop its own prescription.

The prescription of family-based youth ministry creates a foundation for whatever model a church chooses to use to reach its teenagers, recognizing that no one programming strategy will work effectively over the long haul. By focusing on equipping parents and the extended Christian family, churches can maintain an open and flexible stance toward the changes that will be demanded of youth ministry in the twenty-first century.

IMPLICATIONS FOR MINISTRY

1. Before a church begins the process of planning programs for its teenagers, its leadership needs to be intentional about building a foundation for the youth ministry. Equipping parents and the extended family of adults in the church to provide ongoing nurture for the church's youth must be the first priority.

2. As a church begins to develop its youth program, its leadership would be wise to decide early on what their model for youth ministry will be and budget accordingly. As an obvious example, if a church wants a long-lasting ministry to hundreds of youth, that church would be foolish to budget for a part-time college student to run its program.

3. If the church decides not to have a "Fortune 500" style of youth ministry, they should focus on a single area—for example, music, missions, discipleship or families. The leadership should be prepared to support this focused program when criticisms come.

4. There are basically two types of family-based programs—those designed to equip parents to effectively nurture their children in the Christian faith (for example, classes and events for parents) and those designed to build cross-generational friendships between teenagers and adults (such as classes and events for parents and teenagers together).

WILD HAIR IDEA

Take a break from the regular youth program (for a year or more) to get the church's attention fixed on the priority of establishing a long-term plan for youth ministry.

*Happy families are all alike; every unhappy family is
unhappy in its own particular way.*
LEO TOLSTOY, *ANNA KARENINA*

*For young people, the home still ought to be the cradle of values,
but unfortunately a staggering proportion of
them do not live in stable homes.
It is thoughtless beyond imagination for older people to say rigidly,
The child must learn his or her values at home, when there is no home.
Some substitute must be found.
Religious training? It would be wonderful
if every child had the warm, comforting experience I had
in my Sunday School with its songs, its stories,
its bags of candy at the holiday, but many are denied that.
And while religion is an admirable teacher for those connected to it,
it is a silent voice for those who are not.*
JAMES MICHENER, *LIFE MAGAZINE*

*We don't really have a family.
We just have four people who are making sure we all survive.*
FIFTEEN-YEAR-OLD SUBURBAN CHURCH MEMBER

*Today, for example, nearly one child in four in the United States
is born outside of marriage, and the divorce rate in the
United States is perhaps the highest in the world.
Although the impact of this trend on adult happiness may be debatable,
its impact on children's well-being is alarmingly clear.
The mounting evidence of the harm done to children by divorce and unwed
parenthood in our society has now become virtually unchallengeable.*
DAVID BLANKENHORN, *REBUILDING THE NEST*

If I grow up, I'd like to be a bus driver.
FIFTEEN-YEAR-OLD IN A CHICAGO HOUSING PROJECT

*I'm there when Johnny goes out for a loaf of bread for Mama.
I'm there. You're not. I win. You lose. It's all about being there.*
DRUG DEALER EXPLAINING WHY CHRISTIAN MINISTRIES IN HIS COMMUNITY
HAD BEEN SUCH A FAILURE, AS TOLD BY GANG-MEMBER-TURNED-PASTOR
GENE RIVERS, *NEWSWEEK*, JUNE 1, 1998

⬛8 BEYOND THE CLEAVERS

The Challenge and Opportunity of Ministry to Nontraditional Families

One of the biggest occupational hazards for me in youth ministry is the telephone. Since the advent of the "Do Not Disturb" button on our church's phone system, I am no longer a victim of calls that catch me at just the wrong time. But more recently, my trouble with the telephone has not been the calls that come to me but the calls that I make.

I know better. I tell myself over and over again that I know better. But on a fairly consistent basis, I find myself with a phone to my ear and a foot in my mouth. I dial the right number and ask for the wrong people—like when I call a twelve-year-old boy in the family by his sister's name.

But over the past ten years, my most classic phone faux pas (would that be "fauxn pas"?) has gone something like this: My call is to one of our students, Colyer Anderson. As I expect, Colyer is not home, but I do get her mother on the phone. I am ready to seize the opportunity to build a little rapport with Colyer's mom. I look down on the list of parents' names in front of me to get her first name, and I respond pleasantly, professionally, "This is Mark DeVries at First Presbyterian Church. Is this Mary?" After a long pause, the icy edge in her voice is unavoidable, "This is *not* Mary. Mary is Colyer's father's new wife. I am Betty Young, and how can I help you?" Talking around the size ten shoe in my mouth, I leave my message as I fumble my way off the phone.

Besides giving me a crash course in phone etiquette for the new millennium, these kinds of conversations serve as stark reminders of the increasingly complex home environments many of our teenagers grow up in. My first reaction to this situation was to create "niche" programs to reach each of the different kinds of families. It all started with a six-week divorce recovery course that went quite well. I began to think of all the possibilities: blended-family support groups, chemical dependency groups and Twelve-Step groups of every conceivable variety. I even started a group just for teenagers who had been kicked out of school.

But after a year and a half of this diversified "niche" programming, I realized that this kind of strategy was, for me, simply unworkable over the long haul. First, this sort of "something-specific-for-everyone" style of programming would require a hefty budget and extensive manpower to maintain, even if the number of teens participating in each group was limited. Second, I discovered quickly that teens from similar nontraditional situations often don't fit neatly into groupings that can be sustained. Third, many young people from nontraditional families already feel sensitive about being "different." Programming based on "family problems" may keep as many away as it attracts. And finally, it would be next to impossible to design a program with enough "niches" for everyone in the group. Many young people will, by default, fall through the cracks.

Family-based youth ministry, therefore, is not necessarily about creating special programming for young people from each different kind of family. What every teenager needs in order to grow in Christ (that is, a faith-nurturing family or a faith-nurturing extended family) is true *especially* for those from nontraditional families. Need-centered programming may attract them to the youth program, but it will usually not provide them with the kind of foundational relationships with Christian adults that will lead to spiritual maturity.

NOT ALL BAD NEWS

Without a doubt, families today are far different than they were a generation ago. But the changes in the North American family are not completely negative. Clearly, families in our time face increasing threats to their survival, but these threats may, in fact, strengthen some families as significantly as they destroy others.

In a recent "Preparing for Adolescence" class for parents of preteens, I began by asking the group, "Is it harder or easier being a parent now than it was for your parents?" Initially, the response was a unanimous, "Harder!" Then one reflective father said, "But my parents never had classes like these, and they needed them! It's harder for us, yes, but we've also got more opportunities to be trained, and we seem to be much more motivated to learn what to do differently."

You won't have to look far in the "Family and Relationships" section of any bookstore to realize that there is, without a doubt, an intense interest in learning parenting skills. Part of the good news is that most parents these days have a healthy awareness of how little they really do know. The myriad of parenting materials available today only hints at the increasing desire that parents have to do their job well.

And here's some more good news: a Mass Mutual American Family Values Study indicated that 81 percent of Americans view their family as a primary source of pleasure in their life.[1] In another study, 84 percent of men named "family" as the most important facet of their lives.[2] And a *Time/Life* survey documented that today's fathers are investing *four to five times* the amount of time educating two children as their fathers spent raising five children.[3]

Not only are parents more interested in the family, teenagers seem to be as well. One survey asked young people aged thirteen to fifteen what they really wanted in life. Their number one desire was for a happy home life, and teenage boys indicated they wanted this even more than teenage girls.[4]

Five thousand high school students were surveyed by the *World Almanac*. The students were asked "Who is your greatest hero?" Without even being included in the list of choices, "Mom" came in second, and "Dad" came in fourth![5]

In many ways, the more difficult and complex family life becomes, the more it seems to be valued by parents and children alike. I consider working with families at this time in our history to be an unparalleled opportunity for ministry. Parents and their children are increasingly interested in finding ways to connect with each other. And these connections can be the most crucial ingredients in building faith maturity in young people.

ON THE OTHER HAND . . .

Developing a ministry to teenagers from nontraditional families can also be exceedingly difficult. Several years after I arrived in Nashville, I decided to "clean up" our rolls to find out the identity of the crowd I had never met. I found that the majority of the fifty young people who had been completely inactive in our ministry came from families that had recently experienced some kind of major change like divorce, death or remarriage.

Recently I have analyzed the relationship between a young person's family situation and the likelihood of his or her involvement in our program. I discovered that teens who are living with both of their original parents are *two to six times* more likely to be involved in our church than young people who live with single parents or a stepparent.

When a teenager's family is in chaos, our creative newsletters and stimulating programs will not be enough. In this chapter, I want to identify the particular challenges that teenagers from various types of nontraditional families present to a youth ministry. The fact that I do not advocate special, diversified programming to reach these young people does not mean that we can ignore the unique demands of each teenager's home situation. Nontraditional families present a challenge to every church. And in general, young people from these families will require more support and attention (perhaps two to six times more) than young people from traditional two-parent families.

TYPES OF NONTRADITIONAL FAMILIES

Divorce. When my parents divorced, I was just beginning junior high. At that time, it was still odd to be one of the few students who did not live with both parents. I can remember being embarrassed even to speak about it. Today, teens from divorced families may have lots of company, but they can still feel tremendously alone.

Practically all recent studies on the effects of divorce on children indicate that there is, in the words of Andrée Brooks, "frequently a substantial period of emotional and practical child neglect following parental separation."[6] The reasons are obvious.

First, the parents are preoccupied with their own issues of grief and anger and simply have less energy to attend to the needs of their children. Second, the economic adjustments that divorce almost always requires can sap whatever nurture-giving energy a parent has left (the income for a single mother drops an average of 37 percent within the first four months of the divorce).[7] Add to these reasons the chaos surrounding a new routine of being transported from one "home" to another, and it becomes clear that children are often the biggest victims of divorce. The argument that divorce creates few problems for a child's long-term development is simply not consistent with the research in the field.[8]

Teenagers from divorced families often have extra demands placed on their time because of the multiple relationships that must now be maintained and because of adult-like responsibilities that must now be assumed. And because this time often competes with "church time," it is important that our youth ministries not abandon the young

The argument that divorce creates few problems for a child is simply not consistent with the research.

people who may need us most simply because they are unable to participate regularly in our programs.

In an extensive study of the effects of divorce on children, one fact stands out as a stark indictment to churches. *Less than 10 percent* of those children of divorce who were interviewed "had any adult speak to them sympathetically as the divorce unfolded."[9]

Single-parent families. A single parent heads approximately one out of every ten households.[10] But research also indicates that as many as 60 percent of children will spend at least some part of their childhood in a single-parent family.[11]

Often the more "family-centered" a church is, the more difficult it becomes for a single parent to find his or her place. When the majority of a church's groups and classes are designed for couples, it's easy to understand why so many single parents simply drop out altogether. When these single parents drop out of the church, their children almost always stay at home with them.

Although some single parents become incredibly intentional about bringing their children to church, many become sporadic in their own involvement, switching from one church to another many times in the span of a few years. This sort of inconsistency is particularly confusing for their children, who often choose to stay away from church rather than face the embarrassment of adjusting to a new group again.

Though this pattern is not one we can likely change, what we can do is take responsibility to pursue all the students under the church's care, even if those students have not darkened the door in years. A surprising number of times I've watched youth with whom we maintained a connection return as young adults, even though they left our church for a period of time surrounding a season of family upheaval.

Blended families and stepparents. When the two girls walked into the room together, they were noticeably tense. I greeted the girl I knew and asked her to introduce me to her friend. With an irritated sigh, she announced, "This is my dad's new wife's daughter" ("stepsister" was obviously too intimate).

Teenagers from blended families often carry around a subterranean tension that is seldom spoken and frequently left unresolved. Confusion and lack of clarity about parental roles often leave these young people with a feeling of being displaced in their own families.

According to the research of the Baylor College of Medicine, "Children in stepfamilies have more behavior problems, less prosocial behavior, and more life stress than children in nuclear families." Similar research (from Princeton, the University of Wisconsin and Louisiana State University) shows that youth who grow up in stepfamilies or single-parent families are much more likely to drop out of school than those who grow up with both parents.[12] And according to the U.S. Department of Health and Human Services, adolescents who are not living with two biological or adoptive parents are between 50 percent and 150 percent more likely to use drugs or need treatment for addiction.[13]

The American Stepfamily Foundation reported as early as 1990 that one out of three children in our country was living in a stepfamily.[14] These young people have an acute need for adult friends and the sort of identity that comes from being needed in the body of Christ.

Chemical dependency. When a family member has a drug or alcohol problem, it affects all of the other members of the family as well. Teenagers growing up in families with chemical problems almost always pick up some unhealthy relational patterns. In one study, two-thirds of teenagers who successfully committed suicide came from homes in which at least one of the parents was an alcoholic. In another study, that figure rose as high as 90 percent.[15]

For children and youth growing up in a home where addiction is present, they'll find their best hope in sustained relationships with healthy adults who can help those young people see themselves and their family situation more clearly. One way to help is to offer quality "prevention" programming, particularly programming that is done with adults and youth together. Though it's unlikely that chemically dependent parents will attend such events, providing an intergenerational context has two distinct advantages:

1. Because they are nervous about their own children's involvement with drugs or alcohol, even inactive parents may be motivated to *bring* their children (particularly preadolescents and early adolescents) to such programs.

2. While the issues surrounding addiction are addressed, we can also involve adults and youth in community-building experiences together that can enhance the process of helping build an extended family for our teenagers.

Families caring for aging grandparents. Many of the parents of our teenagers will be feeling the squeeze of working, raising children and caring for an aging parent at the same time.[16] Like most nontraditional family arrangements, having a grandparent in the home is a good news/bad news proposition. While the family benefits greatly from the grandparent's presence in the home, the parents, both of whom likely work full-time, may find themselves increasingly exhausted, with less energy to give to the intentional faith-nurturing of their children.

Families in financial crisis. Approximately twelve million children in the United States live in poverty, many of them in crime-ridden housing projects. Adult males are often conspicuously absent, and mothers, when they aren't working, are frequently clinically depressed. More often than not, the family structure has been destroyed, and children grow up with an inordinately high "accumulation of risk factors."[17]

Louis Sullivan's description of the kind of ministry that works with teenagers in urban areas sounds remarkably similar to the priorities of family-based youth ministry:

It is time to remember what has worked throughout our history as African-Americans, a history of overcoming negative circumstances by the force of our character. And what worked was tight-knit families and strong neighborhoods supported by the community of faith.[18]

It is beyond the scope of this book and beyond the reach of my experience to speak in great detail about working with teenagers in poverty. But what I do know about working with children in such settings is that flash-in-the-pan youth programming has limited impact. The one determining factor for behavioral and academic success for young people from disadvantaged neighborhoods has been the level of stability of their families and extended families.

Both parents working and busy families. When both parents are working full time outside the home, children and youth find themselves with parents who have less energy and time available for nurturing activities like talking, family meetings and eating together. In addition to parents working more hours away from their families, we have the increasingly hectic schedule of the children themselves to contend with. It is easy for busy teenagers to relegate their faith to the category of just another "activity" or "program" to add to their frantic lifestyle.[19]

REACHING NONTRADITIONAL FAMILIES

Let's face it. Many of the youth in our ministries come from families that fit into more than one category of "nontraditional." These youth, who often grow up starved for the very assets that will lead them to responsible adulthood, are also the ones who are the most difficult for our youth ministries to retain.

Families suffering financial reversals, families in which one member has a long-term terminal illness, families with foster children, families with a parent in prison, families with children with special needs or families with an emotionally absent parent will all pull teenagers away from traditional youth programming. Realistically, no one church can create a different educational program for each of the varying types of nontraditional families. What, then, can a church do?

Although the death of the traditional family has frequently been overstated (see appendix B), the fact still remains that approximately half of the families in America can now be described as nontraditional.

There's the young person from the single-parent family who is uncomfortable around any group of peers. There's the boy from the Christian traditional family who has been arrested for stealing. There's the student whose parents are getting divorced who carries his Bible to school. There's the daughter of missionary parents who makes fun of anything remotely Christian. No neat and simple patterns.

The most effective strategy for reaching these young people is to provide a consistent personal ministry to each teenager who is a member of the church whether or not he or she ever attends. This can come in the form of a prayer partner program, a mentoring program, or a small group ministry that assigns even inactive youth to the care of a **Professional youth staff simply cannot do this work alone.** small group. Admittedly, building programming that creates a web of cross-generational relationships for every inactive student in the youth ministry will not come easily. And quite honestly, the ministries I've seen that do this well have taken years to build an infrastructure that is flexible, responsive and resilient enough to stay connected to students whose circumstances conspire to pull them away from any connection with the church.

The starting point of ministering to a generation of families that is "beyond the Cleavers" is recognizing that professional youth staff simply cannot do this work alone. There are too many families with too many complex needs. Each requires time that is above and beyond anything a single staff person or program can handle responsibly. As a general rule, programming will not be the key to reaching these youth. Relationships must be built in which their unique situation is understood and taken seriously.

The goal is to build extended families for our teenagers and their nuclear families so that the extended family, in turn, can provide the personal support necessary in each situation. More than anything else, what young people from nontraditional families need are roots into an extended Christian family that will "be there" for them, not simply a team of zany youth workers who provide short-term intimacy with little long-term support.

But in order for those relationships to be built, a wise youth pastor will need to spend time "in the balcony" strategizing how to access and organize a constellation of adults who can surround and support students. These kinds of relationships will simply not be established accidentally; they will require someone—or a group of someones—to design and implement a structure that takes seriously both the vision of engaging every student and the unique characteristics of the setting in which each particular ministry exists.

What young people from nontraditional families need are roots into an extended Christian family.

When I think about the priority of developing both a focused vision and a customized, flexible strategy for discipling every student under our care, I am reminded of a company that went from making millions in profit one year to going bankrupt the next.

The devastated board of directors was shocked. Their audits revealed that during the year that led to the bankruptcy, the company did exactly the same things that made them millionaires the year before. What happened?

What "happened" was not caused by anything *within* the company. It had always run a great business making and selling bobby pins. But when the culture changed around them and hairstyles no longer required bobby pins, this company simply kept doing what it had always done. Because of a vision that was too small, this company folded.

As we begin a new millennium, our world is undergoing enormous change. Families are changing. The teenagers we work with are becoming a new breed, different from any before them. Will our vision be large enough to meet these changes? Or will we wind up like the board of directors, scratching our heads, wondering why "doing it the way we've always done it" has left our ministries bankrupt?

IMPLICATIONS FOR MINISTRY

1. Because most young people from nontraditional families tend to "fall through the cracks" of a traditional youth program, ensuring that someone

is available to administer the "trivial" task of keeping an accurate list of students' names, current addresses and phone numbers is absolutely essential.

2. Every young person needs contact from caring adults, but most teenagers from nontraditional families have an acute need for this kind of contact. The pastor or youth pastor can put together a team of organized parents in the church to create a system in which each young person is contacted at least once every six months simply to check in (the caller is sure to gain information about the family that would otherwise not be learned until the church's next stewardship drive!). If children from nontraditional families are two to six times more likely to stay uninvolved in our programs, perhaps God is calling us to give two to six times the amount of effort to reach them as we do to those who more naturally connect with the church.

3. It is crucial that young people from nontraditional families feel a part of the entire church and not simply a part of the youth program. Three ideas to build this kind of connection:

   a. Youth leaders sit with students during worship on Sunday mornings in "big church."

   b. Youth leaders or other adults in the church invite a teenager to all-church fellowship events (for example, Wednesday-night dinners).

   c. Adults in the church invite teenagers to serve with them in local or out-of-town mission projects.

4. Design the publicity for programs in such a way that young people from nontraditional families get a personal invitation, a phone call or some extra reminder about the event.

WILD HAIR IDEA

Cancel all youth activities (Sunday school, youth group, special events, Bible studies, retreats—everything) for one month to allow the youth leader to visit each young person in the church along with some other volunteer adult.

*Years of work with adolescents persuade me that they are
the last ones in the world to want a freedom, a sense of privacy
and autonomy that deprives them of the advice and counsel,
the warm support and understanding of their parents, and,
for that matter of others (teachers, doctors) who are older
and might have a good deal to say about some of the difficulties
that confront a person of 15, 16, or 17.*

ROBERT COLES, *SEX AND THE AMERICAN TEENAGER*

Interdependence is a higher value than independence.

STEPHEN COVEY, *SEVEN HABITS OF HIGHLY EFFECTIVE PEOPLE*

*The ancient Druids are said to have taken special interest
in in-between things like mistletoe,
which is neither quite a plant nor quite a tree,
and mist, which is neither quite rain nor quite air. . . .
They believed that in such things as those they were able to
glimpse the mystery of two worlds at once.
Adolescents can have the same glimpse
by looking in the full-length mirror on the back of the bathroom door.*

FREDERICK BUECHNER, *WHISTLING IN THE DARK*

*But you want so much to do something for yourself, by yourself,
without your parents being involved, even if it's selling used cars. . . .
A part of you wants to be totally different than your parents.
But another part wants to be just like them.*

TEENAGER, QUOTED IN ANDRÉE AELION BROOKS, *CHILDREN OF FAST-TRACK PARENTS*

*Mere change is not growth. Growth is the synthesis of change
and continuity, and where there is not continuity there is no growth.*

C. S. LEWIS, *SELECTED LITERARY ESSAYS*

*The paradox, therefore, is that genuine autonomy
understood as mature independence rather than
simply isolation from others is best achieved within the context
of a well-functioning family, not in its absence.*

EDWARD ZIGLAR AND ELIZABETH GILMAN, IN *REBUILDING THE NEST*

9 WALKING THE TIGHTROPE

Family-Based Youth Ministry and the Developmental Need for Independence

In my final year of seminary, I chose to focus my studies in the area of youth evangelism. Since there were no youth evangelism courses at my school, in many ways I had to start from scratch. I wound up writing to more than a hundred professors, youth ministry organizations and denominational youth ministry offices looking for leads for information.

Responses varied widely. Organizations like Young Life and Youth for Christ were particularly helpful. They sent extensive materials used primarily in their staff training. Ironically, others wrote back simply to say that they didn't have time to respond to requests like mine (I did wonder where they found time to write me the note to tell me they didn't have time to write me a note).

But by far the most interesting response I received was from the director of the national youth ministry office of my own denomination. He wrote, "We are drawing the line and saying in areas such as evangelism it is high time that youth be significantly incorporated into the overall [adult] program and that there not be a special youth evangelism program."

Throughout this book, I have argued that youth do need to be incorporated into the total life of the church. I have *no* problem with that perspective. But I wonder exactly *how* is this "significant incorporation" actually going to take place? The denominational executive's letter contains a noble sentiment with which I wholeheartedly agree—teenagers *should* be incorporated into the church beyond its youth ministry. But it doesn't take a rocket scientist to estimate how many teenagers actually *have been* "significantly incorporated" into their church's evangelism program through this kind of strategy. I would be so bold as to say that this kind of "incorporation" never happens unless adults intentionally plan for it. As Mark Senter's research highlights,

> A survey of the history of youth ministry shows that the evangelization of high school students, if left to peers, will never get done. Adults have consistently had to structure situations, train student evangelists, and hold the young people accountable to do the job.[1]

One church has designed its entire youth ministry around the no-intentional-plan philosophy. At this church, little or no money is budgeted for youth ministry (except, of course, to buy the denominational Sunday school curriculum). The adults in the church throw up their hands when they talk about "kids these days" and are mystified to discover that so few of them show up for church. The minister and the church officers are particularly shocked and embarrassed to discover that their own children would rather go to Young Life than to the church.

What is this church doing right? Instead of isolating the youth into their own group, this church simply wants young people to be incorporated into the total life of the church. But in their zeal for providing continuity and tradition for their teenagers, this church has neglected another equally important need—the adolescent need for individuation.

A second church's youth ministry is at the other end of the spectrum. This church has an active group of teenagers who are so distinct from the church that a casual observer would hardly recognize that they are from the same "family." The teenagers love being together, and they boast of significant numbers. Quite frankly, the church loves having so many visible teenagers; so when the youth break the rules on trips or at the church, the leadership has a habit of looking the other way. The classic response from the adults in the church is, "Let's not do anything that might make them leave!"

Wherever this group goes, their reputation follows them. They have done damage to hotels and retreat centers, performed dangerous "initiations" and learned to scoff at the rules other groups are expected to obey. This church has given its teenagers wonderful opportunities to "individuate" (separate from the tradition they have received), but those students have been robbed of the continuity and accountability that comes from being connected to a community of faith.

WHAT *DO* TEENAGERS NEED?

One of the dads in our church hit the nail on the head when he described his fifteen-year-old son as "sometimes twenty and sometimes four." Teenagers frustrate us because they are caught somewhere in-between. And if it seems like they are saying and showing that they need two very different things at the same time, it's because they do.

If we design our ministries based exclusively on the expressed needs of our youth, we set ourselves up for frustration. Most (if not all) youth ministers have had the experience of asking a group of teenagers what they want to do, only to find (after days of preparation) that the very ones who passionately pushed for the event decided not to come.

Rather than depending primarily on our teenagers' perceptions of what they want and need, it is our role as adults to know what their primary needs are and to create programs that will be responsive to those needs.

What, then, do teenagers need in order to grow toward mature Christian adulthood? Teenagers have a paradoxical task in faith development. On the one hand, they need continuity with tradition, a faith community to be nurtured in. But on the other hand, they need to step away from their inherited tradition and develop a faith of their own—not their mother's faith, the pastor's faith or their best friend's faith. These two tasks often seem to work against each other. But unless we address *both* of these needs, our youth ministries will be limited in their long-term effectiveness.

THE NEED FOR CONTINUITY

Quite honestly, most "successful" youth ministries do a much better job addressing the need for individuation than responding to the need for continuity. Many youth workers revel in the fact that they are always in trouble for something, always questioning the status quo (although, in most places, teenagers don't need much help in rejecting the status quo!).

Johnny grew up in one of the first youth groups I was responsible for—a youth group lacking in continuity. He hit our youth group running when he was in the seventh grade. *Intense* was the word we often used for him. Wherever our youth group was, Johnny was usually in the middle of it. He was a working machine on mission trips; he prayed with a passion; he sang worship songs with a serious spiritual intensity that I was thrilled to have in our group. I can still picture him in the back of the room at one of our "afterglow" gatherings after Sunday-night church, with his eyes closed tightly in worship.

Johnny was a model of following Christ for the others in the youth group. But as the years passed, and he graduated from high school and college, he began to understand his earlier intense spiritual experiences as something he did "when he was young." Although he still attends the same church sporadically today (as Johnny's parents did when he was growing up), he has lost the spiritual vibrancy that was so contagious when he was a teenager.

We were so busy keeping our youth ministry together that we failed to connect Johnny with normal Christian adults (youth leaders would typically not fit into the category of "normal") who followed God with a passion. I am not suggesting that the style of our youth ministry is the single most significant cause of Johnny's spiritual condition today. But I do know that, although we provided for many of his felt needs, we failed to address his need for continuity.

Recent studies are suggesting that teenagers may be much more open to experiences with their parents (and, by association, with other adults) than has commonly been believed. As a matter of fact, the first issue of the *Journal of Research on Adolescence* dispelled the myth that healthy adolescence requires a strong break with parents. Here are some of the conclusions:

1. Equating the youth years with inevitable storminess is inaccurate.

2. The predictable disintegration of parent-teen relationships (through conflicts) is also false.

3. Teenagers are more likely to support parental values than to be in conflict with them.[2]

Because the current of traditional youth ministry has been so heavily weighted on the individuation side of the balancing act, the majority of this book has emphasized the need for continuity. But on the other side of the tightrope is the teenagers' need for owning their own faith, for separating from and pushing against the tradition that has been given them. The remainder of this chapter will address that need.

Without this balance, a myopic emphasis on one need or the other can actually create rather than solve youth ministry problems. A new program overemphasizing continuity (what some naively assume is meant by "family-based youth ministry") will be no more effective than the old one overemphasizing individuation. The "fall" is simply on the other side.

I like the way my friend Ben Freudenberg, the coauthor of *The Family-Friendly Church* (Group), keeps this balance in place as he teaches about youth programming that is "family friendly." He recommends that youth ministries have three distinct types of programming: home-centered, intergenerational *and* peer-centered. All three are necessary components to a family-based youth ministry.

THE NEED FOR INDIVIDUATION

Several years ago I took a group of teenagers to Frontier Ranch, a Young Life property in Colorado. On the third day, right after breakfast, we were assigned to the ropes course, complete with zip line and high wire.

By the time I made it to the end of the course, I knew had a problem. I was still twenty-five feet in the air, and there was no logical way down. I couldn't go back. The two rugged freshman girls behind me would have laughed.

And then I saw it. Dangling in front of me, just out of reach, was a trapeze. Now I had read enough of those how-to-build-community-by-scaring-the-wits-out-of-kids books to know what was coming next. I was supposed to jump to the trapeze and trust that the sophomore boy holding the rope would not try to seek revenge for the wet willie I had given him that morning. (If you aren't familiar with the term *wet willie,* ask one of the youth in your church to demonstrate it!)

The instructor shouted up the simple directions, "Jump to the bar! It's the only way down!" As a Christian, I decided it was my duty to let the girls behind me go first. One at a time, they went. The girls leaped with no apparent concern for their bodies. I was less than eager to let go of my solid footing. But there was no way to reach the trapeze and stand securely at the same time. Eventually, I did jump, caught the bar and was lowered to the ground without incident.

The Creator designed adolescents to not be satisfied living as appendages of their parents.

What a marvelous picture of adolescence, these "jumping-off" years. Some make the jump out of the security of childhood with relative ease. For others, it is a terrifying step. Safety harnesses (that is, parents and the extended family of the church) should be required equipment for everyone.

The Creator of the developmental process intentionally designed adolescents so that they would not be satisfied simply living as appendages of their parents. The story of Edsel Ford, the son of Henry Ford, is a classic example of the innate need children have to separate from their parents:

> The story of the life of Edsel Ford . . . is replete with examples of how Edsel was thwarted in this attempt [to individuate], turning finally to the world of modern art (something his father knew little about) as a way of distinguishing his life from that of his famous father. The need was so strong that Edsel continued to spend a great deal of his energies fostering modern artists even though the elder Ford scoffed at his endeavors, maintaining that Edsel needed nothing more than the chance to follow in his father's automaking footsteps.[3]

As Erik Erikson, David Elkind and others have argued, the primary developmental task of adolescence is the formulation of a personal identity. These wet-cement years give us the most teachable moments for helping young people establish their own faith identities. These are the passionate years when teenagers try on different beliefs, like they might try on clothes at a department store. If they are going to honestly embrace the Christian faith, they need to do more than simply parrot back to us what *we* believe; they need to make intentional decisions about what *they* believe.

I am particularly grateful for "parachurch" groups like Young Life, Campus Life and the Fellowship of Christian Athletes, because they have consistently provided outlets for teenagers to express their own faith apart from the faith of their parents. Because these groups are seldom linked to a specific church and very few parents force their children to go to these groups, by attending, young people are often saying, "This is what *I* believe."

As a high schooler, I was enthusiastically involved in a marvelous Young Life club. In my idealism, I expressed great frustration over the deadness of my own church (compared to the excitement of a Young Life meeting). There was even a time when I talked with my Young Life leader about starting our own church, because there were "no churches in town that really understood what it meant to be a Christian." Our wise leader, who was himself active in a local church, advised against it.

At least part of my frustration with my church grew out of the passion of my growing relationship with Christ. Wisely, the minister of my "dead church" affirmed my growth and involvement in Young Life. His lack of defensiveness allowed me both to individuate and to maintain the necessary continuity with an extended Christian family in the church. Eugene Peterson's explanation matches my own experience: "Resistance to the church isn't the first step to atheism. It is more likely to be a natural development in discipleship."[4]

The fact that some teenagers seem to go along with everything their parents or youth leaders believe may be less a sign of maturity and more a sign of avoiding the challenges of growing up. Huggins points us beyond the pseudo-maturity of such young people when he explains,

> Too often the teens who find church attractive are the compliant/compulsive kids who possess the iron will to keep all the rules that are given to them in the name of God. This is a tragic irony since the very thing that is supposed to be generating sole dependence on Christ is really strengthening a kid's dependence on himself.[5]

THE HAZARDS OF INDIVIDUATION

Often the process of individuation is very uncomfortable for the keepers of the faith (parents and churches). Some teenagers arrive at their convictions only through a process of rejecting what they have been taught. Admittedly, much of this adolescent criticism and anger is immature, but for many, it is a necessary step. If teenagers do not care enough about their faith to question their parents' or their church's beliefs, their faith will often remain underdeveloped.

C. S. Lewis makes this same argument in *Miracles:*

> Many a man, brought up in the glib profession of some shallow form of Christianity, who comes through reading Astronomy to realize for the first time how majestically indifferent most reality is to man, and who perhaps abandons his religion on that account, may at that moment be having his first genuinely Christian experience.[6]

And again, in *Mere Christianity,* he argues,

> When a young man who has been going to church in a routine way honestly realizes that he does not believe in Christianity and stops going provided he does it for honesty's sake and not just to annoy his parents the spirit of Christ is probably nearer to him then than it ever was before.[7]

This dynamic poses a special predicament for the youth worker. It's possible that as we are successful in our work of moving youth toward mature Christian adulthood, we may very well find our youth become *more* critical of the church than before, because they care more. The process can be unnerving!

When I was a student at Baylor University, I was at the height of my own spiritual individuation process. Everything was an issue worth arguing about. As I look back, I am amazed at how easily I could determine who was and who was not a Christian on campus (I had trouble finding even one Christian teacher!). As an older adolescent, I was able to know and affirm what I believed partly by clarifying who did and who did not believe like I did.

At its worst, this move toward individuation can become a judgmental, "us-versus-them" battleground in which every issue is a witch-hunt worth burning someone for. But at its best, this experience can be a healthy part of establishing one's own faith. This process is *not* mature Christian adulthood, but it is often a necessary step along the way.

Jesus' methods for teaching his disciples addressed both their need for continuity and their need for individuation. Jesus did much of his teaching in the context of the religious establishment and quoted often from the Scriptures of the Hebrew tradition. But Jesus taught his disciples less often by giving them answers that they could memorize and more often by raising questions they couldn't answer, questions that would engage them more deeply in the pursuit of God.

If we hope for our teenagers to grow toward mature Christian adulthood, we must stop programming in such a way that we ignore some of our best students, those who stay away from church because they care about their faith experience enough to question what they have been told. What is needed is a ministry that touches every teenager we are responsible for, whether or not they ever darken the doorway of our church.

CREATING OPPORTUNITIES FOR INDIVIDUATION

Our youth ministries can encourage and support the process of individuation in several ways. To begin with, more of our programs can be designed for the youth themselves to serve and lead.

Giving real responsibility is the doorway into the world of adulthood. And research consistently indicates that when older youth tutor younger people, the tutors gain more from the experience than they give. The same is true in peer counseling programs. It is evident that when young people feel significant and needed, they tend to drop their delinquent behavior.[8]

Recently I had a mother explain to me that her son was unhappy because he was "not learning anything in Sunday school." When students and parents have complained about Sunday school in the past, my typical response has been to react by attempting to "fix" the class with some programmatic adjustment. Sometimes I would change teachers; other times I would actually come and teach the class myself. But all my Sunday school repair solutions met with limited success. By taking entire responsibility for the solution, I was actually part of the problem. I had failed to realize that my over-functioning solutions contributed to the dissatisfaction in the first place! So instead of trying to reinvent the Sunday-school program to keep this boy happy, I decided to offer him a position teaching alongside adults in a children's class.

Most churches have experienced the mass exodus of eleventh- and twelfth-graders from their youth groups. By the time teenagers are sixteen or seventeen, they will make one of two choices regarding the church: either they will become increasingly invested or they will drop out altogether. Older youth in general will not continue being involved *as spectators*, regardless of how exciting the programs may be. In an age when teenagers are virtually unnecessary for the efficient functioning of society (and the church), we can intentionally create opportunities where our older teenagers *are* needed.

We can intentionally create opportunities where teenagers are needed.

A second way we can encourage our teenagers' process of individuation is to support their expressions of moving away. The parents I respect most have made their children's church attendance nonnegotiable but have given their children the choice of what church they would like to attend. I have often said that some of the most mature teenagers from our church wind up at other churches. I have to swallow my pride and give up the expectation that our program should be able to meet every young person's need.

As startling as it sounds, I would have to say that our teenagers who have been active in other churches have often gained more than they have missed and have grown in their faith. I take the same attitude toward our teenagers' involvement in Bible studies at school or Christian summer camps. Though their involvement in these groups may limit the amount of time they have for *our* youth group, this broader experience meets a specific need for our teenagers that exclusive involvement in our church youth group cannot meet.

My pastor in high school understood this dynamic well. He affirmed my involvement with a group of Young Life leaders who were much more conservative than he was. He asked questions and wanted to hear about my experiences, even if he couldn't agree with all the theological conclusions I was making. The result? I invested more deeply in the church than I ever would have if I had felt pushed into such involvement by my pastor.

A third way we can support this process is by creating multiple mentoring opportunities for all the teenagers in our church. Peter Benson's first recommendation to schools is easily transferable to the church setting. He advocates that schools become more "personaliz[ed] . . . so that each and every child feels cared for, supported and important."[9]

There are many young people in my church who have made the choice not to participate in our programs. But there are very few who would refuse an invitation to have lunch with me or with one of their leaders. By providing a context for the building of cross-generational friendships, we can provide an extended family for our teenagers, whether they ever attend a youth event or not.

One final way to provide opportunities for teenagers to individuate is to plan for significant peer experiences for teenagers within the church. Without the foundational connections to mature Christian adults, this sort of peer-centered ministry can be no more than a short-term, flash-in-the-pan experience with no lasting impact. But with the proper foundation, teenagers can help each other significantly on their journey toward independence.

Adolescent separation from the world of adults is healthy and natural. The neglect of teenagers by adults is not.

Adolescence involves letting go of the security that comes with dependence on parents. But teenagers are not fully prepared to be independent either. They need a handrail, what Kenda Dean and Ron Foster call "a blankie," something to hold onto until they become truly independent. Because teenagers are looking for a new family to which to give their loyalty, peers become a temporary family of sorts and, *in the short term,* can exert even more influence on their values than their parents do.

Soon after *Family-Based Youth Ministry* was published, I received a letter from a young man who had grown up in our youth group. His letter, written on the stationery of the church where he was serving as a youth pastor, gave me an important perspective. He told me that he enjoyed the book but that he had a "bone to pick" with me about some of the things I had said. For this young man, who had grown up in a home that was not always supportive of his Christian pursuits, the peer-centered youth group we did have, with all its imperfections, was crucial to leading him toward maturity in Christ.

His letter was a reminder to me that there is nothing wrong with using positive peer pressure as a doorway into the church's program. Family-based youth ministry is not about abandoning traditional forms of youth programming as much as it is about building the foundation of solid connections with mature Christian adults, a foundation that my young youth-pastor friend had built, even in what felt very much like a peer-centered youth ministry.

IMPLICATIONS FOR MINISTRY

1. We can expect that as young people grow toward Christian maturity, some of them may very well go through a time of rejecting at least parts of the faith of their families before they can embrace it for themselves. If the church is prepared for this type of response, they can, in nonanxious ways, continue to love and celebrate God's work in the young people who find themselves moving away from the faith they have received.

2. The natural adolescent desire for separation from the world of adults is a healthy, natural process. What is not healthy or natural is the neglect of teenagers by adults. We must not use the God-ordained process of identity formation as an excuse for the abandonment of our responsibility for the ongoing nurture of the next generation.

3. Youth programs that emphasize student leadership without connecting those teenagers to an ongoing community of faith deprive the young people of the very relationships that can most effectively lead them to Christian maturity. But undergirded by Christian families and the extended family of the church, those same student leadership programs can greatly enhance a young person's growth in Christ.

4. Many churches can easily hire an active high school senior to work five hours a week as an intern for the youth program.

WILD HAIR IDEA

Cancel all youth activities for a month and allow each teenager in the group to find a ministry where he or she can serve in the church during that month. Report back at the end of the month and share ministry experiences.

And all the time . . . we continue to clamor for those
very qualities we are rendering impossible. . . .
We make men without chests and expect of them virtue and enterprise.
We laugh at honor and are shocked to find traitors in our midst.
We castrate and bid the gelding be fruitful.

C. S. LEWIS, *THE ABOLITION OF MAN*

Entertainment reaches out to us where we are,
puts on its show and then leaves us essentially unchanged,
if a bit poorer in time and money. It does not (and usually does not claim to)
offer us any new perspective on our lives or on other matters in creation.

DON MYERS, *ALL GOD'S CHILDREN AND BLUE SUEDE SHOES*

The Church disowned, the tower overthrown,
the bells upturned, what have we to do
But stand with empty hands and palms upturned
in an age which advances progressively backwards?

T. S. ELIOT

All is summed up in the prayer which a young
female human is said to have uttered recently:
"O god, make me a normal twentieth century girl!"
Thanks to our labors, this will mean increasingly,
Make me a minx, a moron, and a parasite.

SCREWTAPE (THE TEMPTER) IN C. S. LEWIS, *THE SCREWTAPE LETTERS*

The Christian home is a mission base when we refuse to shop for churches
after one church has bored or inconvenienced us.
When a family struggles to stay with a church through bad times,
it demonstrates another way of life than that so relentlessly
promoted by the economic exchange model.

RODNEY CLAPP, *FAMILIES AT THE CROSSROADS*

The biggest challenge for the church at the opening of the
twenty-first century is to develop a solution to the discontinuity and
fragmentation of the American Lifestyle.

LYLE SCHALLER

10 A DIFFERENT GOSPEL

Youth Culture Comes to Church

I was twelve when I first visited the ocean. We went to visit family in Galveston, Texas, and arrived just in time for a brief swim in the gulf before the sun went down. My mother warned me that the ocean had strong undercurrents; and, much to my disappointment, she stood with a watchful eye, ensuring that I wouldn't venture out more than knee deep. I promised myself that if I ever got back to the beach without her, things would be different.

When I got into high school, my brave pastor took four carloads of us (our total youth group and then some) to camp on the beach for a weekend. Even commando mosquitoes, clingy sand and 100-degree-plus Texas weather could not spoil this trip for us.

The first morning at the beach, we let the adults set up our home base, and we threw ourselves at the waves with a passion. For hours, we played tackle the kid with the ball, king of the raft, and body surfing. Finally our stomachs screamed loudly enough to send us out of the water in search of food. As we walked to the shore, our group was nowhere to be found. We saw no home base, no familiar cars, no sunburned pastor in sunglasses and Hush Puppies.

It didn't take long for us to realize that, while we were concentrating on having a good time, the current had carried us hundreds of yards down the coast without our even knowing it. And because we were being carried along by the current, we didn't notice its strength.

Strong undercurrents of our culture are carrying along the teenagers we work with, and yet they typically don't even feel it. Unless our youth programs work intentionally to resist these currents, our efforts at discipling youth may, in fact, simply entrench them more deeply in the very values that are in strong opposition to the Christian gospel.

In this chapter I want to identify three dominant characteristics of the culture that serves as far more than simply a neutral backdrop against which children in our time grow up. These are currents that can, in fact, push our young people away from maturity in general and from Christian maturity in particular.

ALL BY MYSELF: THE CONFORMITY OF INDIVIDUALISM

Recently I was at a restaurant that is frequented by students from a local high school known for encouraging "nonconformity." As the students walked in, it didn't take me long to recognize that all the students were from that school. How could I tell? Every one of these nonconformists wore the same uniform—not one required by a school dress code (there was none at this school). In absolute obedience to the "tyranny of the they," these young people dressed *exactly alike!*

Particularly striking were three senior boys with carbon-copy haircuts. They sat at their table with identical posture, manners and vocabulary. These students who prided themselves on their individualism didn't have the power to resist the conformity that individualism almost always demands.

Although the individualist may live with the delusion of fierce independence, he or she is the most likely candidate for codependence or, in Scott Peck's words, "a passive dependent personality disorder." Why?

Individualists, by definition, have freed themselves from loyalties that might in some way tie them down. But liberation from all loyalties beyond self cuts a person off from roots that bring the stability and identity necessary to stand against the currents of our culture. The idea that deep within each one of us there is a genuine "self" somehow completely separate from our roles and relationships is nonsense. If you take away my roles as husband and father and Christian and pastor and friend, there isn't much of a private self to discover!

As Robert Bellah explains, "My 'self' is composed of my relationships and commitments, my 'roles,' if you will. That doesn't mean I lack autonomy. In-

deed, only because of my relationships and commitments can I be autono-
mous at all. If I were isolated, I would be helpless."[1]

Some rejoice over the occasional "return to traditional family values" in
our culture. Realistically, this trend must be understood as one more phase
in the evolving conformity of individualism. After all, family values are "in"
these days. We would be unwise to get our
hopes up. This too shall pass.

Christians carried along by individualism cannot help but create God in their own image.

The persistent current of individualism
has radically changed the character of the
American family. Carl Schneider in the *Michigan Law Review* has observed that family
members today tend to view themselves "as a
collection of individuals united temporarily
for their mutual convenience and armed with
rights against each other."[2]

Individualistic Christians, carried along
more by the culture than by the gospel, come to define all their commitments in terms of *self*-realization: marriage is seen as personal development;
work as personal advancement; and church as personal fulfillment.[3] When
asked why they attend church, the individualist response is always, "Because
I get something out of it." Christian individualists learn to approach God as
a doting old grandfather, a "mush god," perhaps a cross between Big Bird
and Mr. Rogers—the kind of friend who would never require anything and
certainly never say no.

It is this sort of understanding of God that led a college girl to argue ve-
hemently, "*My* Jesus wouldn't think it was wrong for me to sleep with my
boyfriend!" It is this kind of understanding of God that leads musicians who
use blatantly immoral lyrics to thank God when they receive Grammy
awards. Christians carried along by the current of individualism cannot help
but create God in their own image.

Several years ago Vanderbilt beat the University of Tennessee in a barn-
burning, buzzer-beater basketball game. One of our students from Vanderbilt made sure he called his father (a UT graduate) to gloat over the game.
The father's only comeback was, "You have to admit that UT did have the

strongest single player on the court." The son quickly responded, "Yeah, Dad, maybe that player needs to take up tennis. Basketball is a team sport!" Christian discipleship is a team sport. It always happens in the context of Christian community.

One of the goals for our youth ministry is that our teenagers will grow to become independent in Christ, that they will be able to stand alone when their faith calls them to do so. But there is a clear distinction between healthy independence and the (unhealthy) cultural current of individualism.

An independent person has the power to "say no" because his or her identity is grounded in a heritage of secure relationships. The individualist can only do what he or she wants.

The independent person is secure enough to serve or give without being consumed in the process. Individualists (whose only identity is in themselves) will become consumed in validating their identity and proving their worth through service, achievements, relationships and activity.

The individualist can only do what he or she wants.

The pseudo-community in which teenagers grow up, what some have referred to as a "cyber-suckled community," has become a breeding ground for increasing isolation and individualism. Churches that are carried along by the current of individualism can inadvertently train teenagers that being a Christian is primarily a personal and individual affair. The unspoken message to many teens involved in these churches is that their personal faith decisions are all that really matter. This belief is found most notably in the scores of young adults who argue, "I don't need to go to church to be a Christian."

I have often wondered what would happen if football coaches approached their work like most youth ministers are expected to. For example, I wonder what would happen if, when a player was too busy to show up for practice, the understanding coach simply said, "We'll miss you. I hope you'll be able to make it next week sometime." Imagine the players leaving practice and hearing the smiling coach say, "Thanks for coming. I hope you'll come back tomorrow."

If a football team operated like a typical youth ministry, we might expect concerned parents to call the coach, saying, "Can you tell me what's been going on in practice? My son says it's boring, and he doesn't want to come anymore. I was wondering, could you make it a little more fun for them? And by the way, you might want to talk to the coach at the school across town. He seems to have the right idea." The coach might send out quarterly questionnaires about what the players would like to change about the team. (I can just imagine the answers: "shorter practices," "more winning").

Commitment to the church has become implausible to most Christians in our culture.

Responding like a typical youth minister, this coach might first feel guilty that the practices were not meeting the boy's needs, and he would try to adjust his program to suit this boy (and every other boy who complained). Between trying to keep everybody happy and giving every student a good experience, the coach would squeeze in a little football practice. And what kind of season would this coach have? It's a safe bet that the coach wouldn't be the only one who felt like a loser.

But this is the very way that most churches expect to run their youth ministries. To expect that youth be committed to the church with the same level of commitment that would be expected of them on an athletic team would draw the charge of legalism and insensitivity. Our culture has been so carried away by the current of religious individualism that the expectation of commitment to the church has become implausible to most Christians in our culture. Because the god of individualism pressures us to program to the lowest common denominator, we seldom raise the expectations high enough for teenagers to experience real community.

Real community means real responsibility for each other. It means a commitment to be there for each other even when the schedule is tight and the motivation is low. But the typical Christian adult in our culture knows little about commitment to community.

In our city there are five prominent evangelical churches. Like obedient individualists, many of their members move among the churches as easily as they change their clothes. When they feel the need for a little more liturgy, they move to the charismatic Episcopal church. When they are looking for a little more freedom in worship, they move to the fast and loose Pentecostal church. In the mood for more substantive teaching? The conservative Presbyterian church will do the trick. For these enthusiastic Christians, loyalty to a specific community (which can often be quite bothersome) is rejected in favor of finding a place that meets their needs.

Most youth ministers have their files jam-packed with lessons that promise to help build young people's self-esteem. But positive self-esteem is gained by repeated interactions with others who have gone before, by affirmation from and connection to a genuine community.

If we hope to move our young people toward mature Christian adulthood, the discipline of community needs to be a central focus of our program. If our teaching and programs center exclusively on personal, individual faith, chances are they will simply grow fat without growing strong.

Church consultant Lyle Schaller points us to the foundational question the contemporary church must ask:

> Rising from the debris of our lost values is the new value on the individual. The "me" generation has given way to a "me" world. The question is, how will the church, the ultimate "we" organization, adjust?[4]

CAN SOMEONE CHANGE THE CHANNEL?
THE CONFINES OF CONSUMERISM

One of my favorite images of our culture is the "couch potato," the person who invests his or her life on the couch, watching television, experiencing life secondhand. Couch potatoes sit, wait and react. When they get bored, they simply change the channel to something more exciting.

Through consumer-oriented entertainment, our teens have been conditioned to seek pleasure (or the avoidance of pain and boredom) as a goal for life. From kids who lick slimy secretions from toads to get high[5] to others who wear the "party till you puke" philosophy plastered all over their lives, pleasure has become serious business.

A group of teenagers was asked, "What images come to mind for the word 'party' when you think of your peers?" The response: "getting destroyed, totaled, wasted, hammered, annihilated, decimated."[6] What caught my attention about this study was not the typical teenage responses but the way that teenagers describe their images of "partying" in *passive* terms. These descriptions indicate that teens perceive "fun" as something that happens to them.

Next to sleeping, the average teenager will spend more time watching television than pursuing any other activity. Is it any wonder that approximately three-fourths of them think church is boring?[7] After half a century of doing research on adolescents, Merton Strommen makes a fascinating observation:

> I find it significant that [our] national survey of randomly chosen youths in the mid-1950's . . . did not show boredom as a prominent characteristic of church youth. What characterized youth work then? Not entertainment or fun activities organized by a youth minister, but personal involvement and responsibility.[8]

I don't know of any youth ministry that can, week in and week out, ever be as entertaining as a 92-million-dollar movie. Compared to most other options young people have for entertainment, let's face it, we don't have a chance. If we train our youth to expect entertainment from us, we can be assured that when things get a little slow, they will be switching the channel to somebody else's show.

Entertainment-centered programs provide an artificial intimacy, like a crowd at a concert, without the joys or frustrations of real relationships. When attracting teens through exciting programs becomes the goal of a youth ministry, we teach them the Christian life will always be a party. I wonder—have those of us in professional youth ministry been accomplices in raising a generation of Christian teenagers who some refer to as "God's little brats"? I have to believe that a generation that grows up believing they should never be bored, never be uncomfortable, never have to do without will be severely limited in the transforming impact they can have on their world.

I have discovered an interesting phenomenon. Often the most spiritually responsible adults grew up in miserable or nonexistent youth programs, in churches where there was no youth pastor to blame for the problems in the group. These young people and their parents had to take responsibility for their own youth ministries. They had to struggle with failed attempts to get programs off the ground. And these young adults are often the best prepared to live a Christian life that doesn't get neatly fixed in thirty-minute blocks.

Youth ministries that are carried along by the current of entertainment will treat their youth as consumers, and the leaders will do everything they can to keep the customers happy. This fact may explain why the majority of *churched* teenagers cannot name the four Gospels and do not even know why Christians celebrate Easter. Learning the basics of the Christian life takes work and discipline (the very demands that just might keep youth away!).

Most churched teenagers have just enough knowledge of the gospel to inoculate them against ever being transformed by it. They know bits and pieces of the biblical story, but they know the Disney myths much better (every one of them could tell you what happened after the Handsome Prince kissed Sleeping Beauty, but few know what Abraham, Isaac and a knife were doing on the mountain together!).

A Gallup poll discovered that 95 percent of teenagers believe in at least one supernatural phenomenon (for example, angels, astrology, ESP, witchcraft, ghosts, or clairvoyance).[9] And why not? These beliefs require no investment or commitment. They can simply be held passively without any risk or involvement.

Young people who develop a low tolerance for boredom will be unable to practice the disciplines necessary to grow in the Christian life. Prayer, Bible study, fellowship, witnessing, fasting and solitude are all disciplines that have at their very heart the facing of our own boredom and restlessness.

LOOKING GOOD:
THE CULTURAL DEMAND FOR SUCCESS

I found a fascinating report that described the results of crosscultural study designed to determine the prime causes for misbehavior in adolescents. Researchers identified two universal factors associated with misconduct. Not surprisingly, the first was the level of parental monitoring (that is, limited parental participation was a likely indicator of misconduct). The second factor was more surprising.

The study showed that the more a teenager valued "outward success," the more likely it would be for that teenager to misbehave. Youth in each of the three countries studied (United States, Australia and Hong Kong) all reported the same trend. Values like wealth, power, a comfortable life and social recognition were strong predictors of misconduct.[10]

In this culture where human value is often reduced to how much one produces, teenagers are easily seduced into bowing down before the false god of success. But, as the research indicates, teaching our young people to place a high value on success doesn't always have positive consequences.

Teenagers are often victims of a cultural system that tells them they are valuable only *if* they are physically attractive, *if* they are intelligent or *if* they have money.[11] As long as young people depend on these visible signs of success for their self-esteem, they remain dependent and immature.

Consider Henri Nouwen's story. Having written a number of bestselling books on Christian spirituality, he was a Yale professor, a sought-after lecturer, a man of no small stature in his field. His convictions about the nature of the Christian faith, though, led him to leave his prestigious position and join the staff of an institution that cared for adults with mental disabilities.

In his new position, no one recognized him as anyone special, except that he was a part of their community. Nouwen's move represented his refusal to allow his identity before God to be tied up in his ability to perform or produce or succeed. He explains,

> It seems easier to be God than to love God, easier to control people than to love people. . . . The leader of the future will be the one who dares to claim his irrelevance in the contemporary world as a divine vocation that allows him or her to enter into a deep solidarity with the anguish underlying all the glitter and success and bring the light of Jesus there.[12]

For Christians, measurable success can never be our primary goal. Judas was looking for visible signs of Jesus' success. The Pharisees demanded signs to prove that Jesus was speaking the truth. But, according to the New Testament, Jesus never did anything intentional to build a crowd. As a matter of fact, he often tried to do just the opposite. Visible signs of success were not high on his priority list.

If we place success over faithfulness, we will inevitably choose image over substance, in danger of becoming ecclesiastical public relations directors rather than ministers of the gospel.

One of the college students who worked as an intern in our youth ministry was asked by some parents, "What are you going to do when you graduate from Vanderbilt?" He explained that he was considering full-time ministry with teenagers. Later, I couldn't believe what I happened to overhear. One of the mothers in the church said, "How can he do that to his parents after all the money they put into his education?" Image over substance.

Youth ministries teach young people that success is the real priority when they only use good-looking adults for youth leaders. We train them to seek success first when we consistently recognize those who visibly accomplish the most. We demonstrate how highly we value success when the youth minister cannot "handle" having a program that fails. Let's face it. Our young people may learn more about discipleship by watching their leaders struggle than by following the seemingly magical gurus who find success second nature.

Young people need training in living with failure.

Young people do not need our help in learning how to handle success. They need training in living with failure. All the great success stories I know of have more failures in them than successes. Abraham Lincoln, Louis Pasteur and Martin Luther are known for their success but faced failure over and over again. And I'm told that every great songwriter in Nashville has a much larger trash pile than "hit" pile.

When our youth ministries tacitly teach the doctrine of success, we are in danger of raising a generation so afraid to fail that they are paralyzed to take the risks necessary to live the abundant Christian life. When young people leave our meetings thinking, *Those guys are so good. How do they do it? I could never do anything like that!* we have taught them not to risk, because to do so could mean they wouldn't measure up.

Youth who graduate from success-centered youth programs learn to treat God as the most efficient means to their success in life. They learn to pray because "it works" or because "it makes them feel better." These young people grow up to be adults who are surprised by struggles and wonder how a loving God could ever let them suffer or fail.

A ministry that is leading teens to mature Christian adulthood will often find itself going against the stream of these values. I picture the forces of youth culture as in figure 3.

The diagram is most easily understood as a canal through which a child's faith "flows" toward maturity. The thesis of family-based youth ministry is that the family and the extended family of the church are the structures (or walls of the canal) that most naturally move a person toward faith maturity. As a teenager moves into adulthood, the extended family of the church will begin to have the most formative influence on a young person's faith. The primary task of a family-based youth ministry is to "pass the baton" of faith formation to the extended family of the church. Because traditional youth ministry takes place outside these structures, young people in those ministries are more susceptible to the juvenilizing forces of youth culture.

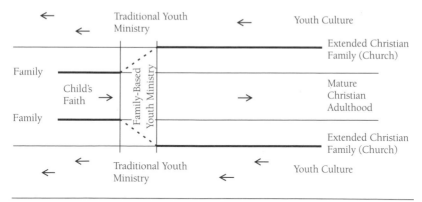

Figure 3. The forces of youth culture

IMPLICATIONS FOR MINISTRY

1. The only way to combat the encumbering influences of modern youth culture is to connect teens to adults who are moving against the culture. These relationships can give young people courage as they go against the flow.

2. It is very appropriate for leaders to ask the young people in their groups to be as committed to the community of faith as they are to an athletic team (for example, showing up for practice even when they don't feel like it).

3. Churches can invite interested teens to participate in community spiritual disciplines that allow them to face their boredom and not run away from it (for example, fasting, concerts of prayer, days of silence).

WILD HAIR IDEA

Have an annual Boredom Fest—a night when everyone is together with nothing planned, no games planned, no materials (like pool tables or Ping-Pong tables). Or take a year to enjoy (as a youth group) another church's Sunday-night programs rather than taking time to plan something new each week.

The failure of youth ministry in the mainline church
has to be viewed, above all, as a crisis in theology. . . .
The truth is that the sickness pervading youth ministry
reflects all too accurately the illness infecting
mainline denominations as a whole: an absence of passion.
Passion—the state of loving something enough to suffer for it—
is what puts the crucified Christ at the center
of our work with young people, and therefore is what
makes our work ministry and not something else.

KENDA DEAN AND RON FOSTER, *THE GODBEARING LIFE*

It is not within our power to place the
divine teachings directly in someone else's heart.
All that we can do is place them on the surface of the heart
so that when the heart breaks they will drop in.

HASIDIC SAYING

God may be one, but it takes two to find him.

MARTIN BUBER

God has so ordained things that we grow in faith
only through the frail instrumentality of one another.

JOHN OF THE CROSS

As long as ministry only means that we worry
a lot about people and their problems;
as long as it means an endless number of activities which we can hardly
coordinate, we are still very much dependent
on our own narrow and anxious heart.
But when our worries are led to the heart of God
and there become prayer, then ministry and prayer become two
manifestations of the same all-embracing love of God.

HENRI NOUWEN, *THE WAY OF THE HEART*

The kingdom and the reality of church as first family deny the right of
biological family to be the whole world for any of its members.
For of course any family that attempts to be the world for itself
in fact creates a stunted, shrunken world.
Paradoxically, a family is enriched when it is decentered,
relativized, recognized as less than an absolute.

RODNEY CLAPP, *FAMILIES AT THE CROSSROADS*

11 GOD CALLING

Thinking Theologically About Youth Ministry

We spent most of our lunch dreaming and talking together about moving our youth ministry to "the next level." After an hour and a half and five glasses of iced tea, we ended our conversation hopeful, enthusiastic, both convinced that our new design was going to increase vastly the scope of our ministry.

As a father of three teenagers himself, my lunch partner had been actively supportive of our work. He was a faithful giver to the church and a diligent student of the Bible. As we walked out of the restaurant together, I was grateful to have someone like this man on our team.

But before we reached our cars, he stopped, suddenly very serious, looked me in the eye and said, "You realize that if this program is going to work, it is going to have to be *flawless.*"

I wasn't quite sure how to respond. At first, I generally agreed, mentioning something about how important it was for us to be faithful with our plans. But sometimes my honesty slips out when I least expect it. I said, "I do need you to know up front that I am not particularly good at perfection."

He looked at me like I had just flown in from Mars.

I kept going. "I don't believe the level of our program's perfection is going to make or break our youth ministry." Eyebrows were furrowing. "As I see it, the Christian faith is not about our perfection but about God working through our imperfection and even our failure. That is the whole idea of grace."

His response was quick, with an air of frustration about having been dragged away from the real topic. With a dismissive gesture he said, "Look, don't bring God into this. We're talking about the youth ministry!"

Now years later, I can understand my friend's frustration. We have all known Christians (ministers in particular) who avoid taking responsibility by theologizing from an ivory tower, who avoid executing strategic plans as if they were unspiritual. But I'm afraid that much of our thinking and planning about youth ministry gets done outside the context of our faith. And when dependence on God's grace is excluded from our thinking, we wind up trusting our human strategies (and our own ability to work those strategies) more than we trust that our youth ministries are, first and foremost, God's business.

A PLACE TO BEGIN

One of my foundational theological assumptions is that we never quite "get it right" when it comes to understanding God. All our language, all our descriptions, are provisional. No matter how well we understand God today, there is a fuller understanding still awaiting us. With this disclaimer as a context, though, I want to offer in this chapter a first draft of a brief theological foundation for family-based youth ministry.

> Our goal is not simply to socialize young people into a religious belief system, as if we could mass-produce mature Christians.

As we think theologically about the process of helping teenagers move toward mature Christian adulthood, we must begin with God's central role. We begin with a confession that all of our methods, all of our programs, all of our systems are not enough to lead a young person to genuine repentance and faith.

Our goal is not simply to socialize young people into a religious belief system, as if somehow, by finding the right production method, we could mass-produce mature Christians. We must not delude ourselves into thinking that we can "make" teenagers into anything, particularly mature Christians. What we can do is provide a context in which they can, to borrow Eugene Peterson's wonderful expression, "acquire a taste for grace."

We have no more power to make a young person grow faith than we have to make a bean sprout grow. All we do is plant and water. We cannot get down inside the seed and pull out a plant. We can simply do the very small, but very important, part of planting and nurturing the seed.

To use another image, a doctor can only bandage and set a broken bone. The physician cannot make the bones grow back together. All he or she can do is work with God's healing process. Though *we* will never be "successful" in making young people into mature Christian adults, we can work with God's process to support them in the growth that only God can bring. In this sense we do not "take Christ to kids." But we do have the privilege of being included in God's revelation of himself to them.

> We have no more power to make a person grow than we have to make a bean sprout

Only when we understand that we, as well as the teenagers we seek to reach, are "under God's grace" will we ever be free from the driven hyperactivity that has become typical of so many youth ministries. God uses us most often *in spite of* our gifts, abilities and hard work, not because of them.

Perhaps this is the reason Jesus sent out his disciples empty-handed. He warned them, "I am sending you out like sheep among wolves" (Mt 10:16). Sheep are defenseless. No matter how many push-ups they do, no matter how much training they have, in a head-on battle with a wolf, a sheep will lose every time. As long as the sheep is depending on its own resources, it can never win.

Jesus introduces this "sheep among wolves" warning by reminding his disciples of the uselessness of any human strategy they might be tempted to depend on. First Jesus tells them, "Do not take along any gold or silver or copper in your belts" (Mt 10:9). A sheep with a bigger budget is still powerless against wolves. Next Jesus instructs his disciples not to take a bag or even a second coat or shoes. There is no bag of tricks big enough for a sheep's encounter with a wolf. In youth ministry, there is no human resource sufficient for the task, no provision for what to do when what we have wears out. Those things we would instinctively reach for to support ourselves (like perfection, hard work and the best human strategy) will not guarantee the effectiveness of our ministries. A generous youth ministry budget, all the right connections, even our bag of methodological and perfectionist tricks will not be enough to ensure our success. The Shepherd offers his sheep no provision other than himself.

MINISTRY BY GOD'S DESIGN

Recognizing God's central role in our ministries (or better yet, our supporting role in God's ministry), the best we can do is to work *with* God's design for faith formation. According to the famous words of the Shema, God's first provision for faith formation is the family:

> Hear, O Israel: The LORD our God, the LORD is one. Love the LORD your God with all your heart and with all your soul and with all your strength. These commandments that I give you today are to be upon your hearts. Impress them on your children. Talk about them when you sit at home and when you walk along the road, when you lie down and when you get up. . . . Write them on the doorframes of your houses and on your gates. (Deut 6:4-9)

God's provision for the Christian nurture of children begins with the family, the people who are there when those children lie down and when they rise up, who are there with their children when they sit down to eat or take a journey. No mention is made in this text of the priests taking responsibility! These early parents (and their Israelite kin) were not told to get their children to meetings or to worship (that was understood). They were commanded, instead, to talk about God and his commands throughout their daily activities.

For most Christian teenagers, Sunday school and youth group have become a substitute for spiritual training in the home. Interestingly enough, the Sunday-school movement itself began as an outreach to *unchurched* poor children. Its founders never intended for it to take over the role of Christian parents. When mothers brought their children to Jesus to bless them, it would have been much more efficient if he had sent them off with Judas to start a "Kids' Klub" program. Instead he interrupted his teaching to adults and came to where the children were and blessed them right where they were . . . with their own parents.

In many ways, family-based youth ministry is not a new model as much as it is a radical return to God's original design. Christian educator John Westerhoff affirms, "No matter where you look in our Judeo-Christian heritage it is the parents who have the prime responsibility to bring up their children in the faith."[1]

There is a table spirituality that is central to our faith. From the Jewish family rituals of the Passover and the Sabbath to the Lord's Supper and even to the banqueting table of our Lord in heaven, the undercurrent of a family meal is consistent. It is startling to realize the lack of programmatic focus in Jesus' ministry. He had no organizational chart, no planning team, no curriculum, and no ten-year long-range mission statement. Jesus' first priority in calling his disciples was "that they might be with him" (Mk 3:14).

THE DISCIPLINES OF COMMUNITY

As I suggested in the last chapter, much of popular religion in our country today has uncritically embraced the overwhelming individualistic emphasis of our culture, a pervasive emphasis evident even in the writings of highly acclaimed Christian authors, one of whom has said, "The ultimate goal of life remains the spiritual growth of the individual, the solitary peaks that can only be climbed alone."[2] Certainly the spiritual growth of the individual is an important *part* of the Christian vocation, and often God does call us to stand alone. But the personal growth of the individual Christian cannot be our ultimate goal. This is the very issue that the Westminster Catechism speaks to in its first question.

Question: What is the chief end of man?
Answer: Man's chief end is to glorify God and enjoy him forever.

As disciples of Christ, our ultimate goal (our "chief end") is not limited to our own personal growth. That goal is much too small. The glory of God and our *enjoyment* of God come first for the Christian. Our own spiritual growth is a natural outgrowth of learning to glorify God.

In the New Testament I find no recorded incidents of God dealing with his people in isolation, simply as individuals. Even Jesus surrounded himself with twelve stiff-necked men. After Saul received the revelation from Jesus on the road to Damascus, Jesus directed him to another person, Ananias, to complete the transaction. Of course, Jesus could have simply given Paul instructions for his future ministry and sent him on his way. But instead, God's design was to connect Paul to the community of faith.

From the very beginning of his ministry, Paul was involved with other believers. When he started churches, he assumed that all believers would be committed to the body of believers in that community. There was no hint of salvation without a link to a specific community of faith. When Paul went to make disciples, he could have held evangelistic crusades directed at individuals, but instead, he planted churches. Apparently he understood that the nature of the life of discipleship involves a practical commitment to a specific community of faith.

Whether churches practice infant baptism or infant dedication, almost always two groups of people in the church make a commitment to provide for the Christian nurture of a child: the parents and the congregation. The youth minister and the youth program must never be seen as substitutes for the parents' and the church members' fulfilling their own commitments.

I remember well the first child I baptized. I was nervous, hoping I wouldn't forget anything and vaguely remembering some comment my mother had made about how easy it was for a baby's neck to break. Everything went beautifully right up to the final words of the baptism, ". . . and of the Holy Spirit." With a sigh of relief, I said, "Let us pray." But just as I began praying, the child, whose mouth was strategically placed next to my lapel microphone, began (I will not attempt to put this delicately) to throw up. Of course, this day just happened to be one of those rare occasions when the sound system was working perfectly. (I don't think the congregation heard much of my prayer.) The parents were embarrassed and apologized profusely as they tried to wipe off my robe. But I remember thinking, *What a perfect picture of the church this is.* We are loved unconditionally by God, and God charges the community of faith to love and nurture each child in the faith whether it is easy and pleasant or not. We do not love these children and young people *because* they are cute and adorable. We love them as a demonstration of Christ's unconditional love for us.

> **We are called to make disciples who are moving toward Christian maturity and obedience.**

Our goal in youth ministry is not simply to get teenagers into a relationship with Jesus Christ. We are called to make disciples—men and women who are moving toward Christian maturity and obedience. One cannot move toward Christian maturity alone. One may be able to become a mature Buddhist monk alone. One may be able to become a master in New Age religion alone. But one cannot be a mature Christian adult in isolation from other believers.

Although solitude is an important discipline of the Christian life, Christian solitude must never be confused with a concern for individualistic, private spiritual experiences. As Henri Nouwen suggests,

> Solitude in prayer is not privacy. And the differences between privacy and solitude are profound. Privacy is our attempt to insulate the self from interference; solitude leaves the company of others for a time in order to listen to them more deeply. . . . Private prayers are selfish and thin; prayer in solitude enrolls in a multi-voiced, century-layered community.[3]

Similarly, Thomas Merton said, "It is in deep solitude that I find the gentleness with which I can truly love my brothers. . . . Solitude and silence teach me to love my brothers for what they are, not what they say." Our genuine experiences alone in the presence of God, then, are properly understood in the context of the community of faith.

Ideally, every young person who makes a commitment to Christ should be eager to become a part of a specific church. But the truth is that most teenagers are no more developmentally ready to make a genuine commitment to the institution of the church than they would be to make a commitment to the institution of marriage.

During the teenage years, interest in institutional religion is at its lowest. It is not so much that young people are against the institution of the church. Most simply don't care. They are at a stage of development when loyalty to relationships plays a much more significant role than loyalty to institutions.

When I was in seventh grade, I was confirmed in my church in Texas. I understood little of the commitment that I was making to God and to his people, but Doris Jones understood. An elderly woman in the church, she made it a point to come to the front of the church after my confirmation, hug me and hand me a five-dollar gold piece from the 1800s. Even if I didn't understand the life-altering nature of the public vows I had just taken to follow Jesus Christ as my Lord and Savior, Doris Jones did.

What became clearer as I grew older was not the strength of my commitment to the church, but the strength and identity I had received because of the church's commitment to me. I stayed in the church not because of my resolve and commitment, but because adults in the church continued to claim me even when I was an embarrassment to them. No one in my church tried to force me into "institutional loyalty." They simply surrounded me with the kinds of relationships that made loyalty to that extended family only natural.

The Christian faith becomes real to most teenagers not because of rational arguments for Christianity or because they try like crazy to hang on to what they believe, but because real people live out the gospel in what may seem like very insignificant ways. A story is told of Bob Mitchell, the past president of Young Life, visiting with a teenager at a Young Life summer camp. This teenage boy had made a decision that week to follow Christ. Bob had been the speaker and was eager to hear what it was that led to the boy's decision. So Bob asked something like, "How did God get your attention?"

The boy said nothing about the content of the messages or the relevance of what he had heard. He said simply, "I guess what really did it was when you remembered my name."

BEYOND THE IDOLATRY OF THE FAMILY

The most sinister idols are the good things: success, popularity, perfection, wisdom, loyalty and the like. Seeing any one of these good things as an ultimate goal can be a much more pernicious temptation for the believer than the much more obvious sins. To borrow C. S. Lewis's vivid imagery in *The Great Divorce:* "Brass is mistaken for gold more easily than clay."

As I have suggested throughout this book, the Christian family *is* God's primary tool for building faith and character in God's children, but the family is not God. Particularly now that family values are all the rage, both in the church and in the political arena, Christians must guard themselves against the temptation to idolize the family. One way to keep the value of the family in perspective is to reevaluate the commonly held hierarchy of priorities. Many teachers and leaders have listed Christian priorities in this fashion:

1. God

2. family

3. work

4. country

5. church

I wonder if this list is a biblical reflection of priorities or a cultural one. For the Christian, does the family indeed belong in second place? And does the extended family of the church belong at the bottom of the list, as an optional priority "if time allows"?

By now I hope you know how important I believe the family is. But I am also clear that the preservation of the family and "family values" must not be of *ultimate* importance for the Christian. When the family—as important as it is—becomes our primary focus, it too can become an idol, as abhorrent to God

A focus on the family can become as abhorrent to God as any golden calf.

as any golden calf. Our primary allegiance is to God and God alone. The family is a good gift from God, an effectual means to the end of bringing glory to God. But for the Christian, nothing, no matter how noble or good, must be allowed to take the place of God or the priorities of God's kingdom.

The nuclear family is the source of our greatest joys, but it is also the source of our greatest pain and problems. I would wager that when therapists talk with deeply troubled persons, they deal with little that is not related to the nuclear family. We can be assured that in addition to any Christian values that are passed on, each nuclear family passes on its own limited perspective and unique brand of prejudice as well.

I am not advocating the kind of "churchaholic" behavior that abandons family responsibilities for the sake of committee-commitment overload. I have seen fathers who would much rather attend their fathering group than pay attention to their children. I have seen mothers who run from committee meeting to committee meeting to escape the pressures of demanding children and a mediocre marriage. And all too often pastors have allowed their marriage and family to deteriorate while they escaped into the much more manageable world of ministry and programs.

Our loyalty to the church is not a tool for escaping responsibility at home. Rather, our connectedness to the community of faith is the very thing that should hold us accountable for our faithfulness to family, work and church. It is this accountability to the broader community of faith that can free us from the limited perspectives and unhealthy patterns of our family of origin.

It may just be that placing the priority of the community of faith above the priority of our family can allow us to keep a stance of openness to what God may be trying to teach us, even if it goes against the grain of what we might have been brought up to believe.

I know it's just youth ministry we're talking about here, but I couldn't help but bring God into it.

IMPLICATIONS FOR MINISTRY

1. The clearest way for a church to reflect programmatically its dependence on God's grace is to establish an intentional prayer base for the youth ministry so that members of the church on a regular basis pray for each young person, each leader and each event. We do not pray because it "works" but because we understand our genuine dependence on God's grace.

2. Participation in the church's corporate worship should be modeled by the leaders, taught by the teachers and expected as normative in the growing Christian life.

3. Each church can provide regular opportunities for the youth of the church to build friendships with the pastor(s) of the church to remind them of their connection to the total church and not simply to the youth program.

WILD HAIR IDEA

Invite the pastor to preach a series of sermons on the idolatry of the nuclear family and the priority of the "first family" of the Christian community.

In times of change, learners inherit the earth,
while the learned find themselves beautifully equipped
to deal with a world that no longer exists.

ERIC HOFFER, QUOTED IN GLENN AND NELSEN,
RAISING SELF-RELIANT CHILDREN IN A SELF-INDULGENT WORLD

Give me a lever long enough and a prop strong enough.
I can single-handed move the world.

ARCHIMEDES

You are a Christian only so long as you constantly pose
critical questions to the society you live in . . .
so long as you stay unsatisfied with the status quo and
keep saying that a new world is yet to come.

HENRI NOUWEN, QUOTED IN FOSTER, *MONEY, SEX AND POWER*

Is it any wonder that American youth put the profession of clergy
near the bottom of a list of occupations they would like to enter,
ranking just a cut above undertaking?

ROBERT LAURENT, *KEEPING YOUR TEEN IN TOUCH WITH GOD*

The Christian church is not exactly known
for setting trends or embracing change.

GEORGE BARNA, *MARKETING THE CHURCH*

If we are going to learn a life of holiness in the mess of history,
we are going to have to prepare for something
intergenerational and think in centuries.

EUGENE PETERSON, *THE CONTEMPLATIVE PASTOR*

I loved coming home to a place where the
first three pews celebrated my coming back from college.

MARY PRICE MADDOX, RECOVERING YOUTH DIRECTOR DESCRIBING
HER EXPERIENCE GROWING UP IN AN INTENTIONAL FAMILY-BASED YOUTH MINISTRY

The best way to nurture firsthand faith in our students
is to occasionally and consciously program no program.

DUFFY ROBBINS, *THE MINISTRY OF NURTURE*

12 MAKING IT WORK

Implementing a Family-Based Youth Ministry

Several years back, I received a curious invitation. I was told that a new book was in the works, a book to be called *The Ten Hottest Youth Groups in the Country*. I was honored that I had been invited to submit a chapter. I sent my chapter in, with some trepidation, realizing that soon everyone would know what I had come to know so well: our youth ministry was, in many ways, anything but "hot." Nonetheless, I looked forward to receiving a copy of the book and reading the fascinating accounts of the truly hot youth ministries in the country.

That was more than a decade ago. And I'm still waiting. I never heard another word from the would-be editor. The book, quite obviously, was never published.

My guess is that the "hottest" youth groups in the country, were, on closer inspection, doing nothing fascinating enough to make the book a decent read. More than likely, when all the manuscripts were in, the editor had in his hands a collection of tedious details, a convergence of hundreds of unspectacular acts of faithfulness.

Youth ministry (and, I suppose, ministry in general), no matter how many years we have under our belts, is a messy vocation. No matter how clear our model is, no matter how tight our evaluation system, no matter how much we invest in training, this is messy work.

But the mess not withstanding, for the past twenty-five years I have lived with one consuming passion in youth ministry. I have sought to find the most effective ways of leading young people toward maturity in Christ. I have searched for the "leverage points of the Spirit," those practices most likely to bring about lasting, life-long change in students' lives.

It didn't take long into my early years of youth ministry to experience the disappointment of watching some of our "most committed" youth group kids head off to college and into adulthood without the sufficient spiritual infrastructure to make it as faithful disciples in the adult world. As I was becoming an expert on what wasn't working, the whole notion of family-based youth ministry began taking shape for me.

During the past ten years, I have been amazed by the broad-based groundswell of interest in this family-based way of thinking about youth ministry. In charismatic groups and groups who are terrified of charismatics, in traditional groups and groups that despise tradition, in denominational groups and in groups that insist on calling their denominations "non-denominational," in conservative groups, liberal groups, and even in groups that have trouble finding any theological common ground, I have found youth leaders drawn to the principles of family-based youth ministry.

Though this vision of youth ministry *has* created a great deal of interest, I'm afraid it has also stirred up good deal of confusion. Some see it as synonymous with abandoning all traditional youth programming. Others see it as a way to place the entire responsibility for the Christian nurture of teenagers onto parents. And a few see it as just another "good thing" to add to their already overloaded job description.

But the one question I've heard more than any other is simply "How?" "How do you make it work?" "How can I get a family-based youth ministry off the ground?" So when my friend Cindy Bunch at InterVarsity contacted me about creating a revised edition of *Family-Based Youth Ministry,* I knew that the most important change to the book would be to add a chapter like this one, a chapter to give some clarity and perspective, to provide a bit of a road map for those who are seeking intentionally to create a family-based ministry in their own churches.

WHY MANY PROGRAMS DON'T WORK

Several years ago, scientists in Canada discovered that the population of rabbits in a particular area of their country had diminished to frighteningly low levels. And loving mysteries, as scientist are wont to do, these curious scholars set out to discover the cause of this dramatic shift in the rabbit population.

Their first assumption was that there must have been an illness that had been killing off all of these rabbits. But they could find no evidence of any such epidemic. Several years later, while they were still scratching their heads over the cause of the decrease in the rabbit population, they noticed an unexplainable *increase* in those same numbers.

At the same time, a different group of scientists began to notice dramatic fluctuations in the area's fox population as well. They, too, investigated the possibility of an animal-specific disease and came up with nothing.

Finally an entirely different scientist read of this quandary and proffered a simple solution, one that ultimately proved to be astonishingly accurate. Having observed the relationship between the fluctuations in the rabbit and fox population, this scientist discovered an inverse relationship between these two groups: As the population of foxes increased, the number of rabbits decreased; and when the fox population decreased, the number of rabbits increased.

He suggested that as the population of rabbits multiplied, they provided an ample food supply for the foxes, resulting in an increase in the number of foxes. But as the fox population increased, they ate more of the rabbits, resulting in a decrease in the rabbit population. And the resulting lower number of available bunny meals caused a decrease in the fox population, which consequently again made it possible for the rabbits to multiply more rapidly. The cycle was self-perpetuating.[1]

For too many years, the attention of those of us in youth ministry has been focused, quite appropriately, on students and their needs. But when our perspective of a problem is limited to what happens *within* a specific group alone, we tend, of necessity, to ignore the powerful changes created by interactions *between* groups. As long as we attempt to "solve" the crisis in youth ministry with a myopic focus on adolescents and their problems, treat them as if their lives happen in isolation from the powerful forces of family and culture, the solutions we develop will always be too small.

WHAT DO YOU MEAN BY *FAMILY-BASED YOUTH MINISTRY*?

If you've ever had the sense that not everyone who talks about family-based youth ministry is speaking the same language, you're not alone. As I've attended conferences and met with family-based practitioners across the country, I have observed two distinctly different understandings and approaches to family-based youth ministry:

- the family-ministry model

- the youth-ministry model

The first step, then, to implementing a family-based youth ministry is to decide between these two different approaches. Churches that fail to consciously make this decision naturally find their implementation of family-based youth ministry easily bogged down in competing agendas and unspoken assumptions. It all begins with getting a grasp on these two approaches.

The family-ministry model is driven primarily by a desire to empower families. No one describes (and more importantly, lives out) this model of family-based youth ministry better than my friend Ben Freudenberg. Ben's perspective[2] is that the church's primary job in youth ministry is to *support* the ministry that rightly belongs to the family. One of the key assumptions behind this kind of ministry is that the real action of the Christian nurture of children and youth takes place not in youth programs or even in the church but in families. Programming for this style of ministry, therefore, is centered not around the church or the youth ministry as much as around individual families. Ben sometimes refers to this approach as "family-centered, church-supported." In larger churches, this model of ministry would likely be run by a "family pastor" who focuses on empowering and equipping parents to fulfill the vows that many of them took for the Christian nurture of their children.

They might also spend a good deal of time on what some family ministry practitioners refer to as "ambulance programs" (such systems as Divorce Recovery or Stephen Ministry that help people in crisis) and "guardrail programs" (such programs as Marriage Enrichment or Parenting Seminars that can prevent later, larger problems in families). This approach is an effective way to assist and support families and to access the incomparable power of the family in the faith formation of their children. The biggest challenge to this approach is in dealing with students whose parents do not and will not, despite the effectiveness of the church's parent-equipping programs, take the initiative to do anything particularly Christian in their homes.

The Youth-ministry model is driven by a focused commitment to see young people grow to maturity in Christ. Over the past decade I have often straddled the fence of my ministerial identity, not quite sure whether I was a youth pastor or a family pastor. Though many family ministers are dear friends of mine and I believe deeply in what they are doing, I have come to realize that I am, by calling and by passion, a youth pastor. And though I am committed to healthy families, it is my passion for seeing young people grow to maturity in Christ that drives my work with families.

In contrast to the family-ministry model, the youth-ministry model *accesses* parents and significant other adults, knowing that this approach will always be the most fruitful means of helping young people grow in Christ. The distinction is subtle yet significant.

In the family-ministry model, the parents are expected to take the responsibility; in the youth-ministry model, the church takes the responsibility. In the family-ministry model, the first focus is on supporting *parents and families* with classes, counseling and support, while in the youth-ministry model, the focus is on moving *students* to maturity in Christ, accessing as much as possible the family and the extended family of the church.

Which of these approaches is really "family-based youth ministry? " Both, of course. Once I realized that I was working with a youth-ministry model, not a family-ministry model, much of the fog surrounding implementation cleared for me.

THE HOW OF FAMILY-BASED YOUTH MINISTRY

This is not a chapter I could have written back in 1994, as much as I would've liked to. At that time, family-based youth ministry was a concept so new that no one, including me, seemed to be able to define what exactly it was we were talking about. But after almost a decade of experimentation and more failures than I care to recount, I now have a working definition, at least for my brand of family-based youth ministry:

Family-based youth ministry accesses the incomparable power of the nuclear family and connects students to an extended family of Christian adults to the end that those students grow toward maturity in Christ.

Almost every youth worker I have spoken to loves the *concept* of family-based youth ministry. But the vast majority of them feel ill-equipped to work with adults in general and with parents in particular. As a matter of fact, a recent Link Institute study indicated that "working with adults" was listed near the top of the list of the "hardest things about youth ministry." And "lack of parental support," was ranked very near the top of the "greatest challenges."[3]

It's the same message I have heard from youth leaders all over the country: family-based youth ministry is a great idea, but show us *how* to do it.

When I talk about implementing a family-based youth ministry, it's important to understand that I am talking less about establishing specific programs and more about creating an ongoing ethos (what might be called a "new normal") in the ministry. In this regard, I love Marv Penner's *Youth Worker's Guide to Parent Ministry* (Zondervan, 2003), particularly the way his nine-step process begins with four steps that are not "programs" at all. Family-based youth ministry is not, strictly speaking, a "model" but rather a foundation that *every* youth ministry needs to ensure its long-term impact. The specific model of youth ministry a church chooses is almost irrelevant.

Suppose, for example, that your church wants to adopt Doug Field's "purpose-driven" approach to youth ministry. You need not choose *against* family-based youth ministry in favor of purpose-driven youth ministry. Instead, you would use Doug's principles as the model for your youth ministry, but undergird that model with the kind of family-based connections that will offer the structures for the long-term faith formation in your youth.

Another church might choose to use the Logos model or a Peer Ministry model. Family-based principles are an imperative foundation for any of these models, because, regardless of the model, every ministry must find ways to build on a foundation of parents providing intentional Christian nurture for their children and students connecting to an extended Christian family of faith-full adults.

Implementing a family-based youth ministry, then, doesn't require that you create a new weekly or even annual program all at once. As a matter of fact, the most effective implementation process takes years (it took us almost a decade) to put in place.

During the past five years I have taught a specific long-term implementation process for family-based youth ministry that borders on being absurdly simple. Here it is:

Year One: Experiment with one family-based program.

Expect limited response.

If the program is well-received, repeat it the next year.

If the program flops, try something else the next year.

Year Two: Repeat what worked the year before (if anything).

Experiment with another family-based program.

Again, expect limited response.

Year Three: Repeat what worked the year before (if anything).

Experiment with another family-based program.

Year Four: By this year, you can expect that some family-based program (or some aspect of some family-based program) will have been well-received.

I jokingly summarize this no-brainer, four-year process in this way:

Year One: Try something. Fail.

Year Two: Try something else. Fail again.

Year Three: Try something else. Stumble on one thing that works.

Year Four: Repeat what works. Try something else.

You get the idea. Since my implementation process essentially involves the creation or experimentation with only *one* new family-based program a year, there is little need for hundreds of program ideas (though they are certainly out there). The most common mistake in the implementation process looks something like this: A youth pastor learns of family-based youth ministry and falls in love with the idea. Without getting buy-in from the key stakeholders in the youth ministry (and often without even finishing the book), this youth worker begins to make dramatic changes in the program in an effort to make it more "family-based." Students and parents experience change overload and strongly resist the changes, slowing the implementation process to a screeching halt.

I have found, in my denomination particularly, that it usually takes only about a year for a style of programming to move into the category of "the way we've always done it." Adding one family-based program a year may seem slow at first, but that is actually an asset. Not having to battle against "the way it's always been done" actually speeds up the process in the long run and typically ensures much more enthusiastic partnership from parents and church leadership. Unless your church already has a "family-based" ethos, my counsel is that you not label these new programs as a part of some new family-based philosophy.

Now almost ten years after the first printing of *Family-Based Youth Ministry*, I have just begun to use this term in my own congregation again. When I first started out, my overuse of the "family based" title resulted in defensiveness and resistance, because, for most parents and youth, it translated "taking away what we like and putting in something we're sure to hate." But now, after years of implementing family-based programming, I simply point to what we do that they love (what now is "the way it's always been done") and let them know that what they're looking at is a family-based youth ministry. And today, they wouldn't want anything else.

As I began the process of building this family-based youth ministry, I found it helpful to categorize this type of programming into two distinct types: (1) completely new, family-based events and (2) what I call "exfamized" events. Let me give a sampling of possible programs in each category.

UNIQUELY FAMILY-BASED EVENTS

1. Parent/youth Sunday school class—We have established a pattern in which each year our youth Sunday-school classes take a break for three weeks and meet with the parents. Much of this curriculum is available in a resource called *Bridges*, coauthored by Nan Russell and me (available at <www.familybasedym.com>); some is included as an appendix in this book. Using the following structure, we provide parents and youth an interactive setting in which to discuss important issues:

- seventh grade—community building
- eighth grade—drugs and alcohol
- ninth grade—sexuality

- tenth grade—communication
- eleventh grade—decision-making
- twelfth grade—independence in Christ

2. *Prayer partners*—This is our version of a mentoring program. Each youth in the church is matched with an adult prayer partner who simply commits to pray for that young person (ideally until he or she graduates from high school) and attend a prayer partner banquet one Sunday night during the year.

3. *Parent/youth retreats*—I've done a number of retreats like this for other churches, with entire families as the participants. These retreats focus on giving parents and youth the chance to laugh and learn together, in addition to the unique opportunity to speak words of blessing to each other.

4. *Parenting-equipping classes*—I've heard these groups called everything from "The POT Party" (for "Parents Of Teenagers") to the "Better Homes and Guardians" class. It may be a "Preparing for Adolescence" class for parents of preteens, or a dad's group or a mom's group centered around a specific topic, or one of any number of prepackaged, video-based parent-training programs (for example, *Active Parenting of Teens*, *Parenting Adolescence*, or my favorite, Jim Burn's *Parenting Teenagers for Positive Results*). The focus of these programs is to create an opportunity for parents to learn together how to be more effective in the Christian nurture of their children.

5. *"Understanding Your Teenager" event*—Wayne Rice has put together an exceptional event for parents, which he (or someone on his team) will bring to your church. Your main responsibility is getting your parents there. For the past few years, I have been privileged to be a presenter for this team and have seen firsthand the impact it can have on a congregation or a community.

EXFAMIZED EVENTS

Several years ago I coined the word *exfamize* to describe the process of taking a program already in place and infusing that program with an extended Christian family of adults. The idea is to work *with* the momentum of an already existing program and naturally expand its influence by dramatically increasing the number of adults involved.

In the fall of 1996, a friend of mine shared a classic example of exfamization. He had participated for the first time in a Promise Keepers event that had a breakout session just for teenage boys; more than four thousand teenage boys were in attendance. After the boys were dismissed, the men were instructed on giving the returning boys a corporate blessing upon their reentry: The men were simply asked to stand and cheer for the boys as they streamed into the stadium. The folks at Promise Keepers had exfamized the breakout session, giving kids not only helpful content, but perhaps more importantly providing them with a corporate blessing from sixty thousand men.

Here are a few examples of exfamized programs that require fewer than 64,000 participants.

1. *Senior Banquet*—Several years ago, we moved from having a banquet with only our graduating seniors and their youth leaders to a banquet that involved parents as well. Now we collect letters from special adults for each student, and each child's parents (or parent substitutes) come prepared to speak a two-sentence blessing over their children.

2. *CRUD Day*—We use this typical wacky youth-group event as a way to welcome the new seventh graders into the youth group on the afternoon of their confirmation. But what makes this event different is not the five thousand water balloons or the mud or the shaving cream (all of which have become predictable in contemporary youth ministry). The distinction is that kids are surrounded by more than 150 adults, each of whom is assigned a specific task at the event.

3. *Sitting service for worship*—One church I know of has a sitting service in which teenagers sit with small children *in worship* and help them find the hymns and follow along. The vertical connection increases attention for both the children and the teenager and communicates clearly that they both belong to the same "family."

4. *Preretreat dinner and parents' seminar*—I recently participated in a weekend event at a church tied to the youth group's annual youth retreat. On Friday evening the kids and parents arrived for a dinner together, followed by a program focused on bringing the generations together. At 9 p.m. the kids were loaded onto a bus and they left for the retreat. The next morning the parents returned for a Saturday morning parenting seminar.

5. *Mission-trip commissioning and sendoff*—We exfamize our youth mission trips in two ways. First, we have a sendoff dinner with parents and youth a week or so before the group leaves. Second, we commission our youth missionaries in a worship service in which they are given a charge to serve Christ faithfully. The congregation prays for them at this time.

In the final analysis, though, family-based programs provide only the context for healthy connections to be made. It is the caring attentiveness of the older generation to the younger that is likely to make the most significant difference in the lives of the teenagers we touch, an attitude that can affect our youth much more deeply than our programs.

I recently heard the story of an altar boy in a small village, who, as he was carrying the chalice before the priest, dropped the goblet, spilling the consecrated wine all over the floor. The priest responded by backhanding the boy, striking him in the face and shouting, "Never come back here again!" The child obeyed.

In a very similar situation, another altar boy in a different church committed the very same mistake, serving before the bishop himself. But this bishop reacted very differently. He winked at the boy and whispered, "You're going to be a priest someday."

The first boy grew up to become Marshall Tito, the abusive, tyrannical head of the communist party in Yugoslavia, who reigned with an iron fist for decades. The second grew to become Archbishop Fulton J. Sheen, the Roman Catholic bishop who, in the 1950s received an Emmy for his work on television, a role in which he positively affected hundreds of thousands.

May we who form the face of youth ministry in this new century influence adults to lead students in such a way that when they grow to be adults, we will know that we have invested well.

IMPLICATIONS FOR MINISTRY

1. Implementing a family-based youth ministry requires a systems approach, thinking beyond the specific needs of teenagers and considering the patterns within families that influence youth along with the patterns within the culture that influence families.

2. Ordinarily, attempting to implement a *totally* family-based youth ministry only works in entirely new ministries or in ministries that are begging for a wholesale change in their approach to ministry with teenagers. For the vast majority of churches a slow implementation process makes the most sense.

3. Fundamentally, every family-based youth ministry must decide whether they want to be a family ministry that has youth as one of its components or a youth ministry that accesses the immense power of families.

WILD HAIR IDEA

Select the first (and only) family-based program you hope to implement this year, but don't refer to what you are doing as "family-based youth ministry" until the parents, youth and church leadership love it.

APPENDIX A

A Matter of Perspective

In 1989 my friend and mentor Robert Wolgemuth and I unintentionally inaugurated the family-based youth ministry at our church with a four-week course for all parents and teenagers. We began the course with the skit "A Matter of Perspective" to help parents and teenagers see their own limited perspectives just a little more clearly.

A MATTER OF PERSPECTIVE

The scene opens on DAD, driving into the school parking lot to pick up his sixteen-year-old son, JASON, after football practice.

DAD: Hey, Jas.

JASON: Hey, Dad.

DAD: Sorry I'm a little late.

JASON: It's all right.

DAD: Ya know, Jas, I've been drivin' this thing around town all day, how 'bout you drive us home?

JASON: What?

DAD: I said, would you mind driving? I've been fighting traffic all day, and I'd just as soon be a passenger and let you drive.

JASON: Yeah. Okay.

JASON steps away from the passenger door and walks around the car. DAD slides into the passenger seat. JASON takes the wheel, starts the car, looks around to be sure it's safe to move into traffic and proceeds. After several seconds the silence is broken as JASON reaches for the radio.

DAD: Hey, we could do without the radio.

JASON: Dad, I haven't heard anything *I* want to listen to all day. I just need to clear my mind for a minute.

DAD: *[laughing]* Clear your mind? With that stuff you listen to?

JASON: *[lightly]* Okay, Dad. Have it *your* way.

A few more moments of silence

DAD: Sooo, how was football practice?

JASON: Not great.

DAD: Well, didja learn anything at school today?

JASON: Daaaaad.

DAD: How 'bout Jessica? What's going on with her?

JASON: She's fine.

DAD: Are you still going steady?

JASON: Dad, we don't go *steady*. We've gone out a few times, okay?

DAD: Well, okay, whatever you call what you do. Are you still doing it?

JASON: *[looks shocked]* Daaaad.

A few more moments of silence.

DAD: *[takes a deep breath, trying to get something started]* Hey, ya know, I was listening to a program on NPR *[JASON mouths the letters NPR]*, and they were saying that automobile accidents caused by reckless teenagers are the number one cause of death in America.

JASON: *[turning toward his dad]* I thought it was heart disease.

Just then the car in front of them makes a quick stop. DAD, of course, is the first to see it.

DAD: *[putting his hand out]* Whoa. Whoa, hey, Jas, careful.

JASON: Hey, Dad, don't worry about it. I saw that.

DAD: Well, it's not *you* that I'm worried about, it's all those *other* guys on the road. *[pauses]* I took that special defensive driving course last month that our Rotary Club sponsored. *[pauses]* You know, I told you about that seminar. I still wish you had come with me.

JASON: Dad, is this going to turn into another lecture?

DAD: Son, I'm just trying to communicate with you.

JASON: Daaaad.

DAD: Well, isn't that what families are supposed to do? You know, communicate?

JASON: You and I just can't seem to talk very well.

BOTH: *[turning to the audience]* We've got a problem!

Both DAD and JASON freeze.

DR.
FREUD: *[facing the audience]* It's not easy to admit we've got a problem. These two have done the right thing in coming to me for counsel. *[turning to JASON and DAD]* Now, in order for me to help you, I need to find out what occurred yesterday after school. So Jason, why don't you go first? Just tell me in your own words exactly what happened.

DAD: Get in the car, boy.

JASON: *[dripping with politeness]* Hello, Dad.

DAD: I've had a lousy day. I know I'm late. But I am fed up with your complaining. So keep it to yourself. Especially the part about how *all* the other dads are *always* on time.

JASON: Hey, no problem, Dad. I know you work hard all day long. I tried to spend the time wisely and get a little homework done.

DAD: Just a minute. *You* drive. I've wanted to test your driving, firsthand. This should give me just the chance I've been waiting for.

JASON: What?

DAD: Don't act so surprised. I've heard about your driving, and I want to see it for myself. Now get over here and drive. And put on your seat belt too.

JASON: *[cheerfully]* I'd be happy to drive, Dad. *[JASON steps away from the passenger door and walks around the car. DAD slides into the passenger seat. JASON takes the wheel, starts the car, looks around to be sure it's safe to move into traffic and proceeds. After several seconds the silence is broken as JASON reaches for the radio.]* Hey, Dad, would you mind if I turn on the radio?

DAD: Forget it. We don't need to listen to that noise.

JASON: Dad, I've really had a hard day today, and I'd like to clear my mind with some good music.

DAD: Clear your mind? With that junk you listen to? Haven't you heard the stories of kids who sacrifice dogs and cats and drink their blood after listening to that music? As a matter of fact, I've read that if you listen to that stuff backwards, your mind turns to kitty litter. If I've told you once, I've told you a thousand times, a mind is a terrible thing to waste.

JASON: *[sincerely]* Well, Dad, maybe I *should* consider adjusting my listening habits.

A few more moments of silence.

DAD: I guess you're ready to start in the big game Friday night. You know it's awful nice to know that—unlike a lot of other dads in the stands—my kid has always been a starter. You *know* how important it is to your mother and me to have you do well on the team. I can just smell those scholarship offers. So how *was* football practice today?

JASON: Not too great. Actually, I doubt if I'll get to start, but I think Kominski probably deserves to play ahead of me anyway.

DAD: *[after a disapproving, uncomfortable silence]* Well, are you still wasting your time and my hard-earned money on this expensive private school?

JASON: Daaaaad.

DAD: And how about that girl, Jessica? Ya know, the last time I saw her she certainly was dressed suggestively. I mean, that skirt . . . and that sweater. Actually, I probably shouldn't tell you this, but from our prayer group at church I've heard stories about her mother, and you know what they say—like mother, like daughter.

JASON: Jessica's real fine, Dad. Thanks for asking.

DAD: By the way, what *do* you do on dates? Are you going steady? Have you given her your class ring? How about that ID bracelet you won at the carnival? You know, I'll bet she'd like to have that. I gave your mother *my* ID bracelet. And why don't you ever bring Jessica over to the house? You know we've got all three of those *Star Wars* videos. I just love the way George Mucas makes all those special effects. And *E.T.?* That Steven Spielman is such a gifted producer.

JASON: You know, we've really only gone out a couple times, Dad. And uh, well, we don't actually call it going steady anymore.

DAD: Well, okay, whatever you call what you do. Are you still doin' it with her?

JASON: *[understandingly]* I don't think so, Dad.

A few more moments of silence.

DAD: Speaking of drunk drivers . . . you know I've been noticing how you've been driving. I was listening to this program on NPR, and they said that teenagers today create more carnage on American highways in one week than Korea and Vietnam *combined*. They said that automobile accidents caused by reckless teenagers are the number one cause of death in America.

JASON: *[turning toward his dad]* I thought it was heart disease.

Just then the car in front of them makes a quick stop. DAD, of course, is the first to see it.

DAD: *[going berserk]* Jaaaassssooooonnnn! You're going to kill us both. I'm going to die!

JASON: It's okay, Dad. I was watching. No need to get too excited.

DAD: Well, I'm concerned that all the rest of these nuts are as crazy on the road as you are. What did you do, go to Kmart to get your license? I tried to tell you that you should have gone to the Rotary Club defensive driver course last month. But nooooo, you were too busy.

JASON: Dad, if you'd like to talk about this in a civil way . . .

DAD: *[interrupting through clenched teeth]* I am just trying to get you to listen to me.

JASON: I'm open to that.

DAD: Don't you know that boys are supposed to respect their dads and take their advice?

JASON: I'd really like to, but sometimes it's hard to get a conversation started with you. You know, Dad, you've got a problem.

DR.

FREUD: *[talking to DAD but facing the audience]* I see, very interesting . . . What's that, Dad? You want to tell it your way? Okay, if you think he missed some details, let's hear what happened from your perspective.

DAD: Hey, Jas. How's it goin', son?

JASON: *[grunts]* Hh.

DAD: Ya know, Jas, I know how much you love to drive. How 'bout you drive us home?

JASON: *[grunts]* Hhh.

DAD: Hey, you'd be the best chauffeur I could ever have. I'm really proud of the way you've learned to be responsible behind the wheel. And I am a little tired from working hard all day to provide for my wonderful family, so I'd like to rest a little and be a passenger this time, if that's all right with you.

JASON: Uh . . . yeah, uh . . . okay.

JASON steps away from the passenger door and walks around the car. DAD slides into the passenger seat. JASON takes the wheel, starts the car, puts the pedal to the floor and recklessly spins onto the access road. DAD is forced back into his seat, his head whipping back violently . . . Several seconds of silence are broken as JASON reaches for the radio. Heavy metal music blares.

DAD: Hey, would you mind turning that down a little? It's not that I have a problem with that kind of music; it's just that I have a little headache from working so hard to provide for my wonderful family.

JASON: Shut up, Dad. It really hacks me off when you try to control my life. It's like living with Nazis in our house. If I have to drive, I *will* pick the music. You don't like it? You can walk. I'm just trying to clear my head, Dad.

DAD: Oh, I'm sorry. Does it help to clear your mind? You know, that's hard for me to understand, but I sure don't want to keep you from anything you really enjoy. I was sort of hoping we could spend some time talking. You know, sharing . . . being transparent and vulnerable.

JASON: *[sarcastically]* Oh, *there's* a great idea. Okay, start one up. I dare you.

A few more minutes of silence.

DAD: Soooo, how was football practice?

JASON: *[shrugging]* Hmn.

DAD: Anything you could tell me about your day at school that would help me understand my wonderful son?

JASON: *[rolling his eyes]* I don't think so, Dad.

DAD: You know that Jessica certainly has an eye for bright young men. How are you feeling about her?

JASON: She's fine. I'm fine. We're fine . . . *[bitterly]* How are you, Dad?

DAD: Do you really like her?

JASON: We've gone out three times, okay? And if you're looking to give me the third degree about what we're up to, forget it!

DAD: Well, okay. I just wanted to know if you're planning to continue your relationship.

JASON: Daaaaad.

A few more moments of silence.

DAD: *[takes a deep breath, trying to get something started]* Hey, I was listening to a radio program, and they were giving some startling statistics about how innocent young people are dying in car accidents.

JASON: *[glaring at his dad]* It's probably more fun than having a heart attack.

Just then the car in front of them makes a quick stop. DAD, of course, is the first to see it.

DAD: *[calmly]* Son, there's a car up there that has stopped. Be careful.

JASON: Would you GET OFF MY BACK! *[The car jerks to a stop.]*

DAD: Hey, son, I know you're a good driver, it's just the other drivers I'm concerned about. I know how busy you are, but I do wish you could have come with me to the defensive driver's school that the Rotary Club sponsored last month. You know, you can never be too careful. I would sure hate for anything bad to happen to you.

JASON: *[his voice sarcastically lilting]* Yeah, Dad. And now you're going to tell me that you learned to drive uphill in the snow in your Volkswagen Beetle on your way to school because you were too poor to ride the bus.

DAD: Son, I do wish we had a better relationship. One where we could really communicate.

JASON: Hey, look. Our *relationship* is as good as it needs to be. None of the other kids' dads try to *communicate* with them. They just give 'em stuff and leave 'em alone.

DAD: Oh, that hurts me when I hear you talk like that. I want to have a strong, loving family. Where we really care about each other.

JASON: Look, just because you couldn't talk to your dad . . . Hey, I don't mind communicating as long as you don't expect anything out of me. Why can't you accept me like I am?

DAD: *[turning to the audience]* You've got a problem.

APPENDIX B

Has the Traditional Family Really Died?

One of the most quoted statistics about today's families is that less than 10 percent of families in America can now be defined as traditional. In 1989, Senator Chris Dodd of Connecticut argued, "There are only one in ten American families today where you have mom at home and dad at work—only one in ten. Ozzie and Harriet . . . are gone."[1]

In a 1988 television interview, Congresswoman Pat Schroeder of Colorado asserted, "Only 7 percent" of today's families "fit the Ozzie and Harriet syndrome." In making her case for a national child-care policy, she claimed that basing such a policy on traditional families was "like saying the highway program must recognize people who don't drive."[2]

Like any compelling statistic, this one has been used by many who were obviously too busy to check the facts. The "less than 10 percent" statistic is simply not true. According to a 1987 Bureau of Labor Statistics report, traditional families (that is, father working, mother at home) account for more than one-third—the largest single category—of all families with preschool children.

Another 15.8 percent of families with preschool children can be classified as semitraditional, with the father working full-time and the mother working part-time (sometimes as little as ten hours a week). My wife, whose primary role is raising children, would not be considered as part of a traditional family because she worked one day a week doing child-care in our church's Mother's Day Out program and did some telephone work from our home.

When the statistics are added up, 49 percent of families with preschool children could be seen as "traditional." In other words, there is a good chance that a significant percentage of the youth we work with have grown up in a traditional family setting.

There actually seems to be a growing desire among families to return to the traditional family model. *Newsweek* took a poll of working mothers and discovered that only 13 percent of them said they actually wanted to work full time. Similarly, a Washington Post survey indicated that 62 percent of working mothers would stay home with their children if they could afford to.

In light of this reality, Steven Bayme's conclusion to *Rebuilding the Nest,* a collection of essays on the American family, offers the needed balance as we design ministries to changing families:

> Stable families, in turn, both provide opportunities for personal growth and hold the key to society's future through the socialization of children. For these reasons, we should be willing to assert our cultural preference for traditional norms such as marriage and the two-parent home while at the same time accommodating and reaching out to those who have chosen to lead their lives within alternative settings.[3]

APPENDIX C

19 MODELS FOR YOUTH MINISTRY
A Highly Biased, Overly Simplistic Perspective

1. *Missions*—This model seeks to make every component of the ministry re-volve around a series of excellent summer (or Christmas or spring break) mis-sion trips. Paul Borthwick (youth-pastor-turned-missions-pastor) and Ridge Burns (Center for Student Missions) are names that could help in this field.

2. *Student leadership*—Ray Johnston, in his book *Developing Student Lead-ers*, proposes a model in which every young person in the church is involved in some form of leadership, such as music, drama, setup, audio-visual and puppets.

3. *Interest-centered*—The typical church-based version of this model is a youth ministry that centers around the youth choir. The Fellowship of Christian Athletes is the classic parachurch version.

4. *Family-based programming*—This model is not identical with *family-based youth ministry* (the title of the compelling, scintillating, captivating, bargain-priced book of the same name), which can and should undergird every model. Family-based programming takes place in a church that has decided to center its youth ministry specifically around programming across generational lines.

5. *Discipleship*—Duffy Robinson's book *The Ministry of Nurture* is the classic resource for this model of youth ministry. This model focuses on creating programming that systematically leads youth through intentional stages (what Duffy calls the "come level," the "grow level" and the "lead

level") of growth toward Christian maturity.

6. *Creative evangelism*—The youth ministry of Willow Creek Community Church (originally called Son City) as I understand it, was built on high-energy, high-tech, high-quality outreach events designed to attract a large number of youth. They may have actually moved beyond this model.

7. *Retreats*—This model is centered around reducing programming so that the major focus of the youth group is a series of retreats. Here, all other programming would feed into and out of these continuity-building retreat events.

8. *Team-based*—This model is based on Ginny Ward-Holderness's books, *Youth Ministry: The New Team Approach* and *Teaming Up*. The typical team-based youth ministry would seek to balance worship, service, fellowship and study, using a rotating team of youth and adult leaders for each of the specific foci.

9. *Mentoring*—Miles McPherson and Wayne Rice have an excellent resource entitled *One Kid at a Time* that covers the waterfront for setting up a mentoring program.

10. *Worship*—Based on Bill Myers's book, *Black and White Styles of Youth Ministry*, the worship model centers the youth ministry around the weekly experience of worship with the entire church family. This model was particularly present in his study of African American churches.

11. *Reconciliation*—This model focuses on building a bridge between churches from different socioeconomic-racial backgrounds. In this model the majority of the programming would be designed for the two groups together.

12. *Assets*—Based on the forty necessary assets for health identified by the Search Institute, this model seeks to find ways to ensure that as many of these assets as possible are provided for youth in the church and the community.

13. *Christian education*—This model puts all the eggs in the Sunday school basket. The focus here is on building an intentionally excellent Sunday-morning program.

14. *If you build it . . .* —This model is the classic Sunday-night youth-group model (based on the original Society for Christian Endeavor). "If you build it" youth ministries simply focus on exceptional programming in the

evening to attract and involve youth in the life of the church.

15. *Confirmation*—Rick Osmer's book *Confirmation* is a helpful, if chewy, resource here, providing significant theological reflection on the whole topic of helping the confirmation experience mark a new beginning of a young adult's faith experience. A youth ministry that is focused on the confirmation model would build its programs around the preparation for the confirmation experience and the living out of the vows made at confirmation. Rich Melheim's Faith Incubators can also provide marvelous resources surrounding the confirmation process.

16. *Church planting model*—Recommended by Mark Senter in *Youthworker*, this model is built on the idea that students from healthy youth ministries be used to begin entirely new churches.

17. *Logos*—This popular transdenominational youth program is used as the heart of many youth programs. Having its roots in the mainline church, this model provides students with a variety of activities and Bible study and usually centers around tables at which there is an intentional "family" atmosphere.

18. *Spiritual practices model*—Currently being developed by Mark Yaconelli at San Francisco Theological Seminary, this model focuses on giving leaders and students opportunities for experiencing God through more classical spiritual disciplines together.

19. *Purpose-driven youth ministry*—Growing out of the thriving Saddleback Church in California, this model is arguably the "state-of-the-art" traditional youth ministry. Doug Fields's book *Purpose-Driven Youth Ministry* offers an insightful and comprehensive approach to discipling students.

APPENDIX D

122 Family-Based Youth Ministry Programming Ideas

Though chapter twelve offers a strategic implementation plan for family-based youth ministry, many people have asked for suggestions for family-based programming. So I've come up with 122 programming ideas. I actually hesitated to include some of these ideas because they seemed so obvious, so uncreative. But by now it should be clear that family-based youth ministry is not about splashy programs or complex strategies. Its key objective (and thus the criterion for success) is simply for teenagers to build friendships with Christian adults.

My experience has been that whenever a group moves from the traditional objective (collecting young bodies in a room) to the objective of helping teenagers build relationships with Christian adults, there will be challenges. The truth is that the majority of churches will simply not be able to find the kind of youth minister who can draw hundreds of teenagers to meetings. There are simply not enough of them to go around.

And very few churches can afford the Fortune 500 style of ministry. Not even those churches that can adequately fund their youth ministries will be able to do everything the parents, the teens and the church's leadership expect. As we move into the twenty-first century, most churches will need to develop selective excellence in their youth ministries. Most churches that try to do everything will find that they end up doing very little well.

As I mentioned in chapter twelve, family-based youth ministry is best begun as an "undercover" or mustard-seed kind of ministry. The great unveiling of a new family-based youth ministry would, in fact, be quite underwhelming. It would be about as exciting as watching a tree grow or uncovering the foundation of a house. Though there will likely be little splash on the front end, this "mustard seed conspiracy" can yield great returns in the long run.

I began creating family-based youth ministry programs with one rule of thumb: if it works with youth, try it with youth and parents together. Just as in youth programming, some ideas worked beautifully; others were less successful. But in general, family-based programming, used judiciously, was almost always more effective (and more fun) than having the adults and the youth apart.

So I present the following smorgasbord of ideas to equip parents and to create intentional intergenerational connections between youth and adults in the church. I will present these ideas in categories of four programming components: worship, service, education and recreation, along with a fifth category of "miscellaneous ideas" that don't fit neatly into one of the first four categories.

WORSHIP

Teenagers' involvement in the worship of the church often yields more significant long-term results than does even the most active involvement in the youth program or Sunday school. For that reason alone, finding ways to involve young people and their parents in a church's life of worship is imperative.

Some churches have incredibly engaging worship services to which young people are drawn, but the average worship experience is less than compelling for most teenagers. But sitting in worship can be much like having a regular place to sit at the family dinner table. This is the place where you learn the normals of the family, hear the stories and come to know that there is a place at the table for you.

Whether young people sit with their parents or in a youth section or the choir, their involvement in worship is powerful formation ground for leading them into mature Christian adulthood. It's in worship that young Christians, week after week, can offer God praise, confess their sins, hear from God's Word and offer themselves in a deeper way to serve God. It's in worship and through the sacraments of God's people that teenagers gain a sense of their connection to a rich family tradition.

Some churches have attempted to appeal to teenagers by altering their worship services, changing the style of music or increasing the variety and decreasing the length of the sermons. During my teenage years, my pastor would ask us frequently what we would like to see changed about the worship service. And to his credit, he tried almost all of our ideas. But I can't say that those changes made much difference to my appreciation for the experience.

The older I get, the more I see the wisdom in Søren Kierkegaard's classic theater analogy for worship. It goes something like this:

> We tend to view the preacher as the performer, God as the prompter and the congregation as the audience. But in genuine worship, God is the audience, the preacher is the prompter and the congregation is made up of the real performers.

If we simply try to appeal to teens by making worship easier or more entertaining, we may end up tacitly teaching them that their first role in worship is to be passive spectators and critical consumers. Implementing family-based youth ministry in worship is simply a matter of finding ways for teenagers to grow into meaningful involvement in the worship of the whole community. Youth pastors can choose to complain that the worship service is simply not fulfilling enough or engaging enough for the teenagers of the church, like a teenager who constantly complains about the food his family puts before him at meals. But that approach usually results in increased frustration and powerlessness. Instead we can choose to focus on helping our kids connect with imperfect people in imperfect worship experiences—not bad preparation for real life as an adult.

Here are a few suggestions:

1. Youth readers—Many churches have a regular tradition of using a different young person to read Scripture in each service.

2. Prayer leaders—A church could invite different youth to lead the congregation in prayer during the service. Pastors could take this opportunity to work with a number of different teenagers during the year.

3. Ushers—Teenagers can work *with* the team of adult ushers on Sunday mornings, taking the collection, passing out bulletins and so on.

4. Youth choir—Although the youth choir does isolate teenagers, it also gives them an opportunity to contribute as a group to the total church. The youth choir can also teach the entire congregation a style of worship music that is significant to the young people of the church.

5. "Adult" choir—Young people can benefit greatly from singing alongside the adults. An adult choir mentor for each teenager in the choir would be the best possible situation.

6. Sunday-school classes writing liturgy—The summer months are great times to let the teenagers pick the Scripture lessons and hymns, write the prayers and any other readings, all related to the sermon for the day.

7. Youth writing and/or performing a drama sketch in worship—Here they can work as a youth drama team or in partnership with adults in the church.

8. Greeters—Teenagers can serve with adults in greeting people as they come to worship.

9. Minutes for missions—Teenagers can report to the congregation about their youth mission experiences, their adult mission experiences or about a local ministry that they are passionate about.

10. Youth Sunday—Many churches set aside one Sunday or more a year for the youth to plan and lead the worship service.

11. Commissioning services—Before youth and their leaders leave for their mission trips, they can be commissioned in the church's worship service and prayed for specifically by the members of the congregation.

MISSION AND SERVICE

More and more public and private schools are finding that active involvement in serving others is an important prerequisite for a complete education. The students I work with have been volunteering through their schools to work at the soup kitchen, collect toys for poor children or participate in any number of service-oriented activities.

The church doesn't need to duplicate the activities its teenagers will be involved in with other groups. The contribution that the church can make is to provide a place where youth and adult Christians work alongside each other in their volunteer service.

It is too easy for young people who grow up in churches with active youth mission programs to learn that Christian service is something *teenagers* do, something, like proms and student government, that they can expect to grow out of. Youth centered service events can, in fact, create passivity in teens who have learned to react by signing up for the mission projects that are marketed the most effectively.

Obviously, genuine Christian service is very different from responding to calculated group motivation. Christian service is proactive, not reactive. At least part of the formula for teenagers' becoming proactive in serving is to allow our youth to see Christian adults living out their faith through service as well. Since parents are the primary faith-shapers for their children, any of the following activities can be strengthened by involving parents.

One of the problems with family-based youth ministry is that most parents think of youth ministry with the traditional model in mind. They are all in favor of their *children* doing service projects because it "builds character," but they are often less aware of their own need to model a serving lifestyle. But unless the adults model this kind of behavior as normal for Christian adults, chances are great that their children will grow out of the serving habit as well.

Most of the ideas that follow simply tie into the existing benevolent projects that a local church normally sponsors. The only distinction is that instead of encouraging adults to volunteer alone, family-based youth ministry advocates that whole families take on some of these projects together or that teenagers and other adults in the church work alongside each other.

12. Habitat work day—Most communities now have programs for building low-income housing with volunteer labor. Youth groups have been doing this kind of thing for years. It can work even better with adults and teenagers together.

13. Vacation Bible School—Often teenagers are recruited to lead Vacation

Bible School. Why not match them up with adults in the church to lead the younger children?

14. Soup kitchen—The local soup kitchens are always looking for volunteers to serve meals. Encourage families or groups of families to sign up and work together.

15. Experience homelessness—If your church does a "Room at the Inn" type program that houses homeless people during the winter months, encourage parents (or mentors) and teenagers to spend the night together with the homeless. If your church doesn't have this kind of program, certainly some church or agency in the city does.

16. Food or care packages for the homeless—Allow groups of families to volunteer to prepare food or care packages for the homeless, or create periodic programs for adults and youth to serve together.

17. Family mission trip in the United States—Any intergenerational youth mission experience can give youth and adult participants multiple opportunities to be together before the trip in planning, prayer and fellowship.

18. International mission trips—Our church sends a group of adults, youth and children to Mexico each year to build low-income housing. The children and youth seem to get much more out of the program when it is not directed at them.

19. Adopt a grandparent—Entire families (or mentor partners) could link up with an elderly person in the church or the community.

20. Visit nursing homes in intergenerational teams.

21. Weekend family mission trips.

22. Adopt international students—Every town with a college nearby is likely to have a number of international students who are in need of American friends.

23. Visit a children's hospital with someone of a different generation.

24. Sort clothes for a local clothes closet.

25. Sort food for a local food pantry.

26. Adopt a missionary (prayer, letters, financial support).

27. Sponsor a child as a family through Compassion International.

28. Participate by families in the church's fundraising efforts (Stewardship, One Great Hour of Sharing, Two Cents a Meal, etc.).

29. Deliver Meals on Wheels in cross-generational teams.

30. Find a need and meet it—In every community and church, families can come up with ways to serve an immediate need (for example, put to gether care packages for the family of a person having transplant surgery, visit AIDS patients, reroof the youth minister's house).

EDUCATION

The traditional Christian education program seems designed to separate families by age. This arrangement is efficient for the church, but in the long run it may rob young people of much-needed opportunities to learn alongside adult Christians.

In our church a number of teenagers have chosen to be involved in adult Sunday-school classes. I have to admit that often their choosing not to be involved in the youth class is a bit deflating to my ego. But in my better moments, I know that what they are gaining through interaction with Christian adults is of much more value than their being a part of a well-attended youth Sunday-school class.

I am not, though, advocating that we do away with Christian education opportunities for teenagers separate from adults. As I suggested in chapter nine, we must recognize teenagers' need to establish a faith distinct from that of their parents. My approach is to offer a combination of teaching youth the basics of Christian literacy in creative weekly classes, supplemented by short-term opportunities for youth and parents to learn together.

A family-based youth ministry also provides training opportunities for parents. In research for their book *The Five Cries of Parents,* Merton and Irene Strommen asked 10,457 parents which topics they had "much interest" in learning about. Seventy percent wanted to learn how to help a child develop healthy concepts of right and wrong; 60 percent, how to help a child grow in religious faith; 66 percent, about drugs; 62 percent, how to communicate better with one's children; 47 percent, effective discipline; 44 percent, more about sex education; and 42 percent, how to participate in a parent support group.[1] Short-term courses on these types of concerns can be foundational in curriculum development for parents of youth.

A family-based youth ministry can offer classes on themes related to the family for teenagers (for example, "Living With Your Parents Without Losing Your Mind"), for parents (for example, Wayne Rice's "Understanding Your Teenager" seminar), for parents and youth together, and for teenagers with other adults in the church. We have found that most effective youth curricula are easily adaptable to groups with youth and adults together.

The following list of ideas is a sampling of possible programs. Most of these programs can work in various settings (for example, Sunday school, house groups, Wednesday-night programs):

31. Parent/teenager course using the Serendipity Bible.

32. Parent/teenager course using "Spice Rack," an interactive curriculum for teenagers, available at <familybasedym.com>.

33. Parent/teenager course on the basics of the Christian faith and discipleship (for example, "Bonehead Bible").

34. Parent/teenager course on spiritual formation (The Companions in Christ series is an excellent resource here).

35. Parent/teenager course on sexuality.

36. Parent/teenager course on drugs and alcohol.

37. Parent/teenager course on music and media (for example, Learn to Discern by Bob DeMoss).

38. Parent/teenager course on decision-making.

39. Parent/teenager course on communication.

40. Parent/teenager course on community building (Serendipity's "Beginnings" is a fine resource for a short-term small-group experience).

41. Parent/teenager course on almost any Christian education topic.

42. Classes with teenagers and grandparent-age members on any Christian education topic.

43. Movie night—Parents and teenagers watching a movie together.

44. Concert—Parents and teenagers attending a Christian concert together.

45. Parenting class: *Raising Self-Reliant Children in a Self-Indulgent World* by Glenn and Nelsen.

46. Parenting class: "Understanding Your Teenager" <www.uyt.com>.

47. Parenting class: Video-based parent training material from Youth Builders <www.youthbuilders.com>.

48. Parenting class: "Talking to Your Child About Sexuality."

49. Parenting class: "Youth Culture Today" (Walt Mueller, Center for Parent Youth Understanding, is a great resource here).

50. Parenting class: "Conflict Management in Your Home."

51. Parenting class: "Drug and Alcohol Abuse Prevention," using local drug and alcohol intervention specialists.

52. Parenting class: "Finding Mentors for Your Children."

53. Parenting class: *Parenting Adolescents* video-based curriculum by Kevin Huggins.

54. Parenting class: *Active Parenting of Teens* series.

55. Parenting class: "Building Faith in Your Family."

56. Parenting class: "What's Hot and What's Not," using a panel of youth answering parents' questions.

57. Dads-only class: *The Seven Secrets of Effective Fathers*, Ken Canfield.

58. Dads-only class: *Ordering Your Private World*, Gordon MacDonald.

59. Dads-only class: *Celebration of Discipline*, Richard Foster.

60. Dads-only class: *The Man in the Mirror*, Patrick Morley.

61. Dads-only support group—We had a group like this develop out of a Wednesday-night class for dads that continued to meet for years after the class was over.

62. Single-fathers class (ideally led by a Christian single father).

63. Single-fathers support group.*

64. Moms-only classes, using books chosen by the mothers (for example, *Almost Thirteen* by Claudia Arp).

65. Moms-only support group.*

66. Short-term divorce recovery course for parents.*

67. Short-term divorce recovery course for teenagers—This course could be held either in conjunction with the course for parents (as we have done in Nashville) or separately with only teenagers (Youth Specialties divorce recovery materials).

68. Support group for teenagers from divorced families.*

69. Support group for blended families.*

70. The Familyread Game—This is a fun variation of the Newlywed Game that lets parents and their teenage children predict how the other will answer humorous questions.

71. Pick your teacher— Let each youth Sunday-school class pick four adult speakers to come to their class and teach on the assigned topics for those weeks, thus exposing teenagers to a variety of adults in the church and giving the youth Sunday-school teacher a much-needed break.

72. Role-play a variety of dilemmas faced by youth and parents.

73. Panel of experts—This idea is more of an educational method that can be used in a variety of settings. This method allows a group of teenagers, a group of parents or a group of families to serve as a panel of experts to respond to questions and create discussion.

74. *One on One* and *Talksheets* (Both of these Youth Specialties resources include great discussion starters for teens and parents.)

75. Lenten/Advent devotionals written by the parents or the youth.

76. PIT (Parents in Transition) seminars for parents of junior highers, high schoolers and collegians.[2]

77. A seminar for parents on "How to Pay for a College Education."

---

*A word about support groups: Support groups for families in crisis are usually *not* the place to begin a family-based youth ministry. The potential volatility of these sorts of situations demands that they be led by a well-trained and experienced facilitator.

RECREATION

By providing our teenagers with recreational opportunities with adults in the church, we can infuse them with hopefulness and enthusiasm about becoming an adult. Often the only exposure that teenagers have to adults is as serious and didactic authorities. Many teenagers never get to laugh with adults.

In many ways, teaching our children to laugh with (instead of at) adults is an essential part of our curriculum. The general principle is that almost any recreation that can be done with teenagers can also be done with teenagers and parents together. Here are a few ideas:

78. Any parent-teen competition.

79. Volleyball.

80. Softball.

81. High ropes course.

82. Bungee jumping.

83. Bowling.

84. Snow-skiing trip.

85. Water-skiing trip.

86. Crazy games (Ideas books).

87. Noncompetitive games (New Games books).

88. Bonfire.

89. Generational song exchange.

90. Hayride.

91. Dance.

92. Bike trip.

93. Talent show/gong show.

94. Concert.

95. Progressive dinner.

96. Picnic.

97. Capture the Flag/German Spotlight or youth group favorite game.

98. Video game night.

99. Board game night.

100. Lock-in/lock-out.

101. Cookout.

102. Rappelling.

103. Caving.

MISCELLANEOUS IDEAS

My friend Jim Burns likes to say that family-based youth ministry is more than a program; it's a mindset. For me, the strategy for building that mindset has focused on incrementally experimenting and adding regular programming beneath our regular youth ministry, while no one is really watching. After seventeen years of experimentation, failure and repeating anything that works, we now have a family-based mindset. Let's face it. You can't (and shouldn't) do many of the programs I'm recommending here in a single year. What you can do is look through the list of ideas and find one you can try out each year until you stumble on something that works.

Finally, I want to offer a few family-based ideas that don't fit neatly into any of the above four categories:

104. Parents' book table with books and other resources that can be checked out.

105. Parents' bulletin board with information about upcoming events, pictures of past events and highlights of present programs for parents.

106. Parents' newsletter—Most youth ministers send a regular newsletter to their teenagers, but very few teenagers keep calendars or newsletters! Why not send the newsletter to the parents every other month? (My friend Deon Kitching, with YouthNet in South Africa, has put together a creative quarterly template called *Parent Focus* that allows youth directors to drop their own information into an already formatted newsletter filled with helpful information for parents. You can contact Deon at <deonkit2000@yahoo.com>).

107. Elder friends—Many churches have a program in which the officers of

the church are matched up with young people going through confirmation.

108. Mentoring—Interested teenagers could be matched with trained adults in the church for one-on-one friendship building over the course of the year.

109. The 70+ Club or Adopt a Grandparent—Some older adults have a tremendous ability to relate to teenagers. They also tend to have a great deal of free time! They can be used as youth leaders, Sunday-school teachers or mentors.

110. Taking parents to lunch—One youth pastor friend of mine makes it a habit to take the dads of the teenagers in the church out to lunch during the year, one at time, and to ask them to share their dreams for their sons or daughters. He hasn't had a quiet lunch yet.

111. Teaching parents how to build a Christian community for their children by inviting youth leaders, pastors, missionaries and Sunday-school teachers to dinner.

112. Using parents on the youth committee—Almost every youth ministry has an administrative committee to approve and support the direction of the program.

113. Parents' roundtable—A weekly support group for parents of teenagers.

114. Parents' committee—As a family-based youth ministry gets going, it may become helpful to develop a committee of parents to give counsel and encourage other parents' involvement.

115. Class parents—A mother or father in each class who is responsible for the planning and organization for that class's special events.

116. Parent/youth planning potlucks—We began one year with a different planning event for each grade. Parents and teenagers together planned the special events for their class for the year.

117. Annual open letter from teens to parents—By soliciting input from teens in Sunday school, the youth leader can compile a letter to all the parents from all the young people and send it out in the next newsletter.

118. Annual open letter from parents to teens—The reverse of 117.

119. Preaching on the relationship between parenting and discipleship.

120. Camping experiences—Young Life has recently developed a family camp program. Doug Burleigh, past president of Young Life, has said, "Over the years we have learned that you don't isolate a kid and minister just to him or her. Kids come in the context of families. So it makes sense to take our beautiful facility at Trail West and minister in a broader context."[3]

121. Send baptismal anniversary cards to remind your students and their parents.

122. Invite students to join the elders or ministers as they take communion to shut-ins in the church.

As perhaps the only institution left that's designed and equipped to work with entire families, churches today face an unparalleled opportunity to not only reach teenagers but impact entire families. But unless we make a shift in direction, the long-term return on our investments in youth ministry will be disappointing. Those churches that choose to place their emphasis on empowering the family and the extended family of the church to do the work of youth ministry may be in for a wild ride. But the return on this kind of investment will be rich indeed.

Happy trails.

APPENDIX E

Bridges: A Family-Based Curriculum

Our journey to create resources that could help mold adults and youth into crossgenerational communities started a little more than fifteen years ago. It all began with a vague uneasiness about the shallow impact of most of what we do in youth ministry. And our uneasiness grew into a single conviction: teenagers learn best when they are surrounded by those who know more than they do, namely their own parents or other adults in the church.

And so we began. Our first experimental group was a year-long, five-or-six-family attempt at putting parents and their teenage children together. We had little idea at that time what the curriculum should be. But our compass was set, even though we weren't terribly sure what we would face on the way.

That first group was full of fits and starts as we tried to determine exactly how to implement the strategy we were so sure of. By the next year, we implemented a new format. Together Nan Russell and I led six different three-week courses for each of our six youth Sunday-school classes, inviting parents to participate. Some classes were packed out; in others, we were tempted to count furniture to boost our numbers.

But by the third or fourth year, the vision became more clear. We wanted to fill our teenagers' "family tables" with a world of caring Christian adults. We realized that these courses weren't about "information," but about the formation that happens when Christian adults and teenagers talk together about the most important issues of their lives.

Back in 1996, Nan and I put a fifteen-session collection of family-based curriculum resources together called *Bridges*. Easily adapted for Sunday-school classes, small groups or large groups, retreats, or stand-alone events, this series was designed to give churches multiple opportunities for bringing adults and youth together in an interactive learning environment.

Because the entire curriculum is now out of print and available only on our website <www.familybasedym.com> or by phone order (615-298-9506), we have included in this edition of *Family-Based Youth Ministry* three complete sessions from *Bridges*, along with some of our favorite *Bridges* ideas. Though these Bridges Bonus Ideas are presented randomly, their common thread is a proven track record for helping youth and adults grow together into a single community of faith.

DECISION-MAKING
Session One: Becoming Wise
Titus 1:15; 1 Kings 3:16-28

OVERVIEW
When parents create for their kids a path in life where decisions require minimal risks, chances are that failure will be reduced, but faith development may be stifled as well. Confidence in our decision-making requires a willingness to fail, to step out on a limb, to discover a wiser way.

The following three sessions invite teenagers and adults to do some perspective taking, to learn the value of becoming wise (not perfect) and to decide to live an abundant Christian life.

PURPOSE
To discover what kind of person makes great decisions and to explore ways of becoming that kind of person.

THE QUICK LOOK
I. **Engaging the Brain**
   Forced Choice
   Introductions
   Mini-Lecture: How *Did* You Make That Great Decision?

II. **Igniting the Heart**
   Brainstorming
   Debating
   Journal Writing: Becoming Wise: Titus 1:15; 1 Kings 3:16-28

III. **Taking It Home**
   Small Groups: Processing the Journals
   Closing Prayer

Materials needed: Journal sheets, pencils

I. ENGAGING THE BRAIN

A. FORCED CHOICE: *Identifying Yourself*
   1. Ask everyone in the group to stand in the center of the room.
   2. Explain that you will be giving them a series of choices.
   3. As the group members make their choices, each person will move to one side of the room or the other to indicate his or her choice. No one is allowed to stay in the middle.
   4. Invite the group to ask questions to clarify the instructions.
   5. As you present the following set of choices, direct group members to move to one side of the room or the other to indicate their choices (for example, "If you think _____, go to this side of the room. If you think _____, go to that side of the room").
      a. Which do you like better? Pizza or Chinese food
      b. An art gallery or the symphony
      c. Being with lots of people or being alone
      d. A fire in the den or a picnic at Niagara Falls
      e. A jeep or a Mercedes
      f. Being a minister or a missionary
      g. A bad sinus infection or a stomach virus
      h. Going to bed early or getting up early
      i. A long sermon or a root canal
      j. Guitars and drums in church or an organ in church

B. INTRODUCTIONS *(10 minutes)*

    1. Get the group into a circle and, if necessary, ask everyone to introduce himself or herself and point out any other family members who might be in the group today. Then have each person tell about one good decision he or she has made in life.

    2. Let the group know that the good decision of getting married is not allowed because other adults in the group may feel significant spousal pressure to say getting married.

    3. Invite the group to ask questions to clarify instructions.

C. MINI-LECTURE: *How Did You Make That Great Decision?*

    1. Ask introductory questions.

        a. How many of you learned to make the good decision you just described by taking a class in decision-making?

        b. How many of you thought through specific lists of right steps for decision-making before you made your good decision?

    2. Move beyond discussing decision-making methods.

        a. Explain that one of the first assumptions of this session is that you don't need a list of decision-making steps to file away somewhere and never look at again.

        b. Explain that this section will focus on what kind of person makes great decisions and on finding ways to become that kind of person. One theme you will hear over and over in these three sessions is that wise people seek wisdom, not just answers to memorize.

    3. Interruption Question: Does anyone have any idea why we have the adults in here?

        a. Allow the group to give answers.

        b. Explain that one of the most significant visions for youth ministry is to create for our teenagers an extended family of Christian adults. This sort of extended family can, in the long run, have a much more significant impact on our teenagers' decisions than simply hearing from one or two teachers on a weekly basis.

4. Tell the group that we will learn some important principles about decision-making while we are together, but that perhaps it is even more important for the parents and kids in this group to get to know each other in the process.

5. Allow the group to ask any questions they might have about the direction of the next three sessions.

II. IGNITING THE HEART

A. BRAINSTORMING: *What Choices Will You Have to Make?*

1. Remind the group of the rules for brainstorming: quantity is better than quality, zany is good, no pooh-poohing someone else's idea.

2. Ask them to name every possible significant decision that the youth in this group will make between now and college graduation.

3. Record all the answers on the board or a flip chart.

B. DEBATING: *What Good Are Mistakes Anyway?*

1. Divide the group into teams of three or four with at least one youth and one adult on each team.

2. Separate the groups into two approximately equal teams (for example, two groups on one side, three groups on the other).

3. Explain that each small group will have three minutes to come up with the best possible arguments they can for one side of a debate. Tell the group that you will give them the issue to be debated in just a minute.

4. Remind the group to use specific decisions that were put on the board during the brainstorming time to prove their points.

5. Invite the group to ask questions to clarify the instructions.

6. The two sides of the debate.

   a. One side will come up with the best arguments they can to prove this proposition: Wisdom comes from making mistakes.

   b. The other side will come up with the best arguments they can to prove this proposition: Wisdom comes from avoiding mistakes.

7. Give the small groups three minutes to come up with their best arguments.

8. The freestyle debate.
   a. Explain that you will serve as the impartial judge.
   b. Give these rules.
      (1) The rulings of the judge are final and irrevocable.
      (2) Never question the judge.
      (3) The judge accepts bribes only in small unmarked bills.
      (4) No one can speak more than thirty seconds.
      (5) After one side has had the opportunity to speak, the other side will have the opportunity to speak.
      (6) Anyone who wishes to speak must first be recognized (raising the hand is a fine indicator) and called on to speak by the judge.
   c. Invite the group to ask questions to clarify the instructions.

9. Begin the debate.

10. Stop the debate while it is still lively. (In this exercise, as much as possible avoid saying, "Would anyone else like to add something?")

11. Process questions (with the entire group).
    a. Who won this debate?
    b. How many of you felt like the answer was somewhere in the middle?

C. JOURNAL WRITING: *Becoming Wise: Titus 1:15; 1 Kings 3:16-28*
1. Distribute the journal sheets (p. 218) and pencils.
2. Give the group three minutes to complete their journal sheets.

III. TAKING IT HOME (10 MINUTES)

A. SMALL GROUPS: *Processing the Journals*
1. Return to the small groups that were formed for the debate.
2. Ask each small group to identify the person in the group with the most hair. This person will be the group leader.
3. Have all the small group leaders raise their hands to make sure

that every group has a leader.

4. Explain that each group will work around the circle two times.

    a. Question for the first time around: What did you write or mark on your journal sheet that would help us get to know you a little better?

    b. How did you put Titus 1:15 into your own words?

B. CLOSING PRAYER: Close the group in prayer or prearrange to have one of the youth close the group in prayer.

Becoming Wise

1. Who is the wisest person you have ever known?

What is it that makes you see him/her as wise?

2. Which of these philosophies is closest to your own attitude toward decision-making?

a. Garbage In/Garbage Out: If you fill your mind with foolish ideas, you will be foolish. If you fill your mind with wise ideas, you will be wise.

b. Memorize the Answers: Talk to lots of people who have been there and find out what they did and imitate it.

c. I Believe in Magic: Handle everything on a case-by-case basis and cross your fingers that everything will work.

d. Make Up Your Own: _____

3. "To the pure all things are pure, but to the corrupt and unbelieving nothing is pure. Their very minds and consciences are corrupted" (Titus 1:15 NRSV). In a nutshell how would you summarize Paul's words in this passage about making wise decisions?

4. The one decision that I really want to make wisely over the next few years is . . .

5. Want to know more? Check out Solomon's decision-making process in 1 Kings 3:16-28. Why would one of the wisest men who ever lived want to chop a baby into two pieces?

DECISION-MAKING
Session Two: Only a Fool
Proverbs (Selected Verses)

PURPOSE
To help the group members develop wisdom by identifying the characteristics of a fool.

THE QUICK LOOK
I. **Engaging the Brain**
   What's That Smell?
   Checking In
   Thinking Through the Smell
   Mini-Lecture: An Introduction to Foolishness

II. **Igniting the Heart**
   Journal Sheet: The Foolishness Test
   Small Groups: I Know a Fool When I See One
   New Small Groups: The How-to's of Foolproofing

III. **Taking It Home**
   Journal Sheet: Wrap-up Questions
   One-Word Prayer

Materials needed: Incense, journal sheets, pencils, paper

I. ENGAGING THE BRAIN

A. WHAT'S THAT SMELL? *(1 minute)*
1. Before the group begins, burn some incense in the room and close the door.
2. By the time the group members arrive, the room should have a noticeable smell.
3. If the smell is too strong, it is just right.
4. If the group resists coming into the room because of the smell, ask them to complete just a few questions before moving to another room.

B. CHECKING IN

　1. As the participants arrive, you should be busy with other concerns (setting up chairs, erasing the board, collating papers). Simply give instructions to the group to come on in and sit down.

　2. As much as possible, play dumb about the smell.

　3. Check-In Questions

　　　a. Ask if anyone in the group knows everyone else's name. (Unless your group is *very* unusual, there will be at least one person, probably a teenager, who doesn't know everyone's name. As a general rule, it is best not to assume that everyone knows everyone else's name.)

　　　b. If someone volunteers, let him or her go around the room and give each person's name.

　　　c. If no one volunteers, go around the room yourself, giving every person's name (you may need the group members to prompt you).

C. THINKING THROUGH THE SMELL

　1. Did anyone notice anything different when you came in?

　2. When you first smelled the incense, did you feel like staying or leaving?

　3. Now that you have been in the room awhile, are you more offended by the smell than you were when you first came in?

D. MINI-LECTURE: *An Introduction to Foolishness*

　1. Remind the group that the focus of this group will not be to give them the right answers, but to help members become wise people. Wise people make wise choices.

　2. Today we will be talking about the dangers of being what the Bible calls "a fool."

　3. Proverbs uses the term *fool* often to describe someone who is lacking wisdom.

　4. Foolishness is like a bad smell.

　　　a. It bothers us more at first than when we have been around it awhile.

    b. When you are around foolish people, you begin to become foolish yourself.

  5. Process Question: What similarities do you see between foolishness and what you smelled when you came in?

II. IGNITING THE HEART

A. JOURNAL SHEET: *The Foolishness Test*

  1. Distribute the journal sheets (p. 224) and pencils.

  2. Give the group up to five minutes to complete the foolishness test and tabulate their scores. Have Bibles available for the group to look up verses they may be curious about.

B. SMALL GROUPS: *I Know a Fool When I See One*

  1. Form makeshift families.

    a. Have all the youth stand and find an opposite adult (girls find dads and boys find moms).

    b. Have each pair find an opposite pair, making groups of mom, dad, son and daughter (if there are no more opposite pairs, similar pairs can be joined).

    c. Have each group of four pick one of the leftover people who are still seated.

    d. Have the groups get into close circles in their groups of four or five people.

  2. Explain to the groups their first task: They have two minutes to come up with the best possible description of a fool (promise to give extra points for creativity). These disclaimers will help set the context:

    a. The groups are not trying to describe healthy foolishness, like the king's fool, who played an important role for the king, or like Jesus, who was considered foolish for going against what the majority seemed to think.

    b. The groups are to describe the negative, self-defeating kind of fool that no one wants to be like.

  3. Give the groups two minutes to do their work.

4. When two minutes are up, give each group thirty seconds or less to give their description.
5. Process questions:
   a. Which group had the most creative description?
   b. Which group gave the clearest description?
   c. If you were to award one million dollars to the best definition (and it could not be your own group's), which group would you give it to?

C. NEW SMALL GROUPS: *The How-to's of Foolproofing*
   1. Setup.
      a. Have all the youth stand and move to a different small group. (For example, one small group to the left.)
      b. The youth should be with the same youth from the previous group but with different adults.
      c. Ask every group to select a recorder, a leader, a reporter and a timekeeper.
   2. Instructions.
      a. Explain to the groups that they will each be given two projects to work on.
      b. Let them know that they will have five minutes to do as much as possible.
      c. Each group can decide which project they would like to work on first.
      d. Invite the group to ask questions to clarify the instructions.
   3. The projects.
      a. If you were to give parents a strategy for foolproofing their children, what would the strategy be?
      b. If you were to give teenagers a strategy for foolproofing themselves, what would the strategy be?
   4. Give the groups five minutes to come up with their strategies (if things don't seem to be clicking in these groups, it is certainly appropriate to have them work less than five minutes).

5. Reporting.
   a. Have the reporter from each group share his or her group's strategies with the large group.
   b. Following each report, ask the large group if they have any questions or comments about what has just been reported.

III. TAKING IT HOME (10 MINUTES)

A. JOURNAL SHEET: *Wrap-up Questions* (*3 minutes*)
Give the group three minutes to complete the wrap-up section of the journal sheets (p. 225).

B. ONE-WORD PRAYER (*5-7 minutes*)
Have the large group join hands for a one-word prayer. Beginning with the leader, have each person in the group offer up one word to God that summarizes one thing he or she desires from God.

Only a Fool

1. FOOLISHNESS TEST

Instructions: Answer each question below using the following scale: 1: never; 2: usually not; 3: usually; 4: always.

_____ Do you hate people who criticize you (including your parents)? (Proverbs 15:5)

_____ Do you think that you are the only one who can find the answer that is right for you? (Proverbs 12:15; 18:2; 28:26)

_____ Do your friends do foolish things? (Proverbs 13:20)

_____ Do you think that being smart (especially in your ability to deceive) makes you wise? (Proverbs 19:1)

_____ Do you talk a lot? (Proverbs 10:8, 10; 29:11)

_____ Do you seem to be getting in trouble all the time? (Proverbs 10:23; 19:29)

_____ Do people say about you, "We've tried everything, and you just won't change"? (Proverbs 17:10; 26:11; 27:22)

_____ Do you have trouble disagreeing without getting mad or mocking your opponent? (Proverbs 29:9)

_____ Do your parents grieve over you? (Proverbs 10:1; 17:24)

_____ Do you like to start fights and arguments? (Proverbs 20:3)

_____ Do you seem to get into fights and arguments that have little to do with you? (Proverbs 20:3)

_____ Do you brag? (Proverbs 30:32)

_____ Do you find yourself talking negatively about other people when they are not around? (Proverbs 10:18)

_____ Do you have trouble learning from anyone but yourself? (Proverbs 23:9)

_____ Total Points

What does your point total say?
14-28: No Fool Here
28-42: Hmmmmm
42 and up: You Be the Judge

2. Wrap-up Questions

a. "A fool finds no pleasure in understanding but delights in airing his own opinions" (Proverbs 18:2). According to this verse, what does a fool take the most pleasure in?

b. If a wise person is the opposite of a fool, what does a wise person take the most pleasure in (according to this verse)?

c. Based on what you have written, who was the wisest person in the group today? Why?

d. What is one choice you want to make this week to foolproof yourself?

DECISION-MAKING
Session 3: Risking Imperfection

Purpose
To encourage the group members to be willing to make imperfect decisions.

The Quick Look

I. Engaging the Brain
Time Test
Mini-Lecture: Making Decisions Without All the Facts
Review Question
Summary Statement

II. Igniting the Heart
Wagon Wheel
Story Time
Journal Writing: Risking Imperfection
One-on-One: Processing the Journal Sheets

III. Taking It Home
A Letter to God
Circle Prayer

Materials needed: Journal sheets, pencils

I. Engaging the Brain

A. TIME TEST
    1. Have everyone in the group stand.
    2. Explain that the group is about to experience a test of their powers of concentration and find out who in the group has the greatest awareness of time.
    3. Have the group members close their eyes. After the leader says go, each member will sit down when they think exactly one minute has passed.

4. Allow the group to ask questions to clarify the instructions.

5. Say go.

6. After everyone is seated, acknowledge the winner (an inexpensive watch would be a nice prize).

7. As a variation, repeat the process but this time provide some form of distraction music, talking, etc.

B. MINI-LECTURE: *Making Decisions Without All the Facts*

1. Many of our decisions are like the one you had to make in this exercise.

2. You never have ALL the facts, but you have to make the decision. Sometimes the longer you wait, the further you move away from the right decision.

3. Today's group focuses on our need to be willing to make what we are calling "imperfect decisions."

C. REVIEW QUESTION: If you could come up with the single most important idea about decision-making we have talked about, what would it be?

D. SUMMARY STATEMENT: We make wise decisions by becoming wise people, not by memorizing the answers or by learning a formula.

II. IGNITING THE HEART

A. WAGON WHEEL

1. Setup.

    a. Have the group move their chairs into two concentric circles with the youth on the outside facing in and the adults on the inside facing out.

    b. Adjust the circles until everyone has a partner of the other generation. (Because you will probably not have an even number of youth and adults, adults may need to be paired with adults, or youth may need to be paired with other youth.)

    c. Have the partners introduce themselves. *Remind the group that they will need to remember this partner later in the session.*

    d. Determine the length of time you will give the group for each answer. The general rule is that shorter is better than longer. For some questions, ten seconds for each partner will be sufficient.

2. Instructions.

    a. You (the teacher) will ask the entire group a series of questions.

    b. Each time a question is asked, you will announce to the entire group who should answer first (the youth or the adult) and call time when it is time to move on to the next question. In the allotted time, both partners should have had time to answer the question.

    c. After you call time, direct the inside circle (the adults) to move one chair to the right.

    d. After the inside group has shifted, give the next question to the entire group and repeat the process.

    e. Invite the group to ask questions to clarify the instructions.

3. Ask the questions.

    a. What are three decisions you made this week?

    b. If you had a major decision to make, whom would you talk to first? Why?

    c. How normal is it for you to involve God in your decisions? And if it is, how do you involve God?

    d. Which are you more likely to do: make a quick decision and regret it, or take too long to make the decision and miss the opportunity?

    e. Do you think most perfectionists (people who try to do everything perfectly) have trouble making decisions?

    f. If someone gave you $10,000 right now, what would you do with it?

    g. If you had to buy a book or a movie in the next ten minutes, how hard would it be for you to pick one out? What would it likely be?

    h. If you could be anyone other than yourself, who would you be?

        i. When would it be okay for you to lie, if ever?

        j. What are the top three things you want to accomplish today?

        k. What did you do with this weekend?

        l. You don't agree with the potentially self-destructive behavior of your best friend. What do you do?

        m. Complete this sentence: The biggest fear I have about making decisions is . . .

        n. Complete this sentence: The biggest decision I ever made as a teenager was . . .

4. Ask process questions.

        a. What was the hardest question for you in that exercise?

        b. Adults: If you were to add up all the different teenagers you talked to recently (not including workers at McDonald's), how far back in time would you have to go to total the number of conversations you had with different teenagers today?

        c. Youth: If you were to add up all the different adults you have talked to recently (not including clerks at stores), how far back would you have to go to total the number of adults you talked to today?

B. STORY TIME

1. Read the story that follows by M. Scott Peck from *The Road Less Traveled* (New York: Touchstone Books, 1980), p. 132.

> If you are a regular churchgoer, you might notice a woman in her late forties, who every Sunday exactly five minutes before the start of the service inconspicuously takes the same seat in a side pew on an aisle in the very back of the church. The moment the service is over, she quietly but quickly makes for the door and is gone before anyone can greet her. Should you manage to accost her and invite her to the coffee hour following the service, she would thank you politely but nervously and then dash away. . . .
>
> If you could keep watch over her, you might see that she works as a typist in a large office where she accepts her as-

signments wordlessly, types them flawlessly and returns her finished work without comment. She eats her lunch at her desk and has no friends. She walks home, stopping always at the same impersonal supermarket for a few provisions before she vanishes behind her door until she appears again for the next day's work.

On Saturday afternoons, she goes alone to a local movie theater that has a weekly change of shows. She has a TV set but no phone. She almost never receives mail. Were you somehow able to communicate with her and comment that her life seemed lonely, she would tell you that she rather enjoys her loneliness. . . .

Who is this woman? We do not know the secrets of her heart. What we do know is that she avoids taking any risks to the extent that she has narrowed and diminished herself almost to the point of nonexistence.

    2. Ask process questions.
        a. Did this woman make decisions based on what she wanted or on something else?
        b. What do you think she was afraid of?
        c. If a teenager were on course for becoming this kind of person, what would that teenager look like now?

C. JOURNAL WRITING: *Risking Imperfection*
    1. Distribute the journal sheets (p. 232) and pencils.
    2. Give the group members five minutes to complete questions one and two on the journal sheets.

D. ONE-ON-ONE: *Processing the Journal Sheets*
    1. Ask each member of the group to return to his or her partner from the beginning of the wagon-wheel exercise.
    2. Instructions.
        a. Each partner will have one minute to share his or her answer to question two and talk about anything else he or she has written in the journal.

      b. The listening partner is allowed to ask questions as time allows.

  3. Call time at the end of each minute.

III. TAKING IT HOME

A. A LETTER TO GOD

  1. Invite the group to complete question three on the journal sheet.

  2. Allow the group to ask questions to clarify the instructions.

B. CIRCLE PRAYER

  1. If it is appropriate for your group, ask them to join hands in a circle.

  2. Have each member of the group pray for his or her partner from the previous exercise.

  3. Go around the group with each person praying one word for his or her partner.

Risking Imperfection

Far better it is to dare mighty things, even though checked by failure, than to rank with those poor spirits who neither enjoy nor suffer much because they live in a gray twilight that knows neither victory nor defeat. (author unknown)

1. Which of these excuses tempt you to stay in the "gray twilight" of indecision?

_____ If I try, I might fail.

_____ People might think I'm stupid.

_____ I'll stick with what I do best.

_____ If I really commit to something, then I'll have to change the way I live.

_____ The dog ate it.

_____ If I say yes to something, I'll have to say no to lots of other things.

_____ I want to keep my options open.

_____ I can't do that!

_____ There are no fish in Arizona.

_____ There's nothing I can do.

_____ I tried it before, and it didn't work.

_____ I'll just pray about it.

2. The most important decision a Christian will ever make is the decision to live first and foremost as Christ's disciple. Where are you today in this process?

_____ Zacchaeus in the tree (Just let me watch from a distance.)

_____ Peter stepping out onto the water (Of course I can do this!)

_____ The sick man by the pool (I've got a few good reasons why this could never work.)

_____ Jonah in the boat (I know what God wants me to do, but I'm headed the other direction.)

3. Write a letter to God, describing where you would like to be in your spiritual life and one risk you are willing to take to get there. (Use the back of this page if necessary.)

Bonus Bridges Idea #1: Silent Auction

1. Instructions.
   a. Give each participant a silent auction sheet (p. 234) and a pencil.
   b. Explain that each person will be given an imaginary $100,000 to spend any way he or she wishes.
   c. Each person must bid all $100,000. Once an amount is written in a particular category, that money will be spent even if the bidder does not win that item in the auction (no refunds on the $100,000 after the session is over).

2. Invite the group to ask questions to clarify the instructions.

3. Give the group three minutes to complete their auction sheets.

4. Review the winners.
   a. As the auctioneer, go through the items on the silent auction sheet one at a time, asking questions like, Who bid on the new BMW? (show of hands), or, Did anyone bid over $10,000? How about $15,000? (continue raising the amount until only one hand is raised).
   b. Announce the name of the winner, allowing the group members time to write that name on their auction sheet.

5. Once all winners have been determined, summarize who has won each item, mentioning the name of each winner again.

6. Process questions.
   a. Did you learn anything about someone in "the other generation"?
   b. Who do you think got the best bargain today?
   c. How many of you wished you had bid differently?
   d. How might you bid differently if you could do this exercise over again?

THE OTHER GENERATION: SILENT AUCTION

You have $100,000 to spend any way you like. There are two catches: (1) Anything you bid, you spend even if you don't win the bid. (2) You can bid on as many things as you like, but you must bid on at least three things. You will have a few minutes to make your bids silently.

_____ A brand-new BMW

_____ A million dollars to give away to charity

_____ A great job

_____ The ability to write

_____ A $20,000 stereo system

_____ A year to do whatever you want

_____ A date with the man or woman of your dreams

_____ A lifetime supply of junk food

_____ A week of silence at a monastery

_____ A great relationship with God

_____ Never being sick a day in your life

_____ Having your children grow up to be vibrant, committed Christian adults

_____ An all-expense-paid trip to Disney World for your family

_____ A condo on the beach

_____ Becoming a rock star

_____ Time to read everything you want to read

_____ A year of no hassles from your parents/kids

_____ Being a genius

Bonus Bridges Idea #2: The FamilyRead Game

1. Setup.

    a. Set up two long tables in the front of the group with eight to twelve chairs behind the tables (depending on the number of contestant parents who participate).

    b. Put a sign or banner (The FamilyRead Game) over the front of the tables to give the group a more festive game-show atmosphere.

    c. Pick four families from the studio audience to come forward. It would make sense to pick families of different configurations (a single-parent family, a blended family, a working-mom family, a traditional family).

2. Assign someone from the audience to be the recorder of answers for each team. The recorders will need construction paper (notebook paper might be too transparent) and dark magic markers.

3. Instructions.

    a. The game will begin by having the parents taken out to a sound-proof booth while their children are asked questions.

    b. Each participant will be asked the same questions. When participants give their answers, the recorder assigned to that family will write the answer on one side of the paper and put the number of the question on the other side.

    c. When all the questions are asked of the teenagers, the parents will be brought back in to see how well they can predict what their children said about them.

    d. In the first round, when the teenagers are asked the questions first, a correct answer is worth five points. In the second round when parents are asked the questions first, the correct answers are worth ten points. The last question to the parents is a twenty-five-point bonus question.

    e. Allow the contestants to ask any questions they might have to clarify the instructions.

4. Questions to ask (pick three questions for parents and three for kids).

For the Teenagers

    a. When was the last time a parent was mad at you?

    b. What would your parent(s) have named you if you had been the opposite sex?

    c. If your parent(s) could go on vacation anywhere for a month, where would they go?

    d. Would your parent(s) say he or she would rather (1) take a nap, (2) climb a mountain or (3) stay around the house?

    e. How hard do your parent(s) have to work to get you to come to church: (1) not at all (2) a little (3) drag me kicking and screaming sometimes

    f. What is your parent's(s') favorite radio station?

For the Parents

    a. How many times did your son or daughter change clothes yesterday?

    b. Who was your son or daughter's favorite teacher ever?

    c. Do your kids think you are too strict, too permissive or just right in your discipline?

    d. What would your son or daughter say right now if asked what they want to do when they grow up?

    e. Bonus Question: What is your son or daughter's favorite music group or singer?

5. Play the game.

6. Process questions.

    a. Do you think the parents know the kids better or the kids know the parents better?

    b. Youth, what kinds of things can parents do to understand you better?

    c. Parents, what kinds of things can your children do to understand you better?

Bonus Bridges Idea #3: Case Study—*Like Three Trains*

1. Before the session begins, ask three outgoing volunteers (mom, dad and son from different families) to act out the story you will read. They will not have any lines; they will simply pantomime what you read. Let the volunteers know that it is okay if they overact. Volunteers may need to be prepped ahead of time.

2. Read the story.

   Mom is at home alone one weekday afternoon, putting laundry away in her fifteen-year-old son's bedroom. The son comes home and finds his mother in his room and lets his mother have it for invading his privacy. He storms off. That night, the son comes in an hour late from a date. Mom gives him a twenty-minute lecture about responsibility, ending with "I don't know how many times I need to tell you!"

   The next day, Dad returns from a disappointing business trip. As soon as he walks in the door, he is assaulted by the mom and the son, each accusing the other. Dad, tired and frustrated from his trip, blasts the son. The dinner table is icily silent.

   On the third day, Dad comes home from the office after work. Having lost a big deal, he has been wondering if he will be able to make enough money to provide for his family. At the dinner table that night, the battle picks up again, and this time, the father sides with the son. Dad asks the son to go to his room while he and Mom battle things out.

   Like three trains on connecting tracks headed for each other at full speed, this family must change gears or redirect its path, or someone will be hurt.

3. Process questions.

   a. How would you rate these three characters from best to worst?

   b. What are the mother and the father in conflict about?

   c. Who do you think is the most responsible for the communication problems in this family?

d. Who do you think is least responsible for the communication problems in this family?

e. How many different issues are stacked up in this particular conflict?

f. Do you think this family is normal for a home where there is a teenager?

g. Who has the most power to bring about change in this family?

BONUS BRIDGES IDEA #4: A VISIT TO ANOTHER MIND— *THE THING ABOUT PARENTS/YOUTH THAT CONFUSES ME*

PROCESS

Distribute the journal (p. 239) sheets and give the group 3-5 minutes to complete them. After the questions on the sheets have been answered, move the larger group into cross-generational teams with at least one youth and one adult in each one. Give the teams 3-5 minutes to talk through their responses.

A Visit to Another Mind

1. I think (check one)

____ it takes more work for teenagers to understand adults than for adults to understand teenagers.

____ it takes more work for adults to understand teenagers than for teenagers to understand adults.

2. The one thing I have trouble understanding about teenagers these days is . . .

3. I can see why my son or daughter has trouble understanding me when I . . .

4. One thing I want to do this week to "pay a visit" to what's going on my son or daughter's mind is . . .

— — — — — — — — — — — — — — — — — — — —

A Visit to Another Mind

1. I think (check one)

____ it takes more work for teenagers to understand adults than for adults to understand teenagers.

____ it takes more work for adults to understand teenagers than for teenagers to understand adults.

2. The one thing I have trouble understanding about parents is . . .

3. I can see why parents have trouble understanding me when I . . .

4. One thing I want to do this week to "pay a visit" to what's going on my mom or dad's mind is . . .

BONUS BRIDGES IDEA #5: FAMOUS PAIRS (OPENING)

1. Setup.
   a. Get enough sticky nametags for the entire group (a few more than you think you will need).
   b. Put a different famous name on each nametag. Every name should be a part of a famous pair.

2. Instructions.
   a. As the participants come in, put a nametag on the back of each person in the group.
   b. Avoid putting names of pairs on people sitting next to each other.
   c. Give out the nametags in such a way that everyone has a partner to look for (that is, if you give out Cereal, make sure that someone else in the group gets Milk).
   d. Explain to the group that each one of them is a part of a famous pair.
   e. Each person in the group can only ask yes or no questions of other people in the group until they determine who they are.
   f. As soon as a person learns the name that is on his or her back, he or she should begin looking for the other part of the famous pair (on someone else's back).
   g. When members of the pair find each other, they can sit down.
   h. Allow the group to ask questions to clarify the instructions.

3. Play the game.
   (Use as many names from the following pairs as you'll need to give a nametag to each group member: Abbott and Costello, Laurel and Hardy, Luke Skywalker and Princess Leia, the Sunday-school teacher and his/her spouse, the youth leader and his/her spouse, the pastor and his/her spouse, Antony and Cleopatra, Bonnie and Clyde, Sonny and Cher, Bill and Hillary Clinton, Ronald and Nancy Reagan, Tacos and Hot Sauce, Peter Pan and Wendy, Sleeping Beauty and Prince Charming, Albert Einstein and Mrs. Einstein, Burger King and Whopper, McDonald's and Big Mac, Samson and Delilah, Mary and Joseph,

Adam and Eve, Cereal and Milk, Peanut Butter and Jelly.)

4. Once the group has moved into pairs, you can have each pair find another pair or two to form a small group for an upcoming exercise.

BONUS BRIDGES IDEA #6: BACK-TO-BACK DRAWING

1. Setup.
   a. Bring enough pencils and photocopies of a simple coloring-book picture for every other person.
   b. Make sure that no one in the group sees the pictures before the exercise begins.
   c. Have each adult in the group find a youth partner.
   d. Ask the remaining group members to each find a partner.
   e. Ask each of the partners to sit back-to-back.
   f. Distribute the coloring-book pictures to one person in each pair, being careful to make sure that the pictures can only be seen by the person it was given to. (Variation: Give the pictures only to the parents on one side of the room and to the youth on the other side of the room.)
   g. Give each of the partners without the picture a blank piece of paper and a pencil (or crayon).

2. Instructions.
   a. The person with the picture will be describing the picture.
   b. The person who is drawing will be trying to duplicate the picture.
   c. Here's the catch: the describer can only describe shapes and angles, but not name anything. (For example, the describer cannot say, "Now draw an arm.")
   d. Invite the group to ask questions to clarify the instructions.

3. Give the pairs two minutes to attempt their drawings.

4. After two minutes are up, ask the partners to show each other their pictures.

5. Process questions.

    a. Which drawings were particularly creative?

    b. Who came the closest to the original?

    c. What was the secret to your accuracy?

Bonus Bridges Idea #7: Picturing Your Faith Foundation

1. Distribute paper and pencils to the group.

2. Explain the exercise.

    a. This exercise is designed to help group members identify their own cloud of witnesses and evaluate whether or not they have the kind of support for their own faith that they would like to have.

    b. This exercise will go in stages. First each person will be asked to draw (no art ability necessary); then the drawings will be explained in small groups.

    c. The key to this exercise will be to keep things moving quickly. If the group takes more than one minute for each drawing and one minute for each partner sharing, the exercise will likely drag out and become monotonous. So keep the exercise moving.

    d. Allow the group to ask questions to clarify the instructions.

2. The five-stage drawing.

    a. Stage 1

        (1) Have each person first draw a circle in the center of the page to represent him- or herself.

        (2) Invite the group members to draw other circles to represent all the people who have been positive influences in their lives as Christians.

        (3) Have them place a name by each circle. If there are too many circles to put a name by each, have them at least put the names in groups and name the groups.

        (4) Once the drawing is done, have each person match up with someone else, and take one minute for the pairs to describe to each other what they have drawn.

b. Stage 2

  (1) At the bottom of the picture, have members draw different squares for each Christian tradition that they have grown up with (such as Christmas Eve services, blessings at meals or bedtime stories).

  (2) When this part of the drawing is done, have each person find someone else in the group, and take one minute for the pairs to explain their drawings to each other.

c. Stage 3

  (1) Somewhere else on the page, have everyone draw a triangle for each institution (such as church, Young Life or a mission club) that has had an influence on their growth as Christians.

  (2) When this part is done, have each person find someone else in the group, and take one minute for the pairs to explain their drawings to each other.

d. Stage 4

  (1) Ask the group members to draw squiggly lines for every negative influence on their faith (for example, people making fun of them for being a Christian, certain friends, specific places associated with negative influence).

  (2) Again, when this stage is done, have each person find someone else in the group, and take one minute for the pairs to explain their drawings to each other.

e. Evaluation Stage

  (1) Have all the group members write the following incomplete sentence at the bottom of their completed pictures: In order to have the kind of faith that I want to have, one change I would like to make in this picture is . . .

  (2) Process questions.

    (a) Which of the stages was the easiest to draw?

    (b) Which was the hardest?

    (c) Having seen each other's pictures and heard each other's descriptions, what component do you think is most often missing from our faith-building pictures?

Bonus Bridges Idea #8: The Silent Treatment

1. Setup.
   - **a.** Divide the group into three generally equal parts.
   - **b.** A specific mixing of youth and adults is not important for this exercise, but each group will need both.
   - **c.** Have each small group line up single file.
2. Instructions.
   - **a.** The groups will be given three challenges to complete in one minute or less.
   - **b.** All groups will attempt to complete their challenges at the same time, and no one will be allowed to speak during any of the challenges.
   - **c.** Invite the group to ask questions, but do not let them know what the challenges will be at this point.
3. The silent challenges.
   - **a.** Line up alphabetically.
   - **b.** Line up by birthday.
   - **c.** Line up alphabetically by the last name of your favorite musician.
4. Call time and check groups.

B. MINI-LECTURE: *Sometimes You've Just Got to Talk*
   1. Some things we can do well without talking to other people. Other things (like the last challenge) are nearly impossible.
   2. Making wise choices, whether we are adults or teenagers, is one of those things that are nearly impossible without talking about it with other people.
   3. There is an unspoken rule in many homes that we call the no-talk rule. When it comes to tough topics, we just don't talk about them, pretending they will go away.

Bonus Bridges Idea #9:
Wagon Wheel on the Topic of Sexuality

A. WAGON WHEEL (*20 minutes*)

1. Setup.
    a. Have the group move their chairs into two concentric circles with the youth on the outside facing in and the adults on the inside facing out.
    b. Adjust the circles so that everyone has a partner. (Because you will probably not have an even number of youth and adults, adults may need to be paired with adults, or youth may need to be paired with other youth.)
    c. Have the partners introduce themselves.
    d. Determine the length of time you will allow for each answer. The general rule is that shorter is better than longer. For some questions, ten seconds for each partner will be sufficient.
2. Instructions.
    a. You will ask the entire group a series of questions.
    b. Each time a question is asked, you will announce to the entire group who should answer first (the youth or the adult) and call time to move on to the next question.
    c. After you call time, direct the inside circle (the adults) to move one chair to the right.
    d. After the inside group has shifted, give the next question to the entire group.
    e. Allow the group to ask questions if the instructions are unclear.
3. Questions.
    a. Your daughter is seventeen. A twenty-seven-year-old man asks her out. What, if anything, will you say or do?
    b. Agree/disagree: Women need to learn to say no because guys do not have the willpower.
    c. More and more teenagers are choosing to wait to have sex until they get married. What reasons do you think most of them have?
    d. You are concerned about the way a close female friend dresses. She is getting a reputation as a tease. What will you say to her?

e. Your fifteen-year-old friend asks you for a ride to the birth-control clinic. What will you do?

f. Rumors are spreading around the youth group that your best friend, the preacher's daughter, has been very loose. What will you do? What would you do if it were the preacher's son?

g. When you think about your best friends' attitudes toward sex, would you say for the most part they are healthy, a little out of bounds or so far out that you wouldn't feel comfortable talking about it here?

h. If you had a serious question about sex, you would most likely: look it up, talk to someone or say nothing and hope you figure it out later.

i. How do you feel about discussing sex with your parents?

j. How do you feel about people living together before they get married?

k. Agree/disagree: Guys are too pushy when it comes to sex.

l. I think the biggest reason teenagers have sex is . . .

m. Agree/disagree: If a single girl becomes pregnant, she should marry the baby's father.

n. Agree/disagree: If a person doesn't fool around on a date, he or she won't get a lot of chances to go out.

o. Agree/disagree: Adults these days are too worried about their children being sexually active.

p. What do most of your friends think about people having sex outside marriage?

q. How do you feel about answering these kinds of questions with the other generation?

r. How much should the church talk about sex?

s. If you had moved in with someone of the opposite sex to live together when you were eighteen, how would your parents have reacted?

t. The most uncomfortable question asked in this activity was . . .

B. MINI-LECTURE: *What Does the Bible Say About Sex? (5 minutes)*

    1. Last week each participant was given a list of Scripture references that deal with sexuality. Invite anyone in the group to comment about anything he or she read. (Don't be surprised if no one speaks here.)

    2. Summarizing the Bible's message about sex.

        a. Sex is a good gift from God (Genesis 2:24; Proverbs 5:18-19).

            (1) God did not have to make us sexual creatures, but he chose to. (God *could* have made us like the insect whose female kills and eats her mate immediately after their mating exercise.)

            (2) God knows far more about sex than Madonna or Bon Jovi (or the currently popular musician).

        b. God designed sex for the free enjoyment of those who make the lifelong commitment of marriage.

            (1) Twenty times in the New Testament the word *porneia*, frequently translated "fornication," is used to describe an act that is not consistent with the Christian lifestyle (see the handout from last week).

            (2) Since it is not a term we frequently use, it is helpful to check *Webster's Dictionary* definition of fornication: human sexual intercourse other than between a man and his wife.

        c. Summary: Sex is God's good gift to be enjoyed in marriage, the context for which it was created.

BONUS BRIDGES IDEA #10: PANEL OF EXPERTS

    1. Before group begins, invite parents from four different families to serve on a panel for this session.

    2. It would be wise to ask parents from different family configurations, including two traditional families (with original mother and father).

    3. Ideally these should be parents whose children have recently left for college or moved out of the house. They need not be parents who have a student in the group.

4. A table should be set up in front of the group with enough chairs for all the parents who have been asked to serve on the panel.

5. Instructions.

    a. You (the teacher) will ask each panel member a few questions to get things started.

    b. After each has answered, the group members may ask follow-up questions.

    c. The group members will write questions they have for the panel and pass them to you.

    d. Invite the group to ask questions to clarify the instructions.

6. Ask the opening questions.

    a. Describe one thing you are glad you did to prepare your child for being an independent adult.

    b. Describe one thing you wish you had done to better prepare your child for being an independent adult.

    c. What issue was the most difficult for your family in preparing your children for adulthood during their junior and senior years of high school?

7. Invite the group to ask additional questions of the panel

NOTES

Introduction

[1]Merton Strommen, Karen E. Jones and Dave Rahn, *Youth Ministry That Transforms* (Grand Rapids, Mich.: Zondervan, 2001), p. 171.

Chapter One: Something's Wrong

[1]George Barna, *Index of Leading Spiritual Indicators* (Dallas: Word, 1996), pp. 43-44.

[2]George Barna, *Marketing the Church* (Colorado Springs: NavPress, 1988), p. 22.

[3]Milton Coalter, "Preliminary Report on the Findings of the Study of the Presbyterian Church in the 20th Century," quoted in the *General Assembly Task Force on Membership Report*, 1991, p. 10.

[4]Tom Gillespie, "The Way Back Leads Nowhere: Report of the Standing Committee on Theological Education," Address to the 200th General Assembly, *The Presbyterian Outlook*, July 18, 1988, p. 6.

[5]Mark Senter, *The Coming Revolution in Youth Ministry* (Wheaton, Ill.: Victor, 1992), p. 21.

[6]Ibid., p. 14.

[7]Mike Yaconelli, *Youth Ministry to Kids in a Post-Christian World,* 1989 Youth Specialties Resource Seminar Video (El Cajon, Calif.: Youth Specialties, 1989).

Chapter Two: Is Anybody Out There?

[1]It is not particularly surprising that in the Link Institute's study of over 2,100 youth workers, only one in five expressed satisfaction with their work (*Youthworker*, November/December 1997, p. 50).

[2]Tony Souder, the director of the Chattanooga Youth Ministry Network, told me recently that his organization just completed a study of 160 different youth ministries in his area. And one of their most fascinating discoveries was that out of those 160 youth ministries surveyed, 112 (over 70 percent) had gone through key leadership transitions during a single eighteen-month period.

[3]Patricia Hersch, *A Tribe Apart* (New York: Ballantine, 1998), p. 22.

[4]Ibid., p. 19, emphasis in the original.

[5]Margaret Mead, *Culture and Commitment: A Study of the Generation Gap* (Garden City, N.Y.: Doubleday-Natural History Press, 1970), p. 45.

[6]Mary Pipher, *USA Weekend,* March 19-21, 1999, p. 12.

[7]Mihaly Csikzentmihalyi and Reed Larson, *Being Adolescent: Conflict and Growth in the Teenage Years* (New York: BasicBooks, 1984), quoted in Quentin J. Schultze, *Winning Your Kids Back from the Media* (Downers Grove, Ill.: InterVarsity Press, 1994), p. 49.

[8]Urie Bronfenbrenner, "The Origins of Alienation," *Scientific American* 231 (August 1974): 60.

[9]Pipher, "Shelter of Each Other," p. 84.

[10]Josh McDowell and Norm Wakefield, *The Dad Difference* (San Bernardino, Calif.: Here's Life, 1989), p. 13.

[11]*Parents and Teenagers,* August/September 1988, p. 8.

[12]Andrée Aelion Brooks, *Children of Fast-Track Parents* (New York: Viking Penguin, 1989), pp. 67-68.

Chapter Three: The Developmental Disaster

[1]Charles P. Warren, quoted in Kari Torjesen Malcolm, *Building Your Family to Last* (Downers Grove, Ill.: InterVarsity Press, 1987), p. 77.

[2]*TV Guide,* February 6, 1989.

[3]Neil Postman, *Amusing Ourselves to Death* (New York: Viking Penguin, 1986), pp. 60-61.

[4]R. Jackson Wilson, quoted in Daniel Singal, "The Other Crisis in Our Schools," *The Atlantic,* November 1991, quoted in *Reader's Digest,* April 1992, p. 112.

[5]Quoted in Charles Colson, *Against the Night* (Ann Arbor, Mich.: Servant, 1989), pp. 21-22, emphasis added.

[6]Walt Mueller, *Understanding Today's Youth Culture* (Wheaton, Ill.: Tyndale House, 1994), p. 205.

[7]The "Just Say No" campaigns were essentially ineffective in the lower-income areas of inner cities. In these cases, the horizontal peer dependence, particularly in gangs, outweighed any message from the mainstream culture.

[8]H. Stephen Glenn and Jane Nelsen, *Raising Self-Reliant Children in a Self-Indulgent World* (Roseville, Calif.: Prima, 1989), p. 208.

[9]George Will, "Slamming the Doors," *Newsweek,* March 25, 1991, p. 65.

[10]Avery Chenoweth, "Parents Learning How to Teach Teens Meaning," *Princeton Packet,* January 12, 1983, p. 7a.

[11]Patricia Hersch, *A Tribe Apart* (New York: Ballantine, 1998), p. 20.

Chapter Four: Sitting on a Gold Mine
[1]Mitzi Perdue, "Research Describes Drugs' Dangers and What Parents Can Do," *The Tennessean,* February 4, p. 98.

[2]Kevin Huggins, *Parenting Adolescents* (Colorado Springs: NavPress, 1989), p. 143.

[3]"Teens and Self-Image," *USA Weekend,* May 1-3, 1998, p. 18.

[4]See Robert and Bobbie Wolgemuth, and Susan and Mark DeVries, *The Most Important Year in a Man's Life/The Most Important Year in a Woman's Life* (Grand Rapids, Mich.: Zondervan, 2003).

[5]Huggins's rationale for the extensive influence of parents is also instructive: "No one else (peers, teachers, even favorite recording artists) has access to a kid like parents do. . . . And exposure always breeds influence. The question many parents must ask themselves is not 'Why don't I have any influence over my teen?' but 'Why do I take so little advantage of the exposure I do have with him?' The answer to the second question is very often the answer to the first" (*Parenting Adolescents,* p. 145).

[6]Merton Strommen and Irene Strommen, *The Five Cries of Parents* (San Francisco: Harper, 1985), p. 72.

[7]*Wall Street Journal,* September 10, 1997, B9.

[8]*Youthworker,* March-April, 2001, p. 10.

[9]Josh McDowell and Norm Wakefield, *The Dad Difference* (San Bernardino, Calif.: Here's Life, 1989), p. 13.

[10]*Parents of Teenagers,* December/January 1990, p. 4.

[11]Andrée Aelion Brooks, *Children of Fast-Track Parents* (New York: Viking Penguin, 1989), p. 88.

[12]H. Stephen Glenn and Jane Nelsen, *Raising Self-Reliant Children in a Self-Indulgent World* (Roseville, Calif.: Prima, 1989), pp. 103-4.

[13]Merton Strommen, Karen E. Jones and Dave Rahn, *Youth Ministry That Transforms* (Grand Rapids, Mich.: Zondervan, 2001), p. 130.

[14]Martin Luther, in *Luther's Works,* ed. Jaroslav Pelikan and Helmut Lehmann, 55 vols. (St.

Louis, Mo.: Concordia Publishing, 1955-1986), 45:46.

[15]Armand Nicholi Jr., "Changes in the American Family," *White House Paper,* October 25, 1984, p. 2.

[16]James Dobson and Gary Bauer, *Children at Risk* (Dallas: Word, 1990), pp. 167-68.

[17]*Youthworker,* January/February 2001, p. 11.

[18]Robert Laurent, *Keeping Your Teen in Touch with God* (Elgin, Ill.: David C. Cook, 1988), p. 119.

[19]Edward Hayes, *Prayers for the Domestic Church: A Handbook of Worship in the Home* (Eaton, Kans.. Forest of Peace, 1979), p. 17.

[20]Marjorie J. Thompson, *Family the Forming Center* (Nashville: Upper Room Books, 1989), p. 23.

[21]Benjamin Keeley studied the religious behavior of both Christian and non-Christian high-school students. His study documented that young people who perceive their parents as deeply committed to their religion are significantly more religious than teens who see their parents as less committed (Laurent, *Keeping Your Teen in Touch with God,* p. 46). A 1990 *Newsweek* article titled "The New Teens: What Makes Them Different?" explained that, in general, teenagers reflect their parents' lifestyles and values. The study found far more congruence than conflict between the beliefs of teenagers and their parents (*Youthworker Update,* September 1990, p. 1).

[22]Roger L. Dudley and Margaret G. Dudley, "Transmission of Religious Values from Parents to Adolescents," *Review of Religious Research,* September 1986, p. 13.

[23]Peter L. Benson and Carolyn H. Elkin, *Effective Christian Education: A National Study of Protestant Congregations: A Summary Report on Faith, Loyalty and Congregational Life* (Minneapolis: Search, 1990), p. 38.

[24]Ibid., p. 66.

[25]Jonathan Edwards, quoted in Clyde A. Holbrook, *The Ethics of Jonathan Edwards: Morality and Aesthetics* (Ann Arbor: University of Michigan Press, 1973), p. 83, emphasis added.

Chapter Five: The Critical Care Unit

[1]Patricia Hersch, *A Tribe Apart: A Journey into the Heart of American Adolescence* (New York: Ballantine, 1999), p. 78.

[2]Peter L. Benson and Carolyn H. Elkin, *Effective Christian Education: A National Study of Protestant Congregations: A Summary Report on Faith, Loyalty and Congregational Life* (Minneapolis: Search, 1990), p. 18.

[3]The same report confirmed that approximately 40 percent of women in their forties have a mature, integrated faith. Although the mothers appear to be much further along than the fathers, the net result is that many of the teenagers we work with do not come from a home where even one parent models living as a mature Christian adult.

[4]Benson and Elkin, *Effective Christian Education,* p. 46.

[5]Ibid., p. 11.

[6]In the 1980s the Lutheran Church sponsored a study of family religious practices. The results showed that only 8 percent of families maintain a practice of sharing, discussing or praying together as a family (Carl Reuss, *Profiles of Lutherans,* quoted in Merton Strommen and Irene Strommen, *The Five Cries of Parents* [San Francisco: Harper, 1985], p. 134). Despite the fact

that family conversations about God have a tremendous impact on the future faith maturity of children, most Christian families simply have other priorities.

[7]Walt Mueller, in *CPYU Newsletter,* Fall 1996, p. 1.

[8]Strommen and Strommen, *Five Cries,* p. 129.

[9]Benson and Elkin, *Effective Christian Education,* p. 38.

[10]Ben Patterson, "The Plan for a Youth Ministry Reformation," *Youthworker,* Fall 1984, p. 45.

[11]Gordon MacDonald, *The Effective Father* (Wheaton, Ill.: Tyndale House, 1977), p. 245.

[12]David Popenoe, "Family Decline in America," in *Rebuilding the Nest: A New Commitment to the American Family,* ed. David Blankenhorn et al. (Milwaukee: Family Service America, 1990), p. 39.

[13]David Blankenhorn, introduction to *Rebuilding the Nest,* p. xiv.

[14]"The 21st Century Family," *Newsweek,* special edition, Winter/Spring 1990.

[15]*Saturday Review,* April 1978, quoted in Jim Burns, *The Youth Builder* (Eugene, Ore.: Harvest House, 1988), p. 35.

[16]Kevin Huggins, *Parenting Adolescents* (Colorado Springs: NavPress, 1989), p. 14.

Chapter Six: Stacking the Stands

[1]John Leland with Claudia Kalb, "Savior of the Streets," *Newsweek,* June 1, 1998, emphasis added.

[2]Greg Johnson and Mike Yorkey, *Faithful Parents, Faithful Kids* (Wheaton, Ill.: Tyndale House, 1993), p. 249, emphasis added.

[3]Monika Guttman, "Resilience," *USA Weekend,* March 5-7, 1999, p. 5.

[4]Judith Wallerstein and Sandra Blakeslee, *Second Chances* (New York: Ticknor and Fields, 1989), p. 112.

[5]Ben Patterson, "The Plan for Youth Ministry Reformation," *Youthworker,* Fall 1984, p. 60.

[6]Earl Palmer, "Perspective," *Youthworker,* Spring 1992, p. 4.

[7]Peter L. Benson, *The Troubled Journey: Profile of American Youth* (Minneapolis: Search Institute/ Lutheran Brotherhood, 1991), p. 9.

[8]Andrée Aelion Brooks, *Children of Fast-Track Parents* (New York: Viking Penguin, 1989), pp. 68-69.

[9]Steven Bayme, "The Jewish Family in American Culture," in *Rebuilding the Nest: A New Commitment to the Family,* ed. David Blankenhorn et al. (Milwaukee: Family Service America, 1990), p. 153.

[10]John Guidibaldi, "The Impact of Parental Divorce on Children: Report of the National NASP Study, 1983," quoted in Merton Strommen and Irene Strommen, *The Five Cries of Parents* (San Francisco: Harper, 1985), p. 28.

[11]H. Stephen Glenn and Jane Nelsen, *Raising Self-Reliant Children in a Self-Indulgent World* (Roseville, Calif.: Prima, 1989), p. 23.

[12]Ibid., p. 19.

[13]Strommen and Strommen, *Five Cries,* p. 64.

[14]Peter L. Benson and Carolyn H. Elkin, *Effective Christian Education: A National Study of Protestant Congregations: A Summary Report on Faith, Loyalty and Congregational Life* (Minneapolis: Search, 1990), pp. 33-34.

[15]Marjorie J. Thompson, *Family the Forming Center* (Nashville: Upper Room Books, 1989), p. 123.

[16]Benson, *Troubled Journey,* p. 11. In Peter Benson's recommendations from the *Effective Christian Education* Search Institute study, he advocates that all youth-serving organizations find ways to connect youth to adult mentors.

Chapter Seven: It Only Makes Sense

[1]Mark Senter confirms this idea: "The high school campus has changed. No longer can people concerned with reaching youth for Jesus Christ expect to have a single program or strategy which is attractive to all of the high school population" (Mark Senter, *The Coming Revolution in Youth Ministry* [Wheaton, Ill.: Victor, 1992], p. 18). One of the keys to the success of Dan Spader's increasingly popular Sonpower model is that he has energetically advocated reducing youth activities so that leaders will have the energy to focus their creativity on evangelism and discipleship.

[2]The only notable exception to this pattern was those young people who, although they did not connect with adults in the church, created their own adult extended Christian family by becoming ministers (including joining the staff of parachurch organizations like Young Life, Youth for Christ, Campus Crusade, InterVarsity or the Fellowship of Christian Athletes) or marrying ministers.

[3]Ben Patterson, "The Plan for a Youth Ministry Reformation," *Youthworker,* Fall 1984, p. 61.

[4]Ibid.

[5]Ibid.

[6]The Search Institute study (Peter L. Benson and Carolyn H. Elkin, *Effective Christian Education: A National Study of Protestant Congregation: A Summary Report on Faith, Loyalty and Congregational Life* [Minneapolis: Search, 1990], p. 62) indicated that only 26 percent of churches reported that parents were involved in the planning or programming of their youth ministry. The study goes on to strongly advocate that primary attention be given to the faith formation of parents.

[7]Wayne Meeks, *The First Urban Christians,* quoted in William Willimon, "The New Family," in *Peculiar Speech* (Grand Rapids, Mich.: Eerdmans, 1992), p. 118.

[8]The Search Institute study (Benson and Elkin, *Effective Christian Education,* p. 56) indicated that only 20 percent of churches have youth programs that promote this sort of intergenerational contact.

[9]Senter, *Coming Revolution,* p. 27, describes these two organizations aptly: "Though extremely different in nature, the two organizations [FCA and YWAM] appear to have one factor in common a well-focused target audience. Neither is attempting to be a full-service ministry."

Chapter Eight: Beyond the Cleavers

[1]Edward F. Zigler and Elizabeth P. Gilman, "An Agenda for the 1990's: Supporting Families," in *Rebuilding the Nest: A New Commitment to the American Family,* ed. David Blankenhorn et al. (Milwaukee: Family Service America, 1990), p. 239.

[2]*Gentlemen's Quarterly: The American Male Opinion Index, Part 2,* 1990.

[3]H. Stephen Glenn and Jane Nelsen, *Raising Self-Reliant Children in a Self-Indulgent World* (Roseville, Calif.: Prima, 1989), p. 12.

[4]Josh McDowell and Dick Day, *Why Wait* (San Bernardino, Calif.: Here's Life, 1987) p. 65.

[5]1991 World Almanac.

[6]Andrée Aelion Brooks, *Children of Fast-Track Parents* (New York: Viking Penguin, 1989), p. 208.

[7]Jolene L. Roehlkepartain, "When Your Ex Refuses to Pay," *Parents of Teenagers,* August/September 1991, p. 22.

[8]David Lynn, "Research Brief," *Youthworker,* Fall 1991, p. 30.

[9]Judith Wallerstein and Sandra Blakeslee, *Second Chances* (New York: Ticknor and Fields, 1989), p. 13.

[10]*Parents of Teenagers,* February/March 1991, p. 5.

[11]*Parents of Teenagers,* August/September 1988, p. 6.

[12]Rick Lawrence, *Trendwatch: Insights That Fuel Authentic Youth Ministry* (Loveland, Colo.: Group, 2000), pp. 97-98.

[13]*Youthworker Update,* February 1997, p. 7.

[14]*Parents of Teenagers,* August/September 1990, p. 5.

[15]Anderson Spickard and Barbara Thompson, *Dying for a Drink* (Waco, Tex.: Word, 1985), p. 74.

[16]One estimate suggests that women can expect to spend an average of eighteen years caring for an aging parent and raising children at the same time (Marty Fuller, "More Parents Are Feeling the Squeeze," *Parents of Teenagers,* April/May 1991, p. 9).

[17]"Growing Up Under Fire," *Newsweek,* June 10, 1991, p. 64.

[18]Louis Sullivan, *Urban Family,* Winter 1992, p. 7.

[19]*Youthworker Update,* September 1992, p. 6. Used by permission from Youth Specialties, 1224 Greenfield Drive, El Cajon, CA 92021.

Chapter 9: Walking the Tightrope

[1]Mark Senter, *The Coming Revolution in Youth Ministry* (Wheaton, Ill.: Victor, 1992), p. 177.

[2]*Journal of Research on Adolescence* 1, no. 1 (1991), quoted in *Youthworker Update,* November 11, 1991, pp. 4-5.

[3]Andrée Aelion Brooks, *Children of Fast-Track Parents* (New York: Viking Penguin, 1989), p. 245.

[4]Eugene Peterson, *Growing Up with Your Teenager,* quoted in Jay Kesler and Paul Woods, *Energizing Your Teenager's Faith* (Loveland, Colo.: Group, 1990), p. 24.

[5]Kevin Huggins, *Parenting Adolescents* (Colorado Springs: NavPress, 1989), p. 215.

[6]C. S. Lewis, *Miracles* (New York: Macmillan, 1947), p. 51.

[7]C. S. Lewis, *Mere Christianity* (New York: Macmillan, 1943), p. 163.

[8]H. Stephen Glenn and Jane Nelsen, *Raising Self-Reliant Children in a Self-Indulgent World* (Roseville, Calif.: Prima, 1989), p. 103.

[9]Peter L. Benson, *The Troubled Journey: Profile of American Youth* (Minneapolis: Search Institute/ Lutheran Brotherhood, 1991), p. 6.

Chapter 10: A Different Gospel

[1]Robert Bellah, "The Invasion of the Money World," in *Rebuilding the Nest: A New Commitment to the Family,* ed. David Blankenhorn et al. (Milwaukee: Family Service America, 1990), p. 234.

[2]Carl Schneider, "Moral Discourse and the Transformation of American Family Law," *Michigan Law Review* 83 (1985): 1859.

[3]Chuck Colson in *Jubilee*, June 1987, p. 8.

[4]Lyle Schaller, "Every Part Is an 'I': How Will the Body Function in an Age of Rising Individualism?" *Leadership Journal*, Fall 1999, p. 29.

[5]*Parents of Teenagers*, December 1990/January 1991, p. 27.

[6]*Youthworker Update*, June 1991, p. 1. Used by permission of Youth Specialties, 1224 Greenfield Drive, El Cajon, CA 92021. Taken from *Oregon Alcohol & Drug Review* 10, no. 3, in *Chemical People Newsletter*, March/April 1991.

[7]Peter L. Benson and Carolyn H. Elkin, *Effective Christian Education: A National Study of Protestant Congregations: A Summary Report on Faith, Loyalty and Congregational Life* (Minneapolis: Search, 1990), p. 23-4.

[8]Merton Strommen, Karen E. Jones, and Dave Rahn, *Youth Ministry That Transforms* (Grand Rapids, Mich.: Youth Specialties/Zondervan, 2001), p. 69.

[9]*Emerging Trends*, Princeton Religion Research Center, January 1989.

[10]*Journal of Research on Adolescence* 1, no. 2 (1991), quoted in *Youthworker Update*, January 1992, p. 4. Used by permission of Youth Specialties, 1224 Greenfield Drive, El Cajon, CA 92021.

[11]James Dobson, *Preparing for Adolescence* (Ventura, Calif.: Regal, 1978, 1989), pp. 21-27.

[12]Henri Nouwen, *In the Name of Jesus* (New York: Crossroads, 1989), pp. 59, 22.

Chapter Eleven: God Calling

[1]John Westerhoff, *Bringing Up Children in the Christian Faith* (Minneapolis: Winston, 1980), p. 7.

[2]M. Scott Peck, *The Road Less Traveled* (New York: Simon & Schuster, 1980), p. 168.

[3]Henri Nouwen in *Christianity Today*, April 5, 1985, p. 32.

Chapter Twelve: Making It Work

[1]William J. Lederer and Don D. Jackson, *The Mirages of Marriage*, (New York: W. W. Norton, 1968), p. 88.

[2]Ben Freudenburg with Rick Lawrence, *The Family Friendly Church* (Loveland, Colo.: Group Publishing, 1998).

[3]*Youthworker*, November/December 1997, p. 50.

Appendix B: Has the Traditional Family Really Died?

[1]Chris Dodd, quoted in David Blankenhorn et al., eds., *Rebuilding the Nest: A New Commitment to the American Family* (Milwaukee: Family Service America, 1990), p. 11.

[2]Pat Schroeder with Andrea Camp and Robyn Lipner, *Champion of the Great American Family* (New York: Random House, 1989), p. 84.

[3]Steven Bayme in *Rebuilding the Nest*, p. 258.

Appendix D: 122 Family-Based Youth Ministry Programming Ideas

[1]Merton Strommen and Irene Strommen, *The Five Cries of Parents* (San Francisco: Harper, 1985), p. 191.

[2]Dave Fries, "Middle School Minister," *Youthworker*, Fall 1992, p. 11.

[3]Marge Atkinson, "Drawing Families Together," *Relationships*, Winter 1990, p. 6.

After eighteen years Mark DeVries (M.Div., Princeton Theological Seminary) continues to serve as pastor to youth and their families at First Presbyterian Church in Nashville, Tennessee. He also travels nationwide speaking to church leaders and college and seminary students on the subject of family-based youth ministry. Contact Mark at

5229 Cochran Dr.
Nashville TN 37220
MrkDeVries@aol.com

First Presbyterian Church
4815 Franklin Road
Nashville, TN 37220
(615) 298-9506
www.fpcnashville.org

Or visit the Family-Based Youth Ministry websites:
www.familybasedym.com
www.ymarchitects.com

- Become a part of the Family-Based Youth Ministry Network
- Order other resources by Mark DeVries

  Bridges: 15 Sessions to Connect Teenagers and Adults
  (coauthored with Nan Russell)

  The Most Important Year in a Man's Life/The Most Important Year in a Woman's Life—What Every Groom/Bride Should Know
  (coauthored With Susan DeVries and Robert and Bobbie Wolgemuth)

  True Love Waits Bible

  Shepherd's Notes: Calvin's Institutes of the Christian Religion

  Shepherd's Notes: Augustine's Confessions

- Download practical youth ministry articles.
- Learn about Youth Ministry Architects and how to arrange for a strategic assessment for a youth ministry in transition.
- Contact Mark or arrange for him to lead a family-based youth ministry seminar, a family retreat, a marriage workshop or a parenting seminar with your church
- Check out the Frequently Asked Questions pages.
- Sign up for a free sample subscription to "Spice Rack," Mark's interactive, biblically based youth ministry curriculum available via e-mail.